Uncommon Sense *for Parents with* Teenagers

Uncommon Sense *for* Parents *with* Teenagers

THIRD EDITION

MICHAEL RIERA, PhD

Ten Speed Press
Berkeley

Copyright © 1995, 2004, 2012 by Michael Riera

Previous editions were published in the United States by Celestial Arts, an imprint of Ten
Speed Press, Berkeley, CA, in 1995 and 2004.

Ten Speed Press and the Ten Speed Press colophon are registered trademarks of Random
House, Inc.

Grateful acknowledgment is made to the following for permission to reprint previously
published material:

CNS Productions, Inc.: Excerpts from *Uppers, Downers, All Arounders, 7th Edition* by Darryl S.
Inaba and William E. Cohen. Copyright © 2011 by Darryl S. Inaba and William E. Cohen.

William S. Mayher: Excerpts from *The Dynamics of Senior Year: A Report from the Frontlines.*

Tribune Media Services: "On Being a Dad: A Teen's Lesson in Lurching" by D. L. Stewart, *San
Francisco Chronicle*, August 21, 1991.

Library of Congress Cataloging-in-Publication Data
Riera, Michael.
Uncommon sense for parents with teenagers / Michael Riera.—3rd ed.
p. cm.
Includes bibliographical references and index.
1. Parent and teenager—United States. I. Title.
HQ799.15.R54 2012
649'.125—dc23
2012012082

ISBN 978-1-60774-346-0
eISBN 978-1-60774-347-7

Printed in the United States of America

Design by Colleen Cain

10 9 8 7 6

Third Edition

To Betty and Pat Riera,
who made it all possible
for Peter, Tim, Dave, and me.
Love and thanks.

CONTENTS

PARENT QUESTIONS

Commonly asked questions,
and where to find the responses:

What is the world of today's adolescent, and do I stand a chance of
 understanding it? / 8–34

Is there a pattern of experiences common to all kids during the two or
 three years of middle school and the four years of high school? / 35–63

What are fair punishments when teenagers break the rules? For instance,
 how effective is "grounding"? / 70–78

Why is my teenager arguing with me at every possible turn and is there
 any way to stop this craziness? / 78–85

I'm concerned about my tenth grader going to weekend parties where
 alcohol and drugs are available. What can or should I do about it? /
 86–101

How do I understand and monitor my teenager's use of social media
 sites like Facebook and Twitter and the Internet in general? Should I
 be worried about her constant texting and cell phone use? / 102–15

ACKNOWLEDGMENTS

Without the assistance of Megan Riera and Joe Di Prisco this book would not have been written. Many, many times I've had to borrow Megan's confidence in me and my ideas. And without Joe's editing and continual questioning skills, the book would have been a shell of what you hold in your hands. I owe a great deal to both Megan and Joe. Thank you.

I also want to thank all of the readers who examined and commented on the manuscript in its various stages of completion—Carol and Bill Twadell, Julie Terraciano, Jane Dirkes, Al Hammer, Bodie Brizendine, John Dyckman, Hadley Hudson, Mario Di Prisco, Guy Stiles, John Erdman, and Lenzie Williams. Your input was essential.

From the first edition to this third edition there are many people to thank: my agent, Peter Beren; all the people at Celestial Arts who first believed in the book, especially David Hinds, Veronica Randall, Colleen Paretty, Kathryn Horning, Fifth Street Design, and Victor Ichioka. In this same vein, thanks to everyone at Ten Speed who did such a wonderful job on this third edition, especially Emily Timberlake and Jane Merryman.

Finally, thanks to a few of the people who have shaped my thinking over the years: Peter Baldwin, Harry Kisker, John Dyckman (again), Robert Green, and Amadeo Giorgi. Thank you.

PREFACE

This text grew out of my thirty years of experience working with more than twenty thousand teenagers and parents in a variety of settings, from middle schools to colleges, from residential treatment programs to college preparatory schools.

For me, adolescence is a fascinating stage of life. I feel most optimistic when around teenagers. If this sounds strange, understand that I typically see their best aspects, the growing-up and reaching-out aspects that are too infrequently seen at home. Adolescence is not a phase of life to be feared; rather, it is one of fascination, curiosity, and unexpected twists, and, as such, it is quite different from the previous stages of childhood and the following stages of adulthood.

What parents need is a translation of this period that makes sense and is useful. The isolation that parents of teenagers often feel is profound. You'll find lots of books on infancy and childhood, but few on adolescence. It is as if we hold our collective breaths from the end of childhood to early adulthood, and then breathe an enormous sigh of relief once adolescence has passed. I hope to replace the isolation, silence, and fear that accompany parenting during this period with optimism and hope.

This book deals with middle and high school adolescents, grades six through twelve, and conveys the range of viewpoints, struggles, and conclusions of the teenagers and parents who have come my way. While I have never heard the same conversation twice, all have carried an implicit desire for understanding that often forms the foundation of a solution.

This is not a how-to book, because all teenagers are not the same. While it is true that they all, more or less, traverse the same terrain, it is equally true that they do so with different styles, idiosyncrasies, and personalities. Just ask any parent who has more than one child. As you come to understand the context of the adolescent world, so will you recognize and admire the uniqueness of your child. Stereotypes of teenagers are misleading and blinding.

MOM (to her son walking in the door after baseball practice): So, how was school today? Anything interesting happen?

SON (as he noses through the refrigerator): Nah, just a typical day. Is there any more orange juice?

MOM: Uh, no. We finished it this morning. So, nothing exciting in school today . . . oh, didn't you have that history test today? How do you think you did?

SON: Yeah, it was easy. Any soda in the garage?

MOM (getting discouraged): No. Your father didn't do the shopping for this week yet . . . how about practice today? Was it a good practice?

SON (as he heads toward his room with a bowl of cereal): The usual.

MOM (a bit exasperated): John, how come you don't talk to me anymore, let alone tell me what happens at school?

SON (mildly surprised, but sort of smug): Jeez, what is this Twenty Questions or something? I'm going to my room; call me when dinner is ready.

(The son then proceeds to his room, where he gets comfortable on his bed, eating his cereal, checking his social networking sites, and listening to music—which, to his mother's ears, is rather loud and somewhat dissonant, and, of course, prompts her to request that he turn it down.)

MOM (remembering to knock on the door): John. John, do you hear me?

SON (waiting just a bit longer than necessary): What? What do you want now?

MOM (opening the door and sticking her head into her son's room): John, please turn the music down. I'm trying to get some work done out here, and I can't concentrate with that music so loud.

SON (with an exaggerated exhalation): Okay, okay! I'll turn it down. (Then, while taking his time and exaggerating his effort, he mumbles just barely loud enough for his mom to hear.) Wouldn't want to do anything to help me relax now, would we?

MOM: Did you say something?

SON (barely turning the music down): Nothing. There, it's turned down. Happy now?

(Mom walks away more perplexed and frustrated than before. Five minutes later the music has miraculously gotten louder, or maybe it is just
   beginning to have a cumulative effect on Mom.)

MOM (knocking on the door again, only slightly harder this time): John.
   John, turn the music down! (Then, after a moment of no response, she
   opens the door.) John, please turn the music down.

SON (in a very irritated tone): Jeez, don't you believe in knocking! I mean,
   don't I get any privacy? I don't just walk in on you and Dad, do I? How
   about giving me a little respect once in a while?

MOM (at the end of her rope and quite exasperated): Just turn the music
   down!

(At this point, World War III is imminent. When Mom does walk back
   down the hall, she is shaking her head and wondering what has happened to her son. She also wonders what she did to deserve this and
   what she did to bring this about. Where, she asks herself, did she go
   wrong as a parent?)

When I tell this story to a group of teenagers, they immediately start
laughing and nodding their heads, because they know this happens in their
family and in most of their friends' homes. However, when I tell the same
story to parents, they first look nervously at the floor and only begin to smile
themselves after a few moments, before looking around to see others smile.
We then begin to examine the story to understand the underlying rationale at
work here along with alternative parent responses that avoid World War III
and the bad parenting/bad kid conclusions. You see, there is a kind of logic at
work here, but teenagers can't articulate it in any consistent manner because
they don't understand it themselves. In fact, once they understand it, they are
by definition no longer adolescents. Thus, parents have to uncover and translate this logic and learn to respond to their teenager on their own.

Parents and teenagers possess dissimilar worldviews, which inform their
behaviors, attitudes, and interpretations of events in very different ways. But
teenagers don't want an adversarial relationship any more than you. In fact,
when I discussed this book with several teenagers, they said, in effect, "If this
book accomplishes nothing else other than helping parents realize that we
are not the enemy, it will have been worth the effort." To this end, when this
point was stressed on one of my first appearances on *Oprah*, I was surprised
and delighted that roughly 50 percent of the follow-up responses to the show

were from teenagers wanting to know where to get copies of the books for their parents!

Ultimately, you are responsible for bringing up your child, and with this responsibility resting squarely on your shoulders, it makes sense to use a variety of resources: discussions with other parents, various articles and books (in addition to this one), reflection on your own adolescence, and professional consultations when appropriate. It is this responsibility that also makes you a critical and discerning consumer. Take the ideas that work immediately for you, modify others, and set the rest aside. But don't set anything aside until you've challenged yourself to understand why you are setting it aside; otherwise you'll be shortchanging your developing understanding of your adolescent.

Parenting an adolescent is not an easy job. However, only in the last decade have parents begun to voice their desire for more practical information about their teenagers. In this regard, I have been surprised by parents' intense yearning for education and ideas to help them understand a broad range of teenage behaviors. I've also noticed that the more general questions asked in a large group setting are often followed up with more intimate questions in the privacy of my office. This book is designed to address both sorts of questions. Sprinkled throughout the text are numerous individual stories, anecdotes, conversations, letters, and quotations from teenagers that illuminate the book's ideas.[1] These stories also tell the reader about what is happening in other parent-adolescent relationships.

This book is question driven. After the first three chapters, which are overviews of the parent-adolescent relationship, the adolescent world, and middle and high school, the book is a series of responses (not answers) to questions commonly asked by parents and other adults who work closely with adolescents. The table of contents reflects the general topics covered; the table of parent questions helps find specific questions addressed in the text. Remember, questions that you feel are not relevant to your situation may indeed hold the seeds to solutions for a host of other problems, which is why reading the entire text is important. You'll notice the questions are responded to in digressive and progressive ways that work together to develop the principles of a positive approach to the parent-adolescent relationship. While this book is not meant as a recipe book of solutions, reading others' successful resolutions will inspire and give you the confidence to design solutions appropriate to your life, your values, and your family. This does not happen overnight, but gradually over time.

This book first came out in 1995, and what you hold in your hands is the third edition, which has been substantially expanded and updated. It incorporates many of the questions that were sent to me in response to the first two editions. My book *Staying Connected to Your Teenager*, published in 2003, expands on ideas presented here and builds on them with the theme of keeping the parent-teenager relationship strong throughout adolescence. In many ways, *Uncommon Sense for Parents with Teenagers* and *Staying Connected to Your Teenager* form a two-part series.

Finally, while this book contains plenty of information, the more difficult task is the emotional stability and maturity it takes to put these ideas into practice. Don't saddle yourself with expectations of perfection; instead, aim for a little improvement each day. Good luck, we are in this together!

Note

1. The quotes from adolescents and parents in this book are not direct quotations; instead, they are samples of the kind of things I have heard consistently during my time as an educator. Also, all potentially revealing details were changed in the interests of confidentiality.

1

From Manager to Consultant

The Essential Shift in the Parent-Adolescent Relationship

Conventional wisdom has cast the parent-adolescent relationship as unavoidably adversarial. Both sides view the other as "the enemy"—a most unfortunate and destructive role in which to be a parent or an adolescent.

This book assumes that conventional wisdom is wrong. In fact, it suggests a very different and more useful picture of the parent-adolescent relationship. But first, where has this adversarial notion come from, and why has it gone unchallenged for so long?

On a typical evening when a group of parents gather to discuss and learn about adolescence, we start with two brainstorming questions. The first: "When you think of the generic teenager, what descriptive words come to mind?" This list, written on the left side of a blackboard, is generated quickly.

Then we move to the second question: "What are some of the daily choices as well as long-term decisions that adolescents face while in high school?" This list also comes easily, though generally not as quickly nor as playfully as the first, and it is written on the right side of the blackboard.

Take a minute to look at the two lists in figure 1 (see next page).

Figure 1

Words That Describe Teenagers	Issues and Decisions of Teenagers
Selfish, moody, idealistic, entitled, unpredictable, funny, lethargic, psychotic, irresponsible, surly, independent, angry, irritable, dependent, demanding, sullen, selectively responsible, manipulative, challenging, sulky, posturing, self-conscious, argumentative, disrespectful, stubborn, sneaky, scared, insecure, narcissistic, vulnerable, hungry, sleepy, and aloof.	Types of friends they want; kind of friend they want to be; sexual relations, sexuality; alcohol and drugs; importance of school and grades; class issues; economic worries; racism; existential identity; relationship to family; figuring out who they are and what they stand for; matching their insides with their self-perceived outsides; college; career; daily violence around them; environmental concerns; ambiguity about all of the above.

Looking at these lists side by side, parents tend to have a number of reactions, best summed up as "Anybody in that condition (words on the left) shouldn't be making those decisions (phrases on the right)." Then, parents are hit with a second, more powerful, realization: teenagers are in this condition, they face these issues, and they must make such decisions. As parents, you need to fully recognize this fact and reconsider your role as it relates to their struggles. This does not mean convincing your teenager to make decisions that are "right" by your standards, nor does it mean sitting by passively with your fingers crossed. It especially doesn't mean doing more of what got you through the previous thirteen years of your child's growth. Adolescence is an entirely different game, and the rules and goals have changed drastically— so drastically, in fact, that the old "tried-and-trues" often make things worse. We'll come back to this point in a moment.

When I engage teenagers in this same sort of brainstorming about their parents, the results are just as eye-opening. One set of questions is used to address three different periods in the parent-child relationship. The first time through, the questions are about an infant, the second time about a third grader, and the third time about a sophomore in high school. The questions are "What do typical parents want for their infant/child/adolescent?" and "How do parents show this in their behaviors and attitudes toward their child?" See figure 2 for their responses.

Figure 2

Infant

Lots of attention, encouragement, play, toys, affection, wanting to be with them, touching, singing, reading aloud, showing off, pride, excitement, providing for, pure joy, "can't get enough" of the infant, total acceptance

Third Grader

Involvement in their life; organizing their activities (dance, music, sports, and so on); encouragement and monitoring in school; teaching, helping with homework; giving responsibilities and overseeing them; gentle criticism; gentle feedback; limits and rules with limited freedom; teaching difference between right and wrong; appropriate expectations

Sophomore

Yelling, lots of guilt, excessive limits and rules, overly controlling, encouragement, choice, unrealistic expectations, support, nagging, punishment, limited praise, harsh criticism, overly interested in their life (excessive and obsessive), "little talks" and family dinners, "too much fun equals trouble," focus on their friends and types of people they are, judgmental jealousy, lack of meaningful contact, conflict, loud arguing, too many questions, no trust

Clearly, teenagers see their parents as helpful and caring through childhood and as intrusive, mistrustful, and controlling in adolescence. Quite a shift of perspective! In fact, it is such a radical shift that teenagers can't even focus on what their parents want for them; they tend to focus exclusively on their parents' negative and restrictive behavior. However, with a little prodding, they can intellectually understand that their parents haven't deliberately chosen to switch from loving and caring to misunderstanding and nagging. Teenagers even get the idea that perhaps parents are not really sure how to go about this whole parenting thing with a teenager. Sure, their parents handled infancy and childhood without too many hitches, but that doesn't necessarily prepare an adult for adolescent parenting. When teenagers understand this, they also begin to see how they can help, even "coaching" their parents in a developing partnership. Teenagers have a lot of influence if they choose to make use of it—quite a mind-boggling concept to most fourteen-year-olds.

Take a moment now to look at both lists (figures 1 and 2). At first, both seem to support the adversarial nature of the parent-adolescent relationship. Consider, however, what happens when your child starts high school. Until this point, you have acted as a "manager" in your child's life: arranging rides and doctor appointments, planning outside or weekend activities, helping with and checking on homework. You stay closely informed about school life, and you are usually the first person your child seeks out with big questions. Suddenly, none of this is applicable. Without notification, and without consensus, you are fired from the role of manager. Now you must scramble and restrategize; if you are to have meaningful influence in your teenager's life through adolescence and beyond, then you must work your tail off to get rehired as consultant. And this is how it should be! Many of the adversarial aspects of the relationship stem from both the parent and adolescent not understanding and appreciating this essential shift in roles.

Since parents have experienced only managerial roles in their child's life, they usually see no reason to change as the child enters adolescence. At a loss to explain their teenager's sudden shift in behavior, many parents take on the managerial role with even more gusto and fervor. This, in turn, is met with resentment and often disastrous results. Other parents have the opposite reaction, becoming passive and virtually abandoning any role with their teenager (no role equals minimal conflict), which also meets with unfortunate results.

From the other side of the relationship, as adolescents become aware that the parent-as-manager role is no longer useful, they focus on freeing themselves, without much consideration for alternative roles. They want more say in their lives and will go to great lengths to get it—even tolerating and rationalizing the guilt associated with upsetting their parents and actively pushing them away. Thus, it is a pleasant surprise for most adolescents when they realize that, if the role can shift from manager to consultant, they can have their cake and eat it too. That is, if their parents relinquish the role of manager, they can have increasing autonomy without abandonment; their parents can actually serve as very useful and important advisers. After all, who knows a teenager's history better than her parents? Who wants only the best for her? Who will consistently take risks for her? Who loves her and forgives her no matter how much she messes up? Who believes in her at least as much as she does? However, these attitude shifts are possible only if parents can assume the new, less-directive, adviser role and if adolescents can trust their parents in this role—a point we'll come back to throughout the text.

As a consultant, you offer advice and give input about decisions when you are asked. Otherwise, you'll lose your client. You don't garner the automatic praise and admiration that you did earlier. And, when your client (teenager) asks for advice, you need to make sure that she really wants it. Sometimes, more than anything else, she simply wants your reassurances that she'll figure it out herself. Sometimes she will temporarily lose belief in herself and ask to borrow your belief in her for a short while.

> It's kind of weird. A lot of times I ask my parents for ideas about what to do about a problem or situation, but then I get upset with them when they start offering me advice! I know they think I'm crazy when this happens. It's just that somehow I need to figure it out on my own, and while I want their help, I also don't want to be treated like a little kid.

Offering advice is not helpful when the real problem is the teenager's lost belief in herself. A rule of thumb is not to take your teenager's request for advice too literally until the third time. Nobody wants a consultant who tries to take over the business. What you are doing is not doing—you are waiting, but not abandoning. As a consultant, you must also save your "power plays" for health and safety issues; everything else is negotiable on some level. Skipping a biology class is definitely not on a par with driving a car after drinking alcohol. Finally, at this stage in your relationship, you are no longer the focus of your child's praise and admiration; rather, you are often the scapegoat for the confusion about what it is to be an adolescent. (See figures 1 and 2 earlier in this section.) As a manager, you were quite content to take their feedback personally, as a reflection of you; as a consultant, you must learn to not take most of their feedback personally, since it is often more about them than about you.

> When my son was seven, I remember how much he used to just hang around me. He would wash the car with me, help me mow the lawn, and ride to the dump with me, insisting all along the way that we honk the horn and wave to his friends. He even persuaded my wife to get him the same kind of jeans that I wore around the house on weekends.

Not only that, he really listened to me, and I could answer the questions he asked. I even overheard him telling a friend that I was probably the smartest man alive! But when he became a teenager everything changed. He challenged me and argued with everything I said. He complained to my wife that he wanted different kinds of clothes: "You know, I'm not fifty years old! I don't want to look like Dad!" Whenever we drove by his friends, he would slump down low in his seat so they wouldn't see him riding with me! He even insisted that I drop him off at the corner for school in the morning, rather than take him all the way to the school where people might see us together. Talk about an ego blow. The only consolation was that I saw lots of other parents dropping their kids off at other corners near the school!

A manager parent tries to ensure that his child makes the "best" decisions. A consultant parent focuses on helping his teenager develop and exercise "decision-making muscles." The outcome is at times less important than the exercise and development of the muscle. Adolescence is, in part, an active training period en route to adulthood. (Of course, few teenagers would agree with this statement, unless they were in a very peaceful, trusting, and introspective mood, which is not all that available to most parents.) Thus, there is room for "bad" decisions that are really "good" decisions. Or, as Mark Twain once said, "Good judgment comes from experience, and experience comes from bad judgment."

To parents, a teenager asserting his or her independence *and* behaving responsibly seem like mutually exclusive issues, but they are actually two integral parts of the growing-up process. With this in mind, parents must work to develop trust in their adolescents' growing judgment, and adolescents in turn must work to keep their parents up-to-date on their developing responsibility skills. Kids see how their increased responsibility leads to greater independence; they realize they can directly influence the world around them. Parents see how increased independence fosters increased responsibility, which in turn fosters optimism and trust in the parent-adolescent relationship. Breeches of responsibility and independence are seen for what they are: missed opportunities not to be taken personally or to be construed as complete failure.

The consultant model also has the advantage of more successfully avoiding the two most common errors in parenting teenagers: treating them like children (overparenting or overmanaging) and treating them like adults (underparenting or abandonment). The first is avoided by understanding that your new role involves much less doing; the second, by being present and actively listening in order to make the most of your "consultations." Or as one high school student put it:

> Be encouraging and interested in your child. Although it's nice not to have nosey parents always pressuring me about what's going on at school, sometimes I feel ignored and neglected when they are indifferent to my daily life.

As a consultant, you willingly give up the illusion of power in favor of real influence. Clinging to pseudo-power over a teenager is what inadvertently leads him into accepting sneakiness and lying as viable strategies within the parent-adolescent relationship.

> Part of my problem is that my parents think they control me completely. I mean, they think I actually follow all of their ridiculous restrictions. They have such an inflated and unrealistic view of me that it is scary. I really wish they weren't so naive about my life; then, at least, we could discuss reality with each other instead of make-believe.

In the long run, the shift from manager to consultant is vital and essential for the parent-adolescent relationship. Throughout this book, the differences in these roles are highlighted. Again, the only exceptions to the consultant role are in situations of health and safety; of course, determining when health and safety are in danger is a matter of perspective, one that most adolescents and parents disagree on. This is also addressed throughout the book. Finally, with consultant parenting I am not advocating laissez-faire parenting; quite the opposite, for consultant parenting is often more demanding and time-consuming than managerial parenting. Here's the payoff, though: it is also much more rewarding for both adolescent and parent.

2

The Adolescent World

What is the world of today's adolescent, and do I stand a chance of understanding it?

This chapter serves as both an overview and a review of the chapters that follow. As an overview, it offers a general framework for understanding and working with adolescents. As a review, it ties all the text questions together. Thus, this section can be read before or after the rest of the text, though preferably before and after.

Let's begin with an example from a parent to keep in the background as this discussion unfolds. We'll come back to it at the conclusion of the chapter.

> Saturday afternoon, Sheila [a junior in high school] was moping around the house. I asked her if anything was wrong and got the usual indecipherable grunt. I let it go; I've learned over the last two years that pursuit in these kinds of situations often ends in conflict. Anyway, she got a bunch of phone calls that afternoon that seemed to worsen her mood. A bit later, when I was putting the cars in the garage, I asked her if she needed the car tonight (I wanted to know whether to leave it out or not). She turned on me and said harshly, "Dad, I don't know, just leave me alone!" Hmm, what line had I crossed this time? But, knowing my request was truly innocent, I got indignant and asked again, adding a

snide comment about her first reaction. This time she simply screamed, "I don't know yet! Why should I have to know yet anyway? My life doesn't have to be planned down to the minute just so I don't inconvenience you! Just leave me alone!"

Needless to say, dinner was rather tense. After about five minutes, Sheila declared she wasn't hungry and was going to her room. Unfortunately, my wife reacted before I could catch her. "You have to eat something. You can't just live on air!" Of course, my daughter turned on my wife and launched into a tirade for several minutes—mostly incoherent stuff, but centered around our trying to run her life. Anyway, it wasn't a pleasant interaction.

Later that night my wife looked in on Sheila and she was in tears— curled up on the bed crying to herself. My wife got her to talk for a little while, but after a few minutes Sheila became quite frustrated and asked to be alone. Later, we invited her to watch TV with us, which she eventually did. But she never did tell us what was going on.

The next day she woke up early and went to volleyball practice, and when she returned she was in great spirits. She was like a different kid! When we asked her about the previous night, she looked confused for a second and then dismissed it with a wave of her hand.

What is going on here? How can we possibly understand this kind of behavior, let alone react to it? We'll come back to this at the end of the chapter, but just keep it in mind as you read on.

In many respects, teenagers appear to be more like adults than children, and often seem to inhabit a mature intellectual world. You must remember, however, that they are not adults. Adolescence contains aspects of both the adult and child worlds, but is not wholly either. Psychologist Theodore Lidz gives a well-rounded description of the adolescent stage of life:

> [Adolescence] is a time of physical and emotional metamorphosis during which the youth feels estranged from the self the child had known. It is a time of seeking: a seeking inward to find who one is; a searching outward to locate one's place in life; a longing for another with whom to satisfy cravings for intimacy and fulfillment. It is a time of turbulent awakening to love and beauty but also of days darkened by loneliness and despair. It is a time of carefree wandering of the spirit through realms of fantasy and in pursuit of idealistic visions, but also of

disillusionment and disgust with the world and the self. It can be a time of adventure with wonderful episodes of reckless folly but also of shame and regret that linger. The adolescent lives with a vibrant sensitivity that carries to ecstatic heights and lowers to almost untenable depths.[1]

Tools for Understanding: Developmental Horizons

The adolescent world is one of complex needs and perspectives. To understand it, one must first examine a variety of adolescent "horizons of meaning." These five categories of developmental changes, taken together, serve as the necessary context for making sense of teenage behaviors and attitudes. They also serve as a guide for parental intervention or nonintervention. For the sake of clarity, the discussion is organized around five developmental areas: physical and cognitive, social, friendship, personal identity, and family and life events. These horizons necessarily compete with one another for attention and often demand different actions or nonactions, which also are often at odds with one another. So, while in the following discussion these horizons are examined one at a time, bear in mind that they are experienced simultaneously.

Horizon 1: Physical and Cognitive

Before puberty, most children have established a fairly consistent and reliable manner of dealing with the world. However, with the onset of puberty and its incessant hormonal changes, this stability is lost. Adolescent girls are roughly two years ahead of boys in terms of physical maturity. Most girls have passed through the initial shocks of puberty by age thirteen, which boys have passed through by age fifteen. As an example of how these changes affect the child, boys typically double in strength from age twelve to age seventeen. Often they literally don't know their own strength. In addition, a torrent of sexual feelings begin to emerge. These uncontrollable physical changes are definitely felt by the typical adolescent.

I was behind all my friends in terms of how fast we went through puberty—far behind. I still remember gym class in the ninth grade. During the winter, we spent most of the time playing basketball, which is a sport I usually like. The problem was that we had to wear tank tops. I still didn't have any hair under my armpits, and I was afraid that someone might notice this and make fun of me. So I always kept my arms at my side, even though the gym teacher constantly yelled at me to raise my arms on defense. But there was no way I was going to lift my arms! I never even changed in the locker room with everybody else. I always got to class early so I could change before anyone else got there, and then I hung around late and got changed after everyone left. I never took a shower. It was definitely the worst part of freshman year for me.

Along with these physical changes is a profound shift in cognitive processes. Swiss psychologist Jean Piaget called this the move from "concrete operational thinking" to "formal operational thinking." This shift can be compared to the difference between watching a movie on a four-inch black-and-white television and seeing the same movie in a state-of-the-art theater with surround sound and interactive capabilities. Concrete operational thinking is limited to the present and to physical reality—what is in front of us and immediately apparent. Formal operational thinking handles abstract concepts, ideas, and possibilities—none of which were part of a preadolescent's worldview. This shift of thinking is obvious in the adolescent's sense of humor. Before puberty, most children's sense of humor is quite literal: when you say, "Look at the clock and tell me what time it is," your child might glance at the clock and playfully state, "What time it is." With adolescents, humor becomes somewhat more sophisticated—at least in the sense that they are not so literal-minded. Also, formal operational thinking opens the way for intellectual debate, conceptual thoughts, and reflective observation. It is a new way of experiencing the world that is quite exciting in its possibilities—and simultaneously overwhelming because of these possibilities.

This shift does not happen overnight. It typically begins around age eleven or twelve and becomes the dominant way of thinking around age fourteen. Thus, your teenager's inconsistent behaviors and attitudes are often the result of rapid switches between concrete and abstract thinking. These are the times when you can have an intellectually interesting and satisfying conversation with your daughter only to turn around and hear her whining like an eight-year-old about not wanting to eat her broccoli. Ninth-grade teachers see this process daily.

> I never had the words to put to this phenomenon before understand-
> ing these oscillations between concrete and formal thinking. In ten
> years of teaching eighth grade English, I've seen a lot of inconsisten-
> cies that I intuitively knew the kids couldn't control, but I never knew
> why. At first, I took it as a professional insult when students couldn't
> replicate their verbal insights about literature into equally insightful
> essays. Then I thought they were just lazy. But one day, after watching a
> particularly earnest student struggle painfully with an essay, I realized
> that he just couldn't do it, no matter how hard he tried! Since then I've
> learned to keep my tests and quizzes fairly concrete for the first part
> of this year, gradually making the shift to ideas and motives over the
> course of the year.

These frequent shifts between concrete and formal thinking can also help explain some of your adolescent's school difficulties. For instance, since all adolescents progress at somewhat different rates, a ninth-grade science class like biology that depends on a certain amount of abstract thinking will, theoretically, be within reach of the kids who have firmly established abstract thinking but be just out of reach of those who haven't yet fully made the shift. Thus, if your child experiences surprising difficulties in a class like this during the ninth grade, it often isn't just a matter of his not working hard enough or socializing too much with friends. Sometimes, his current stage of cognitive development is the problem. (Indeed, the timing of this shift to abstract thinking is one of the reasons many high schools have changed the progression of science courses, now starting first with conceptual physics and then moving onto biology later.)

Abstract thinking brings with it a new relationship to time. To a child, the future is very short-term. Children ask, "What's for dinner?" or "What's on TV tonight?" In this stage, the future is limited to concrete possibilities. Thus, a question like "What do you want to be when you grow up?" can be answered. Adolescents, on the other hand, are more interested in the question "What kind of person do you want to be when you grow up?" Adolescents who have firmly grasped abstract thinking can imagine the future in the present, reflect upon the past, and weigh the short-term losses and the long-term gains of certain decisions as they relate to an imagined future. They can also manipulate ideas in their heads without acting upon them physically. Before adolescence, action is thinking and thinking is action; during adolescence, thinking needs minimal action, because the thinker enters the realm of ideas and imagination. Thus, when adolescents sit in their rooms for several hours listening to music, seemingly lost to humanity, they might actually be using their newfound skills—which are not, unfortunately, as visible to parents as the skills needed to ride a bicycle. (Recall the mother and son dialogue in the preface and the son's insistence that he needed music to "relax.")

This developing self-consciousness that comes with abstract thinking is both a blessing and a curse. The blessing is the ability to learn from events without painful repetition, that is, to extrapolate a lesson from a single instance and apply it to a multitude of similar cases. For example, once students stumble through the various unwritten social mores of high school, they learn these implicit norms of behavior in other settings without having to go through the entire process each time. The curse of self-consciousness is that it also becomes a tool for self-disparagement and guilt, some of which is necessary but much of which is excessive. This means that teenagers not only experience pain in the moment, but they can also reexperience pain for a long time afterward. Even worse, they can reexperience neutral events from other perspectives that put their actions in the worst light. For instance, in replaying the events of a previous night's party, most adults remember the good and the bad parts, though they tend to give relatively too much importance to the faux pas. Adolescents do the same thing, but in the extreme. After all, they are relatively inexperienced with self-consciousness. Thus, they tend to exaggerate the negative to the point of, at times, blinding themselves to the positive. These are the kinds of things they're thinking about when they sit in their rooms, listening to music.

A senior in high school, Nick Parker, summarized this nicely in an article for his school newspaper (*Devils' Advocate*, University High School, San Francisco, California):

> When I get home, I have had a full day of school, and usually a lot has happened. I often sit around for a while, and think about what has happened. I sit there and analyze everything I said and did. I try to figure out what I did wrong and what I did right. I try to discover more about the people I talked to that day. What did she mean by that? Did he know I was just kidding? Did I hit a sore spot, or was she just generally pissed off? These are just basic questions that go through my head.

So much goes on in my head, and no stone is left unturned. That school day cannot be resolved until everything has been completely settled in my mind.

Basically, I cannot do any work until I have dealt with what has happened. Usually this means I have a late start on my work, thus putting me in a position where I have to skip a bit on my homework.

This is where stress comes in. Some people think that their homework must be done, and what they did in school that day shouldn't be dealt with until all their homework is done. When your personal thoughts have not been settled, work is probably the worst thing you can possibly do to relax; hence stress is created.

To sum up, this shift into abstract thinking, accompanied by a rush of hormonal changes, can (and often does) change a person overnight. Imagine waking up in a body that has new physical dimensions and new sexual desires, with a mind that conceptualizes the world in drastically new ways and that carries an overwhelming sense of confusion about all these feelings—all without prior warning! This is the world of the adolescent.

Horizon 2: Social

The social horizon encompasses the social pulls and issues of the adolescent's public world: the people they hang out with, the events they frequent, and the behaviors they engage in or don't engage in.

In high school, the social world takes on a new meaning. For a few teenagers, it becomes the focus of their existence and their means of maintaining and gaining prestige. For others, it becomes the bane of their existence. But for the majority of teenagers, the social world is an intermittent focus in their high school years and beyond.

In middle school, the social mandate is to fit in. The goal of most kids this age is to feel comfortable with, and accepted by, a group of friends. However, in this group, they cannot usually "be themselves" but must instead abide by the group's unspoken rules.

I was getting a slice of pizza, and ahead of me in line were three boys who were about thirteen years old. They all had low-top black sneakers with white socks; knee-length, baggy black shorts; faded T-shirts (two white and one black); skateboards with lots of Day-Glo decals; and the same buzz cuts with slightly longer hair on top. Nothing unusual here, except that after a couple of minutes I noticed the faded writing on the back of one of the T-shirts: "Dare to Be Unique!" That sums up early adolescence: dare to be unique, as long as you have two or three other people to do it with.

This horizon changes quite a bit in the high school years. In middle school, it is important that teenagers have a group to hang out with. Minimally, this means that they have people to eat lunch with and people they communicate with occasionally outside of school. Maximally, this means a set social life in which the established group they belong to makes decisions on parties, clothes, group members, and so on. While most adolescents fit in between the extremes, some do not. For the teenagers who never find a group in which they feel reasonably secure, these years can be painful. The horizon of the social life can consume them, and they may neglect other areas. They either obsess on how to join a social group or decide they don't need a group, either way feeling the acute pain of loneliness and blaming themselves for their perceived failure to fit in. These are not joyful alternatives, especially in the context of developing self-consciousness.

The social world is also where race and ethnic issues begin to surface. In grammar school, kids make friends and spend time with peers regardless of race or economic status. Such differences have little meaning to children. This continues through most of middle school, with one area of notable exception: racial and ethnic slurs. This occurs especially in seventh grade, when students are testing all sorts of norms. Digging deeper, however, one often (not always) learns that these kids do not really understand what these words mean:

> I just never knew what "faggot" meant. I mean I heard it lots of times, but I don't know, I guess I just thought it was an insult. I really didn't know it had any particular meaning.

Or, some will use these slurs as a way of attempting to deepen connections with acquaintances or friends, the idea being that we are so close we can call each other names nobody else could get away with.

> A couple of my friends are black and I have heard them use the N-word with each other—not lots, but sometimes. It seemed cool between them, so I tried it one day. They looked at me strangely, but never said anything so I thought it was fine. It was only a few months later, when we were walking home, that Stanley (one of my black friends) told me how much it bothered him. I was shocked.

This all changes in high school when teenagers notice these differences and are affected by them.

Let's begin with race. Adolescents are wrestling with questions of personal identity (described in detail later in this chapter), and as they turn away from parents, some turn to their ethnic roots as a source of confirmation and information. For many, this is an eye-opening experience; a blinder is now peeled back as they start to understand their lives through their cultural roots. At the same time, ethnic differences begin to assert themselves in the selection—and exclusion—of peers and activities.

> In middle school, I [African American student] hung out with a white guy and two Mexican guys. We were all best friends. We did all sorts of things together: ate lunch, hung out after school, played sports, and watched movies together. But when we got to high school, everything sort of changed without any of us talking about it. It just wasn't the thing to do anymore. We all made new friends and pretty much didn't spend time with each other anymore. I mean, we still say "hi" and play on some of the same teams and everything, but we're definitely not best friends anymore. It is kind of weird that way.

Such ethnic conformity, which is often the implicit norm in many American high schools, simply reflects contemporary society. Some teenagers, however, perceive how race is affecting them and their choice of friends. These students are able to decide to make diversity a criterion in their selection. That is, they intentionally move out of their comfort zone to seek out differences in friends.

> It really hit me in the cafeteria one day. I looked around and suddenly realized that all the blacks were in one corner, the Latinos in another, the Asians in another, and the whites in yet another. It was like there were these invisible dividing lines running through the cafeteria! From

that point on I decided to cross the line as much as possible. I don't want to limit my choices in friends that way.

While ethnic differences are obvious and yet still difficult to address, economic differences are even more elusive for teenagers. Part of the difficulty with both issues is that most teenagers are clear on their intellectual and idealistic stances about race and economics, but cannot reconcile this idealism with the reality of their personal, day-to-day lives. Nevertheless, both issues permeate adolescent culture.

> I don't remember money being a big deal at all in middle school, but in high school it sure is. Well, not the money itself, but what it allows you to do, and by that, who you are friends with. I don't hang around any of my middle school friends anymore, mainly because of money, though I'm pretty sure they don't know that. Actually, I'm not really sure what they think. Once we got in high school, they got into doing all these things that cost a lot of money: skiing on weekends, buying clothes at fancy stores, going to lots of movies, and buying the latest computer games and computers. It was no big deal for them; they just sort of took it for granted. But it was a big deal for me; I can't afford to do any of those things on a regular basis. And when I do, I feel guilty asking my parents for the money because I can see how much it hurts them (whether they say yes or no). And I'm not old enough yet to get a job. So at first I just made up a lot of excuses as to why I couldn't do things with those friends—you know, like babysitting or visiting relatives, that kind of thing. Anyway, over time I found that I didn't have much to talk to them about, since we weren't doing the same things on weekends anymore. Then they stopped asking me to do things with them. I don't blame them. I mean, I said no practically every time. So now I still talk to them and things, but we're not really good friends anymore.

Then there is the subset of adolescents from divorced families who are in joint custody arrangements and constantly move between two very different economic (and sometimes ethnic) worlds.

> Moving between my parents' houses is really bizarre. Basically, my dad shafted my mom in the divorce. He has this big, expensive house with just about everything you can imagine: a hot tub and pool, a housekeeper

and gardener, and an amazing stereo and television system. I don't really
know what he does other than run some sort of computer company.
On the other hand, my mom works as a secretary (she never worked
while they were married because he didn't want her to!). She lives in a
third-story apartment with one and a half bedrooms—guess which one
is mine. It is culture shock every time I go from one house to another! I
mean, in one house I have more than a hundred DVDs, and in the other
we don't even have a DVD player. It really pisses me off. But I'm not sure
who I'm more pissed at: my father for shafting my mother so badly, or
my mother for letting him do that to her so easily.

Like ethnicity, economics is a means of asserting independence for some
teenagers. For students who have jobs during high school, work is a means of
taking control of their lives, because they now have money to spend as they
choose.

The social group is also an important place for self-discovery; eventually, teenagers will learn to step back from the group to make their own decisions and to begin taking conscious control of their lives. But they can only
step back from the group after being a member of it. As adolescents begin
asserting their independence from their parents, the "safe place" of the social
group takes on more and more importance. This group gives them an initial
place to break away to, rather than breaking away from the family and into an
abyss. The importance and draw of the social group are most obvious when,
for one reason or another, a parent disapproves of certain friends or groups of
people. Articulating this disapproval to the teenager invites disaster, and not
articulating this disapproval invites self-criticism.

I know Sean is a good kid. It's just that some of the people he hangs
around with worry me. I don't imagine they are a very good influence
on him. But whenever I mention this to him, he gets very defensive and inevitably storms out of the room. I don't know what to do.
Whenever I say anything, we argue, but if I don't say anything, I feel
like a lousy parent.

As we'll see in more detail a bit later, directly voicing disapproval often
pushes the adolescent closer to the disapproved-of friend. In these instances,
maintaining the friendship is a means of asserting independence from parents.
Unfortunately, it often precludes teenagers from making their own decisions

about the friendship and acting accordingly. If parents can contain their anxiety about the friendship, they create the reflective space adolescents need to make their own decisions. This technique works for a range of subjects, as we'll see throughout the text. For example:

> After junior year, my daughter decided to go back East for a month to visit her paternal grandmother. While she was making plans, I stressed how much her grandmother would appreciate a gift. It didn't have to be anything expensive, just something thoughtful. I even offered to help pay for it. Well, as she procrastinated in her preparations, I got pretty anxious about this gift. But whenever I came near the subject, Linda bristled. The day before she left, I couldn't take it anymore. I approached her, determined to ask directly about the gift. But before I could get it out, she pulled a lovely brooch from her bag and sincerely (and with a fair amount of pride) asked if I thought Grandmother would like it. Needless to say, when she asked what I wanted to talk about, I suddenly managed to "forget."

Horizon 3: Friendship

While the horizon of friendship is an aspect of the previous section, it is also much more than the social world and thus deserves special attention. As adolescents grow older, intimate friendship becomes a more vital aspect of their lives. Friendship is the secure environment in which teenagers can experiment with new behaviors and ways of being; they can learn about themselves through the feedback and reflected appraisals of trusted friends; they can learn how to accept their friends' flaws; they can discover the type of friend they are and the type of friends they want to have; and they can learn the important skills of friendship: support, vulnerability, empathy, honesty, trust, and responsibility. Adolescence, by nature, is a very self-centered time of life, and it is through friendship and concern for others' well-being that this focus on self is punctured—and supplemented with compassion and empathy.

The potential benefits of friendship for the adolescent are profound. My dissertation, on the best friendship in eleven-year-old boys, gave me great insight into all that was in play in these relationships.[2] First, the boys felt unselfconscious with one another and were therefore more open to learning about themselves and the world around them. That is, they were open to feedback.

> It's easy for me to try new things with Paul, because I know he won't make fun of me or laugh at me. So I do stuff with him that I would never do with other kids. He can even tell me things that are hard to hear, but that are true. Like once I was complaining about a grade I got in a class, and after a while he just said, "Stop complaining so much. All you need to do is study harder." And he was right.

Second, the friendship taught them how to resolve interpersonal conflicts. They learned how to compromise and listen to others' views.

> Yeah, sometimes we disagree on things, but nothing very serious. Usually, it's over something stupid. But once we talk about it, we can each usually understand the other's point. Then we can put it behind us and forget about it.

These qualities of unselfconscious expression, giving and accepting feedback, taking personal responsibility and resolving conflicts are vital skills in successfully navigating the teenage years. All are potentially present in strong friendships. Close friendships take the pressure off the family, encouraging the adolescent to leave childhood behind and move gracefully into the adult world. It is inevitable that as children enter adolescence they turn toward friends and away from parents.

The overlap between the friendship and social horizons is also a breeding ground for peer pressure. Most adults fear that peer pressure will persuade their child to take dangerous risks. To understand why certain risky behaviors are worthwhile for adolescents takes a little digging on the part of parents. The main consequence of saying no to negative peer pressure is not just withstanding "the heat of the moment," as most adults think. Rather, it is coping with a sense of exclusion as others engage in the behavior and leave the adolescent increasingly alone. It is the loss of the shared experience. Further, the sense of exclusion remains whenever the group later recounts what happened. This feeling of loneliness then becomes pervasive but carries an easy solution—go along with the crowd. Psychiatrist Harry Stack Sullivan called loneliness the single most important organizing factor of the adolescent and adult individual, and by this he meant that the fear of loneliness organized people to avoid it at almost any cost, as the following examples illustrate —the first from middle school the second from high school.

> One of my friends liked to go into corner stores and steal whatever he could get his hands on. He was popular in the group, so a couple of the other kids started doing it to. Before I knew what was happening, they were teasing me about being the only one not to steal. They kept chal-lenging me to join their "club." Finally, it got so bad that I stole some-thing, just to keep them quiet. I even went back to the store the next day and put it back on the shelf. I hated it.

> I used to not drink at parties. I don't even like the taste of alcohol, so it wasn't all that difficult. Besides, nobody really made a big deal about it. But then, over time, as my friends began to drink more, it got kind of boring. I couldn't relate to what they were doing and laughing about because I was still sober. For a while, I just left the parties early with no big fanfare. But, more and more, I would be left out of the second "party"—the blow-by-blow account of everything that had happened after I had left. All of a sudden, I began to feel more apart from my friends. I was lonely, even though I had several "good" friends. Anyway, that's why I started drinking and continued to drink throughout most of last year. I wanted to belong again.

Horizon 4: Personal Identity

Amid this swirl of cognitive and physical changes, and along with the social and friendship issues, is perhaps the most consuming of all adolescent tasks: self-definition. Adolescents are constantly in the process of defining, to themselves and to the world, just who they are and what they stand for. Obvi-ously, this is a lifelong process, but few adolescents appreciate this timetable. Rather, they expect to answer the question "Who am I?" with the black-and-white thinking of the past.

As teenagers discover who they are, parents can expect to witness lots of experimentation with roles. Initially, this is a very external process. Clothes are the most obvious and simplest way to begin this role exploration. For instance, your daughter may suddenly dress herself only in black. Or, your son may insist upon a very particular type of jeans or shoes. Or, perhaps your daughter will dye her hair in a rather dramatic color or your son will pierce his ear. Most of these behaviors are part of the process of self-discovery, as well as of self-expression. None, in themselves, are to be feared. They are, however, attention-getters (and precursors to what is a more internal and subtle process as adolescents get older). Giving some curious attention to these actions can go a long way in understanding your teenager's world. Besides, at this point, negative or fearful attention will only force her hand into going further (this is similar to what happens when you criticize her friends). Your curiosity, which may be tinged with skepticism, lets your daughter know that you've noticed and offers her the space to arrive at her own conclusions, which, in most cases, will help move her along in the process of experimentation as she creates her sense of personal identity. It's also your chance to help her move from the literal to the conceptual—in this example from the style of dress to the creative mind.

> That's quite an outfit you put together, very creative and unique. I like seeing this creative part of you coming out. It feels good when it clicks, doesn't it? Stick with it.

Along with visible external changes comes an even greater number of internal shifts. As teenagers experiment with different external roles, they must attempt to reconcile these roles with their internal states. For example, your son may choose to play the "jock" role for a while. This helps direct him in dress, friends, activities, and attitude. But at some point he will do an internal check: "Is this me? Does this external image match what I am inside? Is there more to me than this image can contain?" Of course, these questions are part of an evolution that adults accept as lifelong. But to adolescents this process is new, and they think they should be able to find ready answers.

> Summer was so terrific, and I had such high expectations for school, but so far this has been an awful year. Over the summer, I worked at a restaurant with mostly college students and hung out with them in cafés drinking coffee between shifts. It was terrific. They really listened to me and were interested in what I had to say. We talked about life, relationships, politics, and important things. I felt so mature, so in control of my life. But I've lost that since school began. It's like nobody is interested. My parents treat me like a little kid with all sorts of silly restrictions. My friends just want to pick up right where sophomore

> year left off. Everybody is in their own little world and I'm lost! Worst
> of all, I either fall back into my old ways or I stay home alone, miser-
> ably depressed. Actually, I'm depressed either way! How come I can't be
> myself anymore? This really sucks.

For most adolescents, this search for themselves is a relentless two-steps-forward, one-step-backward process. And it is difficult for parents to tell where their adolescent is at any given moment.

Personal identity also involves spiritual explorations and questions—this is most commonplace in sophomore year. If raised in an organized religion, adolescents often begin questioning their faith, perhaps even breaking with it. On the other hand, those who are not raised within a religion may seek some sort of belief system, both as a means of self-determination and as a source of solace in difficult times. Some teenagers will explore various modes of spirituality, such as spirituality of nature, without embracing a formal religion. Still others explore a spirituality of community—witness the Grateful Dead phenomenon of the 1960s and '70s. None of these are necessarily good or bad; often they are simply changes, frequently in a different direction from the family. In this sense, exploring and developing personal identity is a two-step process, with the first step defining "who you are not" (which in most cases is your parents), and then moving toward defining who and what you are.

Another important aspect of personal identity is gender. As research shows, boys and girls have quite different educational experiences. Briefly, when boys and girls move from elementary to middle school, both experience a drop in self-esteem; however, girls experience a disproportionately larger drop that stays constant throughout high school. This is alarming. While the solutions are not easy, there are some things that parents can do. First, it is important to maintain the same expectations for girls and boys, especially in the kinds of careers they choose. In this arena, teachers must also maintain the same expectations for both sexes, and they need to encourage and insist that girls stay actively involved in class discussions. Without attention and consistent invitation to participate, girls' class participation often decreases over the four years of high school.[3]

> It's really kind of strange. I [senior girl] remember that during seventh,
> eighth, and tenth grades friends always used to kid me about talking
> so much in class. I had an opinion about everything and wasn't shy
> about letting people know it. I even used to disagree and argue with

my teachers during class, and I was often right! But during junior year,
I somehow got timid, and started speaking less and less. Now [senior
year] I hardly talk at all—I'm so afraid of saying the wrong thing and
making a fool of myself. It's just easier to stay in the background and
listen to what everybody else says—they all seem so sure of themselves.

Second, it is essential for girls to have female role models who are successful across a variety of professions. Boys and girls develop differently, and,
as a result, girls need female models of success, rather than trying to succeed
through the male process of success.

Conversely, while we are focused on helping girls to find, use, and trust
their voices, we are seeing that boys have their own trials and tribulations at
school. Recent statistics on the educational experiences of boys and girls are
pointing out that girls outperform boys at every level of schooling—elementary
through college. In addition, boys are five times more likely to be diagnosed
with ADHD than girls.

As parents, this means we need to maintain high expectations for our
sons as well as work with them on delayed gratification, which is discussed in
chapter 8. We also need to pay attention to how they are using technology with
a sense of how it plays into ADHD-like behavior, which is also discussed in
chapter 8. Finally, we need to advocate for them in schools, especially in envi-
ronments that ask them to sit passively for forty-five minutes at a time, all day.

Adolescence is a time when teenagers are beginning to wrestle with their
value systems, needing to try out a variety of approaches rather than accepting their parents' verbalized values. While necessarily drifting from parents'
values, teenagers are simultaneously noticing the differences in what their
parents say and do. And when push comes to shove, they will point this out to
you—usually without much tact. Teenagers are very observant, and they now
trust their eyes more than their ears. What you do affects your kids' values
more than what you say.

I know I'm supposed to tell the truth and face the consequences and
everything. But it's not like my parents are any more responsible than
I am. They're pretty hypocritical, which really pisses me off! . . . Like
they're constantly on me to tell them exactly what time I'll be home.
They even hold me to the minute! But when they have to pick me up or
take me somewhere they are never on time. Just the other day I asked
my mother to give me a ride to meet a friend at a movie theater, and

she said fine. Well, when it was time to leave, she was on the phone and even though I told her we had to leave, she kept on talking. Of course, I got there late and didn't get to sit with my friend—we didn't even see each other until the lights went on when the movie was over! My mother couldn't understand why I was so upset. She said she was sorry, but then she expected everything to be fine, like it hadn't been a problem at all!

So does this mean you have to be perfect? Not at all. It does, however, imply that you are responsible for yourself. Adolescents don't need perfect parents; in fact, they are probably better off with less-than-perfect parents (who are more reflective of the real world). But they do need parents who acknowledge their own faults and shortcomings as well as their values and strengths. This parental responsibility creates space for the adolescent. When parents don't accept responsibility for their own actions, the teenager gets stuck with the blame. That is, when you don't clean up your messes by apologizing for an overreaction or harsh words, your teenager holds on to all those bad feelings. And nobody holds on to blame gracefully, especially when it isn't rightfully theirs. Thus adolescents begin, subtly, to learn various attitudes of irresponsibility. They become pseudo-responsible: they learn how to justify themselves, how to avoid acknowledging fault, and how to place blame on others, both appropriately and inappropriately. However, when parents accept responsibility for themselves and their actions, adolescents have room to be more honest with themselves. They learn to first acknowledge their own faults, which allows them to improve themselves and ultimately to define themselves and feel more in charge of their lives. This is essential to developing a strong and secure personal identity. However, this is not an overnight process. Developing responsibility takes time and a fair amount of trial and error. (See chapter 7 for more on this topic.)

Horizon 5: Family and Life Events

Teenagers' relationships to various members of their family are a significant backdrop to all that they do. This backdrop includes family history, expectations (both explicit and implicit), and family composition. Significant events in a family's history, such as divorce, death, a prolonged illness, or economic crisis, shape many of an adolescent's decisions, choices, and attitudes. If the event happened prior to adolescence, issues related to it will very likely resurface, usually during times of stress. I remember well one student who used to come by my office just prior to exams, at the end of first and second semesters. Her first visit was before first semester exams in her sophomore year and her last was just before graduation. She usually came by for one or two meetings at a time. Beginning with the first visit, and with all subsequent visits, she talked exclusively about her parents' divorce when she was eight years old. She never mentioned anything about exams. And with each meeting she picked up exactly where she had left off—whether it had been a week or four months since the last visit. In this manner, she reinterpreted the experience of the divorce as an adolescent. That is, with her more-developed thinking and relationship skills, she needed to and did develop a more complex and thorough understanding of the divorce and its effects on her.

All of us have what I call "stress buffer zones." Under ordinary circumstances, we can tolerate added levels of stress without significant ramifications. But when, because of past or current traumas, the stress buffer zone is partially used up, teenagers are quite vulnerable to both new and old stresses (see diagram 1). Adolescents are most susceptible at fairly predictable times: exams, proms, beginnings and endings of romances, anniversaries of traumatic events, and holidays, to name a few.

Diagram 1: Stress Buffer Zone

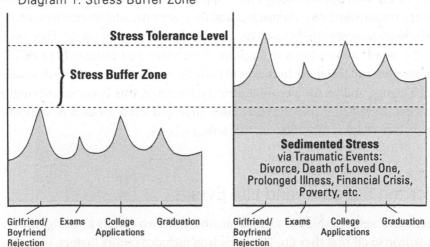

These are the times when an old event is most likely to come up for reexamination, both consciously and unconsciously. If it surfaces consciously, the teenager might talk or write about the event, ask questions for clarification,

or reflect on the event in introspective moods. If the event surfaces unconsciously, the adolescent might show unwarranted moodiness, "act out" nega-
tively, or make sudden significant changes in eating or sleeping patterns.
We'll come back to some of these events and how adolescents deal with them
later in the text; for now, it suffices to say that teenagers see the world differently than they did as children, and it is only natural and healthy that they
reexplore significant events from the past.

Back to family relationships: in the early adolescent's world, parental
expectations set the standard for pleasing or "good enough" behaviors. These
expectations cover the areas of grades, looks, extracurricular activities, habits, friends, and so on. They become clear to the teenager in primarily two
ways. The first is in explicit priorities stated by parents: attitudes like working
hard, being honest, telling the truth, getting good grades, living a balanced
life, and taking responsibility for one's actions. The second way expectations
become clear is implicit, learned by watching what parents (and other family
members) do, regardless of what they say. These realizations are confusing,
but necessary, for the adolescent (recall the "Friendship" section). They begin
to see their parents as real people—complete with human foibles, inconsis-
tencies, and bad habits. This realization is at first terrifying. Suddenly, the
people who several years earlier seemed omnipotent are exposed as really no
different from the rest of the adult world or from the teenager—except that
the parents are older and more experienced.

> It's really weird. When I was a little kid, I wanted to be just like my dad;
> I thought he was perfect. But then one day reality hit like a sledgeham-
> mer. We were at the hardware store together and when we went to pay
> the cashier, she overcharged him. He said something, and she got all
> upset and acted like a jerk. She even called him an asshole under her
> breath. But instead of standing up to her, he just said "forget it" and
> paid the overcharge! On top of that, he apologized on the way out! I
> couldn't believe it—he had wimped out. It completely blew my mind,
> and I was pissed for quite a while. When he asked me what was wrong,
> I couldn't say anything. I mean, what am I going to say—"No, noth-
> ing's wrong with me, Dad, the problem is that you're a wimp"? That was
> probably the worst part. He didn't even get it.

Now, for the first time, many adolescents feel truly alone, and may for a
brief while turn on their parents in angry rejection for being human. They

are scared and vulnerable. And if vulnerability isn't safe, anger is the easiest alternative. In anger, one is active and seemingly in charge, instead of being in the more passive and potentially humiliating state of vulnerability. And teenagers, more than any other age group, will go to extremes to avoid humiliation and vulnerability.

If parents can accept this fall from grace as inevitable rather than a personal attack, then they can learn a great deal about themselves. After all, some of this adolescent feedback hits the bull's-eye. This change is also a clear sign that the parent-adolescent relationship needs to become more consultant and less managerial. If this shift can happen, family relationships become fertile ground for the teenager to learn compassion and acceptance.

While many of these contradictions in a parent's behavior are fully human and fairly harmless, some are quite damaging, mainly because they inadvertently reinforce adolescents' negative beliefs about themselves.

> Well, you know how hyperconscious I am of my weight. And I was getting much better lately about not picking myself apart. That is, until last night. Sometimes I just can't believe that my parents are either so stupid or so mean. I took a break from studying at around nine and went downstairs for a snack. There wasn't much, but there was some ice cream in the freezer. So I made a small bowl for myself. It was really not that much. As I was walking up the stairs, I passed my father, who eyed the ice cream, looked at me, and again looked at the ice cream. Then he said, "Are you sure you want to be eating that? If you're not careful, the fat will sneak up on you!" He said it in a joking way, but it felt like criticism. I just gritted my teeth and went to my room. A little later I sneaked down and finished all the ice cream, just to spite him! But ever since then I've had a guilt hangover. There is no way I can win. And I'm right back to thinking I'm fat again.

Family composition also plays a vital role in how teenagers perceive themselves and how parents perceive them. The eldest child tends to be the trailblazer in the family. Thus, the eldest child and the parents enter the uncharted territory of adolescence together. With the next child, parents believe, often erroneously, that what worked with the first child will work again. Younger kids have the advantage and the disadvantage of entering charted territory with parents. At least parents have an idea of what to expect; on the other hand, they may be blind to essential differences between children. Also, if the eldest child was very successful (or very unsuccessful) at living up to the parents' expectations, the younger child feels pressure to do the same: Do I attempt to outdo my older sibling? Do I not even attempt that set of expectations and instead carve out my own niche? Or do I play it safe and stay average: "Nothing ventured, nothing lost"?

> It's very frustrating. My older sister was a real sneak. She got in all sorts of trouble. By the time she graduated, she had been caught skipping school too many times to count, had been caught stealing an exam, and had gotten arrested for drinking and driving! But the problem is I'm nothing like her—and my parents refuse to see that. They are watching me and waiting for me to screw up. When I try to talk to them about this, the only answer I get is that they're not making the same mistake twice. I wish they could see that I'm a pretty good kid and deserve a little trust. I don't stand a chance until I get out of this place.

Or the teenager may have the problem of living up to an older sibling's successes.

> My sister and brother were real stars in high school: she was an All-State soccer player and he was valedictorian of his class. But I'm not like either one of them. I'm average at both sports and school, and that's fine with me. Really! I'm much more focused on people. In fact, all of my friends turn to me for help with their problems. Even though I'm a peer counselor for the school, my parents don't seem to notice. They're just always on me to get better grades and to do better in sports. Ninety percent of our fights have to do with them pushing sports and academics down my throat.

Then there are the only children, who frequently carry the weight of the entire family's expectations. Because they can't see how siblings are treated, they frequently personalize nonpersonal events.

> I love my parents and everything—it's just that sometimes it's too intense with just the three of us. It's like they notice everything about me! And if something goes wrong for me or we have a fight, it's like a national disaster. Like when I didn't get a role in the school play, they treated me like they expected me to have a nervous breakdown

or something! I mean I was disappointed, but not nearly as much as they were. It was so weird that for a while I thought something was really wrong with me for not feeling worse about not getting a part! Sometimes I wish they had had another kid; it would take a lot of the pressure off me. But then again, when I'm in the right mood, I like all their attention.

Finally, in any family, there is always the dynamic created when the last child leaves home. Aside from what the adolescent goes through (discussed later in the book), this change deeply affects all parents. Now, after raising children for the past eighteen to thirty years, they must again focus on their relationship with one another.

> My parents have been a little edgy with each other lately, and I think some of it has to do with my going to college next year. I'm the youngest, so after I leave it's just the two of them. They've focused so much energy on me and my two brothers that I think they're a little unsure of what to do with all that energy once I leave. I know they still care for and enjoy each other, but still, some things are going to change.

And, these realizations are even more complicated for teenagers raised by single parents.

> Going away to college is going to be tough on my mom. I'm a little worried about her. Ever since my dad left [ten years ago], it has just been the two of us. She's been great, but she's been so obsessed with what's best for me that I'm not sure she'll know what's best for her once I leave. I know she hates her job—the only reason she keeps it is so that we can live in this big apartment and so I can go to private school. So I'm not sure what she'll do when she has the freedom to quit and start another career. Also, we've been like best buddies the last couple of years, and I'm worried that she doesn't have many friends to talk to once I leave.

Ideally, the family is the taproot that supports the adolescent through the winds, breezes, and periodic gales of adolescence. A strong and acknowledged parental commitment to their adolescent along with the determination to let her grow into her own person is what every teenager needs. There may

be times when you don't believe it, but you and your feelings about your teenager are very important to her.

> My parents were great throughout high school. They always let me
> know that they love me, even when I was being impossible. They were
> also always willing to hear the truth about my life, even if they didn't
> agree with what I was doing. We talked openly about tough issues like
> alcohol and sex, and they weren't afraid to let me know exactly what
> they thought, though they gave me the room to make my own mistakes.
> But when things were the worst with friends, boys, and school, I knew
> I could always count on my parents, even if they disagreed with how I
> was handling the situation.

The Logic of Adolescence

At this point, each horizon has been illustrated with examples of its influence
on adolescent behavior. But clearly, the horizons are not distinct; each over-
laps and competes with another. Thus, adolescent decisions are not always
what they appear to be. A teenager may make a decision out of free will and
then change his mind when he discovers he is doing what his parents prefer.
Thus, he may do the opposite of what he wants simply to assert his independence from his parents. Unfortunately, he buys this sense of independence at
a high price, unwittingly giving up the confidence and personal power that
come with making the choice he wants. It gets complicated quickly.

Let's ground all this in concrete terms by returning to the example at the
outset of this chapter (see page 8). What could have made Sheila, the moody
adolescent, act the way she did from Saturday afternoon to Sunday morning? Several explanations may apply. From a social perspective, she may have
been worried about being included with her friends in their Saturday evening
plans. Thus, she was anxiously waiting for the phone invitation and couldn't
offer a simple yes or no response to her dad's question about the car. To
answer him would mean exposing her social vulnerability to her dad at a time
when it was causing her a great deal of anxiety. And since for most adolescents it is easier to be angry than vulnerable, Sheila simply directed her anxiety back at her father (and later her mother) in the form of anger. But why the

sudden mood change on Sunday? Perhaps at volleyball practice she learned that all the plans fell through and everyone stayed home for the evening, so she wasn't left out after all.

From a romantic perspective, perhaps Sheila had said no to her friends in order to leave the door open to say yes to a guy she hoped would call and ask her out. Or, maybe she left the door open to phone the guy herself and ask him out, or at least talk on the phone for a while. Thus, her angry responses to her parents might stem from her doubt and the tenuousness of her plans. She could end up empty-handed—home with her parents on a Saturday night. And what about the change on Sunday morning? After not hearing from the guy on Saturday evening, she may have heard from her friends (who also play on the volleyball team and who saw the guy in question at a party the night before) how he had asked them all about Sheila and had really hoped she would be at the party with them.

From a sexual perspective (addressed more fully in chapter 9), perhaps Sheila had had sex several weeks ago and on Saturday was over a week late with her period. She would then be extremely anxious and wouldn't know where to turn: Should she turn to her parents, to the guy involved, to her friends, or to Planned Parenthood on her own? Should she go out or not? And Sunday—well, she got her period at volleyball practice.

From a family perspective, perhaps her friends were planning on doing something that Sheila wasn't ready for—drugs, drinking, or older guys—and she resented her parents for her doubt and misgivings about going out with her friends. And possibly the next day at volleyball practice she learned that the plans had fallen through miserably or that they were botched and every-one had gotten in big trouble. Either way, she felt good on Sunday about her decision to stay home.

Brainstorming numerous explanations like this shows that all are quite logical. I suggest coming up with four or five viable explanations about your adolescent's behavior before settling on any one, and, in truth, you won't know which (if any) is accurate until sometime in the future. The point is that these possibilities afford you the explanations that adolescents can't yet offer. In turn, the explanations help you handle your anxiety while giving your ado-lescent the space to work through her anxiety. Or, as Ben Furman and Tapani Ahola say in *Solution Talk: Hosting Therapeutic Conversations*, "Uncommon, imaginative explanations are often excellent catalysts for finding solutions."[4]

In Closing

At the conclusion of one of my recent daylong workshops on the nature of adolescence, one of the participants, a very experienced and respected teacher, approached me. He said that he was now more amazed than ever that, given what is happening in teenagers' lives, they learn any math in his class. It is indeed quite a feat. Or, as poet John Ciardi said: "You don't have to suffer to be a poet. Adolescence is enough suffering for anyone."

As we've seen so far, adolescence, at least in this country, is a preordained existential crisis. It is the first such crisis of teenagers' lives; they are unable to put it into the perspective that experience affords. Adults who have that perspective tend to underestimate the impact of various events on teenagers' lives. Flunking a test and getting dumped by a boyfriend or girlfriend within a couple of days is analogous to an adult's losing a job and a spouse in the same time period. While "first loves" are a romantic memory from an adult perspective, they are a traumatic and angst-ridden experience for the adolescent. Remember that adolescence is the process of coming into one's own, but it is by no means a graceful unfolding. It is more like wrestling into one's own.

Many teenagers feel as if they are juggling two lives simultaneously: the leftover kid's and the emerging adult's. Or, as one student put it: "I've been under the influence of confusion ever since I entered high school! When will it stop?" As teenagers develop self-consciousness and the resulting fear of humiliation, parents should think about how to allow teenagers the graceful way out of situations. This is one of the hidden intentions of this book—to help you, the parent, help your teenager develop and maintain grace in a most awkward time of life.

Before moving on, let's take a moment to reexamine the after-school interaction described by the mom in the book's preface—her monosyllabic son, John, coming home after baseball practice at school. If she made use of what was addressed in this chapter, she might have taken a different approach to John. In this regard, when your teenager comes home after school, I suggest thinking like the consummate martial artist. That is, a great martial artist never combats force with force, rather she joins and redirects, eventually using her attackers' energy back on themselves. Here goes.

> MOM (to her son walking in the door after baseball practice): So, how was school today? Anything interesting happen? *Even though she knows he probably won't answer the question, she knows he needs her to show interest.*

SON (as he noses through the refrigerator): Nah, just a typical day. Is there any more orange juice? *This is what she expected, so no disappointment.*

MOM: Uh, no. We finished it this morning. So, nothing exciting in school today . . . oh, didn't you have that history test today? How do you think you did? *Knowing he would be hungry and thirsty, she could have cut him off at the pass by directing him to some other juice or drink in the refrigerator, which would have eliminated the next couple lines of interaction. If she were really graceful, she could even suggest he get a snack and head to his room to relax for a bit—that would leave him perplexed instead of frustrated! And as he headed to his room, she could have capped it off with: "Go ahead, just touch base with your friends, listen to some music, and relax for a while. I'll let you know when dinner is ready, in about 45 minutes." Now, as he closed the door, she would walk back down the hallway with a bounce in her step and a smile on her face. He would take the time that he needs to decompress, though possibly might first search the room for a hidden video camera!*

Now, let's turn our attention to some of the questions asked most frequently by parents. The first deals with the norms of middle school and high school.

Notes

1. Theodore Lidz, *The Person: His Development Throughout the Life Cycle* (New York: Basic Books, 1968) 298.

2. Michael Riera, "A Phenomenological Analysis of Best-Friendship in Preadolescent Boys" (San Francisco: California Institute of Integral Studies, 1992) PhD dissertation.

3. Greenberg-Lake: The Analysis Group, Inc. *Shortchanging Girls, Shortchanging America* (Washington, DC: American Association of University Women, 1991).

4. Ben Furman and Tapani Aloha, *Solution Talk: Hosting Therapeutic Conversations* (New York: W. W. Norton, 1992).

3

The Middle and High School Experience

Is there a pattern of experiences common to all kids during the two or three years of middle school and the four years of high school?

There are some predictable issues that arise during the middle and high school years, though each adolescent navigates these in different ways and at different times. What follows is a rough sketch of middle and high school, year by year, but as always, the only thing you can count on is that your teenager won't follow the pattern exactly. In reading the descriptions of middle and high school back-to-back, you will notice that the developmental pattern of high school is in some ways a redo of middle school—though much more complicated, with abstract thinking and sexuality added to the mix. Middle school lays the foundation for what lies ahead in high school. That is, the better adolescents are able to handle the middle school years, the better prepared they (and we) are for what follows.

The Middle School Years[1]

Sixth Grade

Sixth grade is a constructivist period in every student's life. Because sixth graders are faced with a new school, new faces, and new academic demands, they must construct new and more complex social lives and personal identities based on their successes and failures in elementary school. During this time, they also test out ways for dealing with big-picture issues they will face later in adolescence—they lay the foundation for the person they will become—while simultaneously dealing with the pragmatic details of middle school.

> For just about every sixth grader the biggest single issue during their first week of school is remembering their locker combination and learning how to operate said locker. It never fails. So rather than fight it we've built it into our sixth grade orientation with an hour on "Locker Basics."

Sixth grade is also the time when students face greater demands and higher expectations all around them, from academics to extracurriculars. And, again, they must balance this with the logistics of being a middle school student.

> Honestly, it took me a month just to figure out the darn schedule. For the first few weeks, I just remembered who the kids were in each of my classes and followed them. I actually followed one person into the restroom before I realized he wasn't going to class! It just took a long time to figure out the schedule and where the classrooms were. I still haven't figured out how to remember what books to bring to which class, so I carry just about all my books around with me in my backpack. It hurts my back, but at least I don't get in trouble for not having my book, or worse, look stupid in front of all my classmates.

Fortunately, most middle schools have come to recognize the transition from fifth to sixth grade as a half-step into middle school. For example, instead of a different teacher for each subject, many have combined math and science with one teacher and similarly bundled English and history together as a course in humanities. This combines aspects of elementary school (one teacher for multiple subjects) with middle school (a rotating schedule based on subjects).

One of the underlying goals of all middle schools, and starting in sixth grade, is teaching students organizational skills. This means that schools work to help students develop and train *executive function,* a term you will hear bandied about quite a bit during your child's adolescence. In general, it means achieving skill and control over a variety of cognitive aspects: attention, planning, inhibition, reasoning, and mental flexibility. While this work begins in middle school and continues throughout high school, most people do not reach full executive function until their early twenties. Therefore, when it comes to your sixth grader's organizational skills, or lack thereof, be patient. With time and compassionate persistence, they will develop.

> I've worked as the learning specialist in a middle school for the last seven years and I've found the best way to diagnose students' level of executive functioning is by a close examination of either their backpack or locker. It's all there! Horrifying much of the time, but all there for the curious observer to read. When missing homework assignments (that have been completed but not turned in) show up crushed at the bottom of the student's backpack, you start to wonder whether more than just organizational skills are at play. But for the majority of students, their backpack is the physical manifestation of the process of learning organizational skills through trial and error.

The most frustrating area where the lack of strong organizational skills plays out is with homework. Whether it is not remembering to do the homework assignment in the first place, forgetting assignments at home, losing them between their locker and the classroom, or doing the homework but not turning it in, most middle school students suffer from a lack of organizational skills. Take heart, though—most sixth grade teachers understand this and work closely with their students on developing the skills they need to turn in homework successfully.

> I know that my students roll their eyes at the way I make them color code their notebooks and write down assignments in the same place day after day. They just shake their heads, but they all do it because they know I check it—every day! I also know that these same students come

by to visit once they hit high school to thank me for teaching them how to get and stay organized.

By the end of sixth grade, most students have adapted to the routine of multiple classes with multiple teachers and a larger and more diverse social world. They are ready to emerge from the cocoon of sixth grade.

Seventh Grade

A cliché describes the month of March as coming in like a lion and going out like a lamb. The opposite is true of seventh grade. In this sense, it is a deconstructivist year, when much of what was built in the previous year comes apart. Social connections dissolve—cyberbullying occurs between close friends, respectful students suddenly utter phrases you never imagined coming from their mouths, and limits are tested to the extreme. Seventh grade, for many students, is an extended regression in the service of the ego. That is, much of what has been built up needs to come apart so that it can be reconstructed with a stronger and wider foundation upon which to build their adult personality—a process that begins in eighth grade. Which goes to say, seventh grade is a messy year.

> I was looking forward to seventh grade because sixth grade had been wonderful. I thought it would only get better. Boy, was I wrong! My best friend turned on me, I got suspended for something I didn't do, and my parents just nagged me about my schoolwork the whole time.

Much of what underlies seventh grade has to do with power: What does it feel like to have power and who gets to use it? In general, this plays out differently in boys and girls, but not always. With girls, the power comes out most frequently in their interpersonal relationships. With boys, it plays out most often through physical interactions. And added to this mix is that some boys and girls awkwardly (read: inappropriately) rely on social networking sites like Facebook in their coming to grips with interpersonal power, often with disastrous results. (For more on this, see chapter 8.)

Seventh graders experiment with a coarse version of power, often having to do with how far they can push limits, with friends, family, and school. Sometimes this means being mean to one another.

I don't know why I do it, but giving some kids a hard time makes me feel better about myself, for a little bit at least. It's like a boost of energy. Sometimes I feel bad afterward, but not too often.

This is the harsh reality of this year for parents—kids often try to bolster their self-esteem through disparagement. And then they get good at not letting themselves see or feel the incident from the other person's perspective. It's only when we hold the mirror up to them that the pieces fall together, and they have access to their empathy.

We were driving home from school—after my son got suspended for some awful remarks he made to a classmate. He was sullen in the seat next to me, but I was determined, so I told him we weren't going home until he talked about what happened and answered some of my questions. We drove around for an hour before he finally understood that I was serious. Eventually, he opened up and told me everything that happened. It was worse than I thought. Finally, I asked him how that would feel if someone said all those things to him, and I slowly repeated what he had said to his classmate. I repeated this a couple of times, until I noticed that he was beginning to well up. I pulled over just as the tears started to fall. "Dad, that would be horrible if someone said those things to me! I didn't mean to hurt him. I'm so sorry."

I hear this sort of story more often than you might believe. The average seventh graders' world is so centered around themselves that many do not even realize how much they can and do hurt one another.

They also exercise their power by challenging teachers in inappropriate ways.

I don't know what it is about seventh grade, but all of a sudden it feels like my teachers don't have a clue. All they do is lecture us about not teasing and not talking and not goofing around—the whole year is just a bunch of "not's."

Of course, the irony in all this is that seventh grade is also a year when kids are often hyperfocused on fairness. They are like heat-seeking missiles, finding any and every instance of unfairness on the part of adults to students. Their disapproving anger might be directed at teachers for surprise quizzes or unexpected materials on a test, at administrators for insisting they help pick up trash after lunch even though they already pick up their own stuff, or at coaches for letting some players get extra playing time. In this regard, it's essential to understand their fairness radar points only outward, away from them—they're not yet able to turn the critical eye upon themselves.

Finally, seventh grade is a time when many kids "fire" their parents as managers of their lives, which calls for some quick shifts on the part of parents (who seldom see their termination coming).

> One day everything was normal—she talked to me, helped me around the house, and looked forward to spending time with me. Then the next day it was gone. I think she would rather watch paint peel than be seen in public with me. Worse, she looked at me like everything I said was the dullest or most stupid comment she ever heard. And no matter what I said and how kind I said it, she picked a fight at every turn. She's exhausting, and I'm beginning to understand the concept of boarding school!

Eighth Grade

More similar to sixth than seventh, eighth grade is another constructivist year. This time your child pulls together his or her experiences from middle school to prepare for the next transition into high school. Whether their middle school is part of a larger school or a stand-alone, eighth graders are now the oldest (and biggest) kids in their middle school. They are getting more comfortable with their bodies—most have reached and are well into puberty—and they have a grip on their social world, for better or worse.

> I don't know, it's kind of like I've got it figured out. I mean I graduate in a couple of months, but I'm already bored—I'm ready to start high school. Nervous, but ready.

In general, they soften with one another during this year. Gone are the majority of the mean and hurtful exchanges that occurred in the name of power. In their place are efforts to reconnect with distant friends. It is also the year when sexual relationships become more commonplace. A few friends or classmates may have had relationships in seventh grade, but now in eighth, while still not the norm, it is not so extremely exceptional as it was a year ago.

Last year if someone had a boyfriend it was a big deal, like they were
instant celebrities or something. But this year, well, it's a big deal at
first, but then it's like nobody really pays that much attention.

In the process of reconstructing themselves, some eighth graders are
capable of moments of extreme kindness and care. Whether it is rallying
behind a friend having a tough time, wholeheartedly embracing a service-
learning project, or standing up for a cause they believe in, eighth graders are
capable of compassionate action.

I saw this movie on how cattle are raised and slaughtered so we can
have meat whenever we want it for dinner, and it just got to me. I just
stopped eating meat and started trying to convince my family that we
should all give it up. Not only is it bad for us, but it's inhumane the way
the animals are treated. I even did a science project on how red meat
isn't good for us.

On the minds of most eighth graders is high school, which is just around
the corner. For those not attending the local high school and applying to an
independent or religious school, the transition into high school is even more
complicated. They must apply, risk not getting in, and deal with friends going
to different schools.

Where I live, the public school is not that strong, but there are lots of
other choices for high school. My four best friends and I are all applying
to these private schools, but we won't know until April who gets in and
who is going where. We could all end up at different schools or the same
school, but will probably spread out between a few different schools.
That will be weird. Sad not to have them around, but it will be good to
meet some new people, too. It's all mixed up.

By the end of eighth grade, your relationship with your child has reached
a more even keel, and everyone is looking forward to the new start that high
school provides.

Table 1: Summary of the Middle School Years

	Sixth
Physical and Cognitive	Going through growth spurts; who am I in this sea of new faces?; how does anyone keep track of all these different classes and this crazy schedule?; still grounded in concrete thinking; executive function abilities not up to the challenge.
Social	Lots of new faces and personalities; trying to find a group to be with; who do I eat lunch with?; is anyone else having trouble getting their locker to work?
Friendship	More interested in being around others than in friendship; friendship often an alliance of mutual interest or mutual disparagement of others; I miss my friends from elementary school; or I'm tired of these friends and want to meet some new kids.
Personal Identity	Up for grabs and less important than finding a place to fit in; don't want to stand out from the crowd, so more interested in blending with the various group identities out there.
Family Events	Still close to parents, and often like spending time with them; will cuddle with mom or dad while watching a movie; early signs of your eventual termination as manager.

Seventh	Eighth
Making leaps both physically and cognitively, with some forays into abstract thinking; some huge physical discrepancies between kids, with some well into puberty and others not even close; growth spurts are physically painful, cause awkwardness, and seem even worse because of developing self-consciousness.	Getting more comfortable with their bodies and minds; oldest and biggest in their middle school; more access to abstract thinking and able to reflect on their own behavior more consistently; by the end of eighth grade, feeling they have outgrown middle school both in body and mind.
Testing power in relationships, often physical with boys and interpersonal with girls; both testing the limits of social networking; groups often formed by mutual disparagement of others; dramatic year; What would happen if . . . ?	Having the hang of it now; knowing their way in and around school; at the same time, tired of all the cliques, though they don't do much about it; waiting for ninth grade.
Not sure what friendship is or even who my friends are; trying different types of friends; often with friends, testing traditional family values and limits; what am I looking for in a friend?; can I really trust anyone?; what kind of friend am I?	Friends of a qualitative difference compared to sixth grade; friends take on more meaning, often more meaning than family in determining behavior; a second family.
More clear on who they are not, while simultaneously open to new activities and possibilities; wanting to push identities onto others.	Beginning to question, from a positive place, who they are and who they want to be; still letting activities and friends define them somewhat, but getting an inkling that there is more; looking more to find activities that are meaningful to them.
Parents are typically experienced as an embarrassment, especially when peers are around; you as parents must decide how to handle getting fired; and they send huge mixed messages, late at night still snuggling and at midday glaring across the table.	Much more conciliatory toward family, in part as consolidation of middle school experience and in part due to the thought of high school, where again they will occupy the bottom rung of age and status; if parents make the switch from manager to consultant gracefully, this is a calm period, if not battles loom around every corner.

The High School Years

Ninth Grade

This year begins with the transition from the known world of eighth grade to the unknown world of high school, a transition similar to the move from fifth to sixth, and a precursor to the one from high school to college or work. In eighth grade, your teenager was part of the oldest group of kids in the school. He was familiar with the terrain of the school, knew the faces of his classmates, understood the unspoken rules of the school, and was looked up to by the kids in the lower grades. In ninth grade, the typical teenager is met with a sea of change: an unfamiliar campus, many new faces, a vague understanding of the explicit rules of the school (never mind the implicit ones), and the stress of occupying the lowest rung on the seniority ladder—he is a freshman.

Socially, this means teenagers must get to know and become established with a new group of people. Finding a social niche that includes a safe group to eat lunch with is typically high on the priority list, just as it was in sixth grade.

> By far the worst part of the day during freshman year was lunch. I never knew who I was going to eat with. I didn't have any one set of friends, so I had to decide every day where to eat and who to eat with. Of course, my biggest fear was that I would have to eat alone, which would have been the absolute worst. Honestly, I would start worrying about this at about ten every morning! For a while, I even gave up lunch and just went to the gym to play basketball, but I got too hungry afterward, so that didn't last.

Once ninth graders have found a place to fit in, they begin to search for the place where they can fit in as themselves, a long evolution that often includes moving away from their initial social group.

In ninth grade, there is often a split between boys and girls. The girls typically receive a warmer reception and earlier acceptance into the school, especially by the junior and senior boys. In contrast, because of their lack of physical maturation, ninth grade boys often stand out compared to the older boys. This can also play out socially in terms of who gets invited to parties and who doesn't. Either way, at this point, both boys and girls come face-to-face with qualitatively and quantitatively different social and party scenes than they experienced in middle school. The choices are much more varied and the options are much more viable.

> High school is so different from middle school. It's like two different worlds. All of a sudden I know kids who drive, there are lots of parties with alcohol and drugs, and some kids seem to stay out all night. Everything just seems so much faster and more exciting, but it can be a little overwhelming too.

This increased pace of life and availability of alcohol and drugs is true throughout high school and college, and most students confront these issues somewhere along the line. (See chapter 7 for more on this topic.)

Entering high school also coincides with heightened sexual energy and awareness. Teenagers become attuned to the "group mind" of what the norms and expectations of high school are; to be sure, this group mind is not the accumulated wisdom of the ages, but the grandiose stories and exaggerations of the typical American high school.

> From freshman year on, you get the feeling that everybody has more sexual experience than you. From the first day, I felt behind. And sometimes there was this urgent sense to just have sex to get it over with—to get caught up with everyone else. But one night I stayed up late talking with a couple of friends and we talked honestly about sex (I guess because it was so late and we were all a little punchy). It was shocking! I was sure that they were both much more experienced than me, but it turned out that I was actually more experienced than either of them. Then we talked about how none of us had ever lied about what we had done—but then again we never corrected mistaken assumptions either!

Teenagers acknowledge and develop a relationship with their sexuality, a development that continues well beyond high school. However, if your adolescent is one of the roughly 5 to 10 percent of the population that is gay, you can expect this aspect of his or her life to dominate others for a considerable period of time because of the internal and external conflict homosexuality still generates in American culture. (See chapter 9 for more on this topic.)

With their rapid physical changes, new sexual energy, developing self-consciousness, and the need to find a social niche, it is no wonder that the typical ninth grader is quite self-absorbed. This is perfectly normal, if occasionally disconcerting, and much less fraught with the anxiety experienced in seventh grade.

> I took my daughter out to dinner the other night to spend some one-on-one time together. Well, the dinner was fine and our conversation seemed to flow smoothly. She was even listening to what I had to say. But after a while, I couldn't help noticing how she kept glancing over my shoulder every few minutes for a few seconds at a time. Later, when she went to the bathroom, I looked behind me, fully expecting to see a school buddy or perhaps a handsome guy. To my surprise, I saw a giant, wall-mounted mirror! She had been looking at herself!

The move from middle to high school includes a significant shift in academic expectations. Students face an increased workload and degree of difficulty. Teenagers have to figure out where they fit in academically, given the number of new classmates and teachers they encounter.

> All through junior high, I got mostly As and a few Bs without ever having to try too hard. But in high school I've been working much harder and only getting Bs and Cs. Everyone around me seems so much smarter than I'm used to, and lots of the kids are ahead of me in terms of what they already know, depending on which junior high they came from. And the teachers expect a lot more too.

A large part of freshman year is spent leveling the playing field. Students are getting caught up with one another in terms of the facts they know, while also filling in the gaps around basic study skills and learning what it takes to succeed in high school.

> For the first time in my life, I have to really study. I can't do my homework in front of the TV anymore! Now I sit at a desk in quiet. I'm also having to think and understand instead of just memorize. Sometimes it's a real drag. Sometimes I even get headaches.

Most important, ninth graders begin to wrestle with attitude and priority shifts. They have to decide how important academics are to them. Academic success demands greater effort, so students must decide if they are willing to meet those demands or if they are going to sacrifice academic achievement in favor of the other aspects of their lives that are also placing higher demands on them than ever before.

> Sometimes it feels like too much: all my teachers give more homework than I've ever had before; my basketball team practices more often and much harder; and I'm on the phone more than ever. I don't know what is most important anymore.

Finally, things are changing at a faster rate than ever at home, specifically in relationship to parents. Adolescents now want more say over their lives and less say from their parents. This is rarely a graceful process. It is usually awkward, with the teenager only able to voice what he doesn't want, not what he does want. We'll cover this more completely in the sophomore year, when such behavior is most evident. But for now, during your teenager's freshman year, he'll probably still tell you that he loves you.

Tenth Grade

With the first year of high school under the belt, sophomore year provides a welcome relief. Tenth graders now understand more or less how the school works and where they fit in, both academically and socially. The boys' physical maturation is catching up to the girls'. Both genders are either having more success in extracurricular activities and sports or are slowly coming to grips with reality—no, they realize, they won't be the next basketball or tennis superstar. They are also seeking reassurance in, and control of, their bodies. This can mean weight lifting (and in the extreme, steroids) for the boys and food consciousness (and in the extreme, eating disorders) for the girls. (Many girls flirt with eating modifications at this point, most notably through dieting and exercise—see chapter 17 for more on this topic.)

After finding a group to spend time with during the ninth grade, many teenagers begin to reassess their friendships and what they are looking for in friends during the tenth grade. Many yearn for closer friendships, in which they are honest with feelings, ideas, and opinions—where trust and faith are

the dominant values. With abstract thinking skills in place, teenagers con-
strue these friendships in fairly idealistic terms. Past and current friendships
are reexamined with this perspective. Few are able to withstand the scrutiny.
Fortunately, many friends seem to undergo this reflective process at roughly
the same time, so with persistence and negotiation, deeper friendships are
forged. Often these changes continue well into junior year.

> When I look back at the beginning of freshman year, it's pretty embar-
> rassing. I was so naive! I have new and better friends now who I hadn't
> even met then. I still talk with some of my old friends, but it all seems
> so superficial. I guess we all changed in different directions. It's not like
> anything had happened; we just changed.

And some kids, as they learn more about their new friends, make a conscious decision to move away from these friends.

> I thought I had good friends at the beginning of last [freshman] year,
> but they've done some things that I don't agree with, so I don't spend
> much time with them anymore. They were really mean to some kids
> that wanted to hang out with us—acting nice to their faces but laugh-
> ing behind their backs. It was awful! I still spent time with them until I
> found some new friends, but I couldn't wait to get away from them.

At home, relationships change in dramatic ways for most tenth graders
(and their parents). Many experience home—more specifically, the privacy of
their own rooms—as their only safe haven. Otherwise, home is a fairly volatile place. (Recall the mother and son dialogue on page xviii where, in the
end, both feel bad about the interchange, but neither knows how to go about
changing the pattern that has developed.)

A major part of the problem is timing and expectations. When teenagers
come home from school, they often need to "detox," just like adults do when
they come home from work. Give them the space or at least expect them to
take it (and don't take it personally when they do take the space—see Nick's
comments in chapter 2, page 13). At the same time, seize the moment if they
do want to talk, but don't expect it and don't hold it against them the next
day: "You told me all about your day yesterday, why not today?" As a general
rule, if the conversation is forced and guilt driven, it's probably detrimental

to your relationship. If the conversation is freely offered, it's valuable to your relationship.

I recently got a call from a mom who took this idea to heart. Instead of resisting her daughter's desire for privacy, she now encouraged it. "Hard day today? Why don't you get some juice and go listen to music in your room for a while. It'll help you relax. I'll call you in about an hour for dinner, and we can catch up then." Since she has embraced this new approach, things have quieted down significantly between her and her daughter, and the flow of information between the two has also improved.

Realize that it isn't normal for sophomores to come home and want to brief their parents on the details of their life. In many ways, high school is an elongated process of entering adulthood, which includes keeping certain aspects of one's life to oneself and sharing those aspects when one chooses to do so. Sophomores learn the hard way: sometimes they share too much, but far more often they share too little, mostly in an awkward effort to claim their independence. The key is that, when they do choose to open up, you respond with your best listening skills.

> I was having big problems with my boyfriend and with my soccer coach, but instead of talking to my friends, I talked to my mom. I know this sounds like a weird thing for a teenager to do, but it's just that only my mom would be willing to listen to everything I had to say and not feel obliged to give advice. She's cool that way.

Remember that many of your former methods of parenting aren't working anymore, and in fact, often make things worse. Most sophomores feel this dramatically and desperately want more independence in their lives, all without losing you as an ally.

Consider this example. Stemming from teenagers' desire to assert their independence, every high school across the country has at least a couple of sophomores or juniors who experience what I call "the Party from Hell." The kid's parents are out of town for the weekend, and she invites a few friends over for a small party. Of course, the small party lasts for about ten minutes before two hundred of her closest friends hear about it and crash, seemingly all at once. Eventually, neighbors call in the police to halt the festivities, but usually not before several thousands of dollars in damage has been done: jewelry stolen, furniture destroyed, cars scratched, gardens ruined, and so on.

It was pretty ugly for a while. My parents were so pissed that they didn't speak to me for days. I felt like such a jerk. But, to make a long story short, it really worked out for us after a while. They grounded me for three months, and every day one of them left work early to meet me after school and stay with me. They took away my phone and Internet account. At first, I went crazy and seriously thought about sneaking out at night and running away. But I never did, and I'm not really sure why. I guess part of it was that after the first few days they didn't rub the party in my face anymore (except for a few times); they just stuck to the punishment. Eventually, I got all my old privileges back, but it took a while. I'm real glad my parents didn't give up on me, like I've seen so many others do with my friends. And that was weird: none of my friends could understand why my parents were being so hard on me. They all thought it was way too extreme. It was hard for all of us, but it was worth it. But don't get me wrong, I wouldn't recommend it for other kids!

Fortunately, in this example both the parents and their teenager recognized that an underlying cause of the disaster was the difference in expectations of trust and honesty. The son hadn't trusted his parents enough to ask permission to have the party, and the parents had overindulged their son by giving him more freedom than he could handle. Afterward, their only recourse was to take the necessary time and energy to build that trust and honesty.

The preceding examples lay the groundwork for what a fair number of students experience as the "sophomore slump," which usually occurs in the latter part of tenth grade. Your teenager struggles to define herself and make her own choices. She wants to decide what is important to her and the kind of person she wants to be, yet at the same time she feels held back in making these decisions. She is both excited and cautious about taking control. A parent doesn't stand much of a chance under these circumstances. If you offer too much direction, she rebels; if you give her too much space, she rushes out past the limits. More than anything, she needs to feel that she is making meaningful decisions about the direction of her life.

I got in a lot of trouble for lying to my parents over the weekend. Actually, I got in trouble because I got caught lying. Anyway, I know that I blew whatever trust they had in me when I got caught. Now I have to earn back their trust. It's just that somehow I have to do it in a different way and as a different person. I have to be myself rather than just be out to please them. It's a little strange, but I know something has changed in me and I can't ignore it.

In the extreme, some sophomores consider transferring to another high school, in part for the new environment and in part to assert authority over their lives in a meaningful manner. Amazingly, even the largest of high schools is "small and boring" to most sophomores in the midst of this slump.

> It came out of the blue. In March of her sophomore year, Lisa said
> she wanted to change schools. I was shocked. But rather than resist,
> I helped her think through the process of making such a decision,
> including visiting other schools and talking to teachers at her current
> school and potentially new schools. I also told her that I would prefer
> that she stay where she is, but if she really wanted to transfer and could
> make a good argument for her case, then we would go along with her
> decision. In the end it was a close call, but she decided to stay.

Sophomores who consider transferring are essentially going through a reevaluation process that is vitally important, and one that all adolescents go through on some level. If the transfer question nags at them and they don't seriously explore it or are prohibited from exploring options, they'll often float through the remainder of high school without any solid conviction or commitment. If, however, they explore this question fully, in all its ambiguity and anxiety, chances are much greater that they'll become more deeply committed in their final two years of high school.

This reevaluation process can take numerous forms: changing friends, quitting or joining a sport, quitting or taking up a musical instrument, and so on. The solution to this crisis lies in teenagers making decisions and taking actions in areas that they feel are meaningful. And for now, during her sophomore year, your teenager will probably assert her independence by seldom telling you that she loves you—she has to reevaluate this assumption for herself. It's part of her existential crisis and her declaration of independence.

Eleventh Grade

Junior year represents a significant change: your teenager is now officially an upper-class student. Physically, juniors have a much more accurate sense of and are more comfortable with their bodies. Cognitively, they are well versed in their abilities to think abstractly. This is most evident at home, where your teenager often challenges your ideas and rationales for a variety of behaviors.

> Up until last year, I had no trouble holding my own [intellectually] with my daughter. But during this year [eleventh grade], things have changed, and I've got to scramble quite a bit to stay even with her. She asks some very tough questions that, along with some perceptive observations, are difficult to sidestep. For instance, I stress honesty in relationships. And the other day she overheard me fudging an answer to my boss on the phone. Later that night she confronted me on it. At first, I tried to rationalize it away, but she quickly undid each rationalization until I was eventually quite frustrated and vulnerable. She finally just shook her head and walked away. It was an uncomfortable role reversal.

For juniors who are considering college, a new pressure is building steam: getting into college and the importance of grades during the critical junior year. College admission offices place great emphasis on the junior year and first semester of the senior year, as they believe they are the best indicators of a student's academic capabilities.

In social matters, most juniors have achieved relative comfort and are taking advantage of what is offered. With a driver's license and periodic access to a car, their social world has expanded. Now they are able to meet a crosstown buddy for a movie at a moment's notice. This access to a car is at times perplexing for parents who realize that on most weekend evenings your teenager has no specific destination in mind when he asks to borrow the car.

> I'm not sure where we're going. Sean is going to pick us all up and we'll decide from there. We don't even know what is going on yet, so how can we know where we'll end up?! We'll just figure it out as we go. It's no big deal! You know, I'm not a little kid anymore.

This year is also the time for both more intimate and more diverse friendships. On the one hand, many juniors are looking for closer and more satisfying friendships, building on those they had in sophomore year. They want to get beyond superficial acceptance with one another, but they're not sure how and with whom it is safe. Most are quite ripe for a significant romantic figure in their lives. On the other hand, they often want to spend time with diverse people: those who are different from them, and who were unavailable during freshman year because of restrictive friendship groupings. Teenagers are becoming more curious about people and their beliefs—though probably not with members of their own family. You may hear about a "brilliant statement" made by your daughter's English teacher or best friend's parent, only to somewhat gallingly realize that you told her the same thing several months ago and were met with utter disdain!

> Tracy is my youngest of four, so I'm long over the ego blow that goes with being the parent of a teenager. I know she is deaf to my most insightful offerings. But I also know that she adores her history teacher and hangs on every word he says. So I call him every few months and plant a few insights for him to offer should the time arise. I don't really care where she hears most of this stuff, as long as she hears it somewhere.

In their personal worldviews, juniors tend to be idealistic and somewhat romantic in the face of reality. This is both wonderful and painful to watch. They now must learn some of the hard lessons of human nature while you stand by, unable to help. These necessary life experiences come in a variety of places: first loves, best friends, academics, sports, dramatic or musical performances, and writing, to name a few. During these times, teenagers develop a stronger personal identity while remaining fragile. All the while, they discover and explore appropriate, and sometimes inappropriate, vehicles for their passions.

Finally, because they spend more and more time away from home, juniors gain a clearer picture of the players in their family. Many begin to see their parents first as human beings and second as parents. They recognize and identify shortcomings and strengths in their immediate family. This is a harsh reality for family members until your teenager learns compassion and acceptance for loved ones, which usually doesn't happen until late senior year or, most likely, several years after high school is over.

After my first year at college, I remember realizing, with a lot of surprise, how much more intelligent and civil my father had become since my junior year in high school. . . . I guess we both changed.

As mentioned in the "Tenth Grade" section, many teenagers undergo some sort of brief existential crisis in the latter stages of high school. Over the years, a number of students I've known have addressed this in what have been called "letters of independence" to their parents. In these letters, they congratulate their parents on raising them well and inform them that their duties now must shift. They are declaring their independence, and they are doing so in a thoughtful and mature manner. In short, these letters start a whole new dialogue between parent and teenager, and, most of all, allow all to gracefully participate in this new relationship. What follows is the type of letter I might write to students before they write their own letter of independence:

Dear _____:

This letter is an attempt to summarize what we discussed in our most recent conversation.

It seems that you and your parents are engaged in a struggle over your life—more specifically, who is in charge of your life. Your parents, in their efforts to help you succeed and be happy, are, according to your perspective, overmanaging and overdirecting your life. They are not trusting you with the decisions that you need to make, the decisions that you feel you must make in order to direct your life in a satisfactory manner.

Because they are overmanaging, you are left in the defensive position of simply trying to get by. (You've also taken to a bit of undermanaging in order to get their goat.) Unfortunately, this position doesn't encourage or allow you to start making your own priorities and decisions about what is important to you. By now, you know very well what is important to your parents and the other adults in your world. These are the "shoulds" that fill your head and increase your feelings of guilt. Let's look at a few specifics.

Homework: Your parents constantly stress the importance of homework and good grades. They periodically "pop" into your room to check on how things are going, which often infuriates you. They also direct you when to do homework (of course, in your best interests, so that you can manage it all), while simultaneously criticizing your lack of time-management skills. Somehow they expect you to learn time-management skills without making any errors along the way. All in all, their attitude is one of mistrust in your ability and willingness to study on your own. For you, this is particularly infuriating, as you care a great deal about your schoolwork and doing well. But with all their overmanaging, your own cares and concerns have gotten pushed to the side. You hardly ever think about what you want—you usually spend your time thinking more about what you don't want.

Social Life: Your parents want you to have friends, but they don't want friends to interfere with your academic life. They will routinely say no to weekend nights out so that you have time to get your homework done. Unfortunately, they operate from a purely rational framework. For example, if you have plans for Saturday night, then they insist you do your homework on Friday night, even though few if any students are capable of doing quality homework on a Friday night, given the accumulated stress and exhaustion caused by the week.

Time: To protect you from your poor time-management skills, your parents pay too much attention to how you spend your time. They routinely order an end to phone calls, direct you to your room after dinner to study, and nag about your homework progress. In short, they limit your ability to learn time management through the consequences of your own actions—good or bad.

Your Body: Again, with the best of intentions, they try to help out by reminding you not to eat too much, commenting on your style of dress, and offering unsolicited advice about appearance; none of this feedback gives you any sense of freedom of choice. Instead, you are often left in a reactionary and defensive position. Also, their indirect criticisms hurt you quite a bit.

Your Voice: By talking over you, your parents are in effect diminishing your ability to make and voice your own opinions about yourself, the future, and the world in general. Worse yet, this does not allow you to decide for yourself, in your own voice, what is truly important to you. In the long run, if your priorities aren't in your own voice, the necessary commitment and motivation you need to meet your goals are missing. This leaves you more worried about your parents' reactions to your life than about your own reactions to your life.

So, as we discussed, all this has left you feeling depressed because you are living your life for others, with a genuine lack of joy and self-direction in your life, always feeling like your "fuel tank" is near empty.

Still, it is clear that your parents love you and want what is best for you. The question is, Can they get out of your way long enough and gracefully enough for you to discover and achieve what is best for you? Fortunately, this is where you have more influence than you might realize.

The point of this type of letter is not to decide who is right or wrong; rather, it's to encourage teenagers to take a lead in their lives and include their parents in a genuinely supportive role, which is good for everyone. If juniors and seniors don't have meaningful authority in their lives, they frequently turn to irresponsible authority: risk taking, drugs, alcohol, unsafe driving.

During junior year, your teenager may again tell you that he loves you, but on second thought, he's probably too busy.

Twelfth Grade

Senior year is what most students have been waiting for. Now it is their turn to grab the reins of leadership at school. Their high school has become their home, and they are comfortable there, though perhaps a bit restless too. In fact, much of senior year is spent alternating between these feelings of comfort and restlessness.

Because senior year is their last year of high school, many teenagers feel the need to somehow make this final year extra meaningful so they don't walk away from these years "empty-handed." A sense of meaning and accomplishment, if it hasn't come already, can come in a number of areas: sports, drama, academics, college admission, school newspaper, yearbook, prom committee, relationships, employment, student government, community service, or clubs. The important point is that, by the conclusion of senior year, teenagers need to have found a place where they feel they have left a mark. With these goals motivating them, many enter senior year inspired to make this a different kind of year, and a better one than the previous three—which is a lot of pressure to put on oneself.

> Senior year for me was a huge turning point. I became more outgoing
> and confident, and I really discovered who I am as a person. Remember,
> senior parents, we aren't abandoning you—in fact, we'll really miss you
> next year!

In this year, friendships take on even greater importance than in previous years, as the social scene is well known and well practiced. In fact, by the
end of the year, it is so familiar a scene that it becomes old for most. Some have
significant sexual and romantic relationships prior to or during this year,
while others are pained to have not had such relationships. (See chapter 9.)

At home, a great deal of ground has already been covered in the first three
years. Teenagers have achieved a certain amount of autonomy, and how that
was achieved is important. If it was a more or less graceful shift, then parent
and teenager are getting along fairly well and slowly preparing themselves for
the inevitable separation that comes with graduation.

> Her sophomore and junior years were pretty rough. But to everyone's
> credit, we all hung in there so that by senior year we were actually on
> good terms with each other. It was kind of ironic; here we were say-
> ing hello to each other for really the first time—just as we were getting
> ready to say good-bye.

On the other hand, if a teenager hasn't secured a reasonable amount of
autonomy or if her parents have given up on her, then her senior year is a continuation and escalation of the previous years' problems.

For college-bound students, the first semester of senior year means a
lot of stress—in terms of schoolwork, college applications, and personal and
family pressure. Non-college-bound students are also feeling stress, but from
slightly different sources—postgraduation decisions about employment, living situations, and, of course, personal and family pressure. They also feel
the stress of being excluded when they listen to classmates plan for college
(even if not going to college is their own choice). These students experience
their stress at a different rate than college-bound students. College-bound
students feel the bulk of their future-related stress in the first semester; non-
college-bound students experience the bulk of their future-related stress in
the second semester, when their peers are relaxing after having heard back
on their college applications.

For those aspiring to college, the academic pressure of the junior year continues to intensify throughout the first semester of senior year. Suddenly, everyone is interested in their future: Parents ask about school choices, inquiring about application deadlines and essays, stressing the importance of this semester's grades. The adults around them (teachers, relatives, and friends' parents) want to hear the list of schools to which they're applying. Remember how vulnerable adolescents are during this time. They are completing applications and putting themselves on paper for public judgment. It's a huge endeavor, all around.

I once spoke to a parent who, anticipating the stress and drama around the college admissions application and selection, decided to join in wholeheartedly. He chose to go through the same process as his son! He got information from various schools, made a list of his favorites, narrowed the list down according to the probability of admission (using his own high school grades and SAT scores), and completed the applications for all of them. He figured that school was a full-time job for his son, so that doing the application process in addition to his regular job was comparable to what his son was going through.

> Applying to college is huge, much worse than when I applied to college. Just to be sure of getting into a school that I would be willing to attend, along with a few long shots, meant applying to seven schools. My son and I were both burning the midnight oil the night before they were due! At first, he was skeptical of what I was doing, and we hardly ever spoke of it. But when he saw that I was serious and not demeaning toward him, he began to get curious. From then on, we spent time commiserating on how difficult the essays were; we even critiqued each other's essays along the way. All in all, it didn't give me any more control or direct influence over the process, but it did provide two unexpected benefits. First, I developed a real empathy for what he was going through, which indirectly brought us closer in a manner I hadn't imagined. Second, I felt actively engaged in his applying to college, which allowed me not to intrude so readily on his business.

I heartily recommend this exercise for interested parents.

For students who are not college-bound, the steps are similar, though a bit less formal. Instead of colleges, they are thinking of jobs and living situations. And there is no set application or deadline for these decisions.

It's all kind of hard to think about, because it seems so unreal. School
just sort of ended, and then there was nothing to do. My parents were
all over me to get a job, but I had no idea what I wanted to do. So, for the
most part, I got together with my friends at night and partied, though
there was this weird tension between those going to college and those of
us who were staying home.

College-bound or not, getting "senioritis" during the second semester
of senior year is a common experience for most high school students. To get
through the intensity of first semester, most seniors dangle the carrot of second semester in front of themselves. They imagine this as a time of ultimate
relaxation and enjoyment: the academic pressure is off, friends have time for
one another, and they're the leaders of the school and running all the major
functions.

The majority of students think that second-semester grades are virtually ignored by colleges (unless they are absolutely abysmal), so they feel they
have earned the right to kick back academically—and no amount of yelling,
cajoling, or bribery is going to change that mind-set. Parents and teachers
have minimal influence over this phenomenon once it has set in, primarily
because the antidote must occur before second semester is under way. That
is, if education is seen as an end unto itself, then a shift of focus away from
grades and toward curiosity and self-directed learning is often successful.
This is why projects and independent studies of the students' own choosing
work out well during the second semester of senior year. If, on the other hand,
education is viewed as the means (grades) to the end (college), then once their
college decision is secured they are, in effect, on vacation.

Longtime educator William Mayher had a student who described
senioritis well:

> Senior slump begins with the receiving of the first acceptance letter
> from college. I've been slumping since about February. School is no
> longer an academic hardship; it is a social gathering. It's a place where
> friends meet and go out to lunch and plan parties. School becomes a
> place to thrive on your freedom. We are finally released from the bond-
> age of a rigorous, forced secondary education. One loses the ability to
> concentrate, think, or comprehend what is taught. It's a time to day-
> dream, doodle, fall asleep, or not even show up.[2]

Table 2: Summary of the High School Years

	Ninth	**Tenth**
Physical and Cognitive	Girls are ahead of the boys; how do I fit in?; do I dress/talk/act right?; lots of emerging sexual energy; shifting into abstract thinking; need to develop study skills; new relationship with teachers.	Boys beginning to catch up; anything considered "normal" is tolerable, but anything else is dismal; some girls flirting with eating disorders and boys "bulking up"; lots of sexual energy; still unsure of how to relate to adults; are academics important to me?
Social	Lots of new and unfamiliar classmates; must find a niche; where and with whom to sit at lunch?; party scene, yes or no?	I have people to hang with, but are they real friends?; do I want to transfer?; party scene, yes or no?; natural groups via interests: sports, drama, school government, and so on.
Friendship	Want people to spend time with; groupings by similarities; initial anxiety to have friends; cling to old or make new friends?	Do my friends want the same kind of friendship as I do?; are we changing in similar or different ways?; life would be terrific if only I had a boyfriend/girlfriend!; need good friends as I grow away from family.
Personal Identity	Am I myself?; seeming lack of structure (compared to middle school); loneliness and grief over lost identity of middle school; developing self-consciousness; emerging sexuality.	Do I like who I am?; whose fault is it?; I want and should be in charge of myself, shouldn't I?; what is important to me?; who am I, besides not my parents?; sexuality and extreme self-consciousness.
Family Events	Begin to feel the need to renegotiate relationships with parents; old events are reconsidered, such as divorce and issues of custody; talk to friends about family events.	Can't wait to drive; serious renegotiating of parent roles; they are fired as managers and working hard to become my consultant on my terms; I can talk about family issues with my friends.

Eleventh	Twelfth
Boys are caught up; everyone becoming more relaxed, in fact working very hard to be relaxed; eating and body image issues; future pressures in present; what is after high school?; college and work questions: external and internal pressure around the importance of this year; whose decision is this anyway?; lots of sexual energy.	Beginning to feel comfortable; the oldest and biggest in the school; lots of sexual energy; work like hell and then life's a beach; reality of college and future; I will be judged; leaving secure and known academic environment— both good and bad.
I'm here, for better or worse; getting bored with social scene, strong desire for closer friends; more serious experimentation.	Leaving secure social environment— both good and bad; somewhat bored with present and anxious about the future.
Close friendships often changing or deepening; life would be terrific if only I had a boyfriend/girlfriend!; changing relationships to adults and authority figures.	Very close to friends and have to leave them; what will our friendship be in the future? Can I ever make new friends as close as these high school friends?
Idealistic and often romantic in face of reality; stronger sense of self, but it is so fragile and everchanging; lots of shoulds and guilt at unmet expectations; strong sexuality.	Reflecting and learning, and reacting and behaving; I'm just getting a handle on myself; I'm either ready to go or scared to go—probably both.
I'm driving and experimenting more; want to be seen as more adult and responsible; can seriously question parents and their choices.	I'm leaving home; preparing the way for the new relationship with parents—the post–high school relationship; reexamining past issues of family prior to next phase of life.

Not too many teachers remain empathetic with a student displaying this attitude in their classroom. Thus, rather than being regaled and extolled for their achievements (as many seniors fantasize), they are often chastised and reproached by both faculty and parents. Hardly what they expected: the most respected adults in their lives are annoyed and upset with them. In this vein, I know of several seniors who have expressed concern that their teachers take their behavior personally, when it is seldom intended that way, no matter how outrageous it appears.

> [When I skip class] I wish teachers would just mark me absent for the class and give me a zero for the day. I understand the consequences, but I don't need to be lectured as if it is a personal attack on them or something. I don't need that guilt along with everything else I'm feeling.

Second semester is not just another semester; it is a qualitatively different experience for students. The end is not only within sight, it is unavoidable. This means simultaneously reengaging with friends and disengaging from the school and friends; it means preparing to leave a familiar environment to establish themselves all over again in a new place; it means trying to have all the fun necessary to indeed make these "the best years of their lives"; and it means feeling compelled to understand themselves better than they already do. Again, one of Mayher's students said it well:

> It's difficult to pinpoint, but it's a weird period of ups and downs. One moment it can be diagnosed as spring fever; you feel elated, feel the desire to "get out." The next moment you are down, lethargic, lacking energy. The paper you have to hand in to graduate seems to be an impossibility. Whether up or down, you feel an overall lack of ability to concentrate. Your mind wanders; you think of the prom, of graduation, of leaving your friends. How can you realistically concentrate on the "core collapse theory" with those ideas racing around in your head?
> . . . After attending this school for as many years as most of us have, it no longer matters whether you have enjoyed your experience here or not. Graduation is painful. You are leaving the familiar to go out into the unknown (corny as that sounds). What I think that most people don't realize is that senior slump . . . goes beyond ceasing to care about grades you get on tests and what you're learning in school. . . .

You don't stop learning when you hit senior slump; rather, you use the fact that the pressure is off you to learn more about yourself. I know I feel the need now more than ever "to find myself" before I go to college. It's like a giant mishmash; you have to untangle yourself from your high school years, find the pieces of you that are mixed up with everyone else, collect yourself, and go to college. At the same time, you know that you have left something of yourself there in the mishmash because you can't find every piece, but you learn to accept this. That's what senior slump is all about. It's not a disease; it's a healthy, normal reaction to what's happening all around you.

So, as a parent, what are you apt to see at home? First of all, your teenager will push for greater independence in the form of more lenient curfews, going out on school nights, going on weekend trips with friends, and doing less and less homework—all with more moodiness than usual.

Second, most seniors develop a greater focus on friends and crises in their lives. Emotional catastrophes often appear that demand their immediate attention and that they are hesitant to explain. It is common for family and personal difficulties that have remained in the background throughout high school to suddenly command center stage as the senior year winds down, and typically it is friends that they turn to first and foremost.

By the end of this year, your teenager is once again telling you that she loves you, but usually over her shoulder as she heads out to meet friends for coffee.

Notes

1. In this section, I describe the typical middle school model, which includes sixth, seventh, and eighth grades—as opposed to the junior high model, which only includes seventh and eighth grades. While many sixth graders enter middle school on the cusp of adolescence, most leave sixth grade having made that transition—often to the shock of unsuspecting parents.

2. This quote, along with several others in this chapter, is from William S. Mayher, *The Dynamics of Senior Year: A Report from the Frontlines*. Tarrytown, NY: Hackly School, 1989.

4

Limits and Structure

Are there any rules or guidelines that are guaranteed to work with teenagers?

Like just about everything else about teenagers, this question doesn't have a direct or simple answer. The question is really one about limits and structure, which are family specific and are difficult to discuss usefully in the abstract. But for now, let's define what we mean by "limits and structure," at least in terms of parenting. Basically, these terms refer to providing security for adolescents through consistency, clear expectations, appropriate guidelines, direct feedback, acknowledgment, and the separation of consequences and character lessons. Only when teenagers experientially understand and trust the structure around them are they able to fully develop. The structure provides the safety in which they can momentarily suspend the inherent self-consciousness of adolescence; in other words, the structure contains the effects of anxiety on their development. This in turn opens the door for genuine curiosity, self-reflection, and learning.

Now, what does all this mean in practical terms? First, what it *doesn't* mean is that you use the same rules and limits with your tenth grader that you did when he was three years younger. His world has changed, so the rules and limits must reflect these changes. Throughout a person's growth, infancy through adulthood, structure and limits need to evolve to reflect each developmental stage. For instance, you wouldn't negotiate with a one-year-old about bedtime. Nor would you insist that your seventeen-year-old get in bed by 9:00 p.m. every night. These are not developmentally appropriate limits.

Ideally, limits and structure form the foundation of the stable platform that adolescents use to launch themselves into adulthood. Realize that these rules include not only the actual guideline, but also the consistent enforcement and follow-through. Consistency between words and action is crucial, because no matter what you say about limits, it is what you do that truly matters.

> My parents are pretty clear with me about rules and expectations. But whenever they tell me something, I do the translating myself. Like if they say to be in by midnight, I know that if I'm in by 12:15, nothing is said; at 12:30, something is said and nothing is done; after 12:45, something is said and done.

Here, while words and actions don't quite match up, there is an underlying consistency that the adolescent understands. Without this, there is no way for the teenager to accurately "translate." In fact, consistency is so important that in some instances consistent "bad" parenting is better than extreme inconsistency between "bad" and "good" parenting.

> By most standards, I guess my parents are pretty awful. They don't seem real interested in me other than the grades I get and the free babysitting I provide for my sisters. They hardly ever check up on me or ask about where I go at night. They always say to be in by 1:00 a.m., but they're never around to check, never mind enforce it. I don't think they want to be bothered. The only times they get upset are when I get in trouble at school and they get called, and of course when I leave dirty dishes on the counter. It isn't much compared to most of my friends, but at least I know what to expect. At least they're not constantly changing the rules on me depending on their mood at the time, like with some of my other friends. It is hard, but I'm learning to accept it. They're not going to change, that's for sure!

A good example of an enforced limit versus a legal limit is the fifty-five-mile-per-hour speed limit on urban freeways. While the actual speed limit is fifty-five miles per hour, many people have internalized an enforced speed limit of sixty to sixty-one miles per hour. Thus, if you get a ticket for going sixty-four miles per hour, you'll be upset, but you won't feel unjustly treated. But if you got a ticket going fifty-seven miles per hour, you would feel unjustly treated.

It's best to make sure that the guidelines and rules you set for your adolescent are consistent with your own values. They ought to be what you feel are appropriate and thus have little trouble enforcing. Too many parents set unreal expectations for themselves and their teenagers.

> At first, we tried to be the perfect parents. We read all the how-to books
> and talked to lots of other parents about homework time, curfews, driving privileges, and so on. Very quickly we had a clear set of rules that
> I'm sure the experts would have been proud of. But just as quickly that
> nice set of rules became undone, mainly because in our hearts we didn't
> really believe in them. Oh, we believed in them in theory, but in our
> day-to-day reality we wouldn't follow them. We had set our expectations too high. For example, at first we said, "No talking on the phone
> until all your homework is done." But in reality both my wife and I call
> our friends after dinner and before we do any leftover work from the
> office, so that didn't seem fair. Also, it is more important to us for our
> daughter to learn how to be responsible for herself and her homework
> than to learn to follow our rules blindly. So we've edited our initial rules
> down to the ones that are important to us. Maybe we don't have the
> "best" rules in the world, but at least they're honest ones.

Unrealistic guidelines lead to inconsistent communication and enforcement, which means instability for the adolescent. Given the nature of the teenage world, instability is a handicap. (See chapter 2.)

Establishing an appropriate structure is complicated by the fact that adolescence is a very different stage of development from others. You can't simply upgrade the strategies and structures that worked from infancy through late childhood; they must be reworked for teenagers. In addition, you need to make room for real input from your adolescents. Through negotiation, they learn to have more say and autonomy over their lives, a critical task at this stage of life, and eventually to take on responsibility.

So, how does one decide on appropriate limits? The easiest way I know of is to work backward. Start by imagining the time your teenager leaves home, either to go to college or to start her work life, when she is roughly eighteen years old. At this point, she will be pretty much on her own, at least relative to her life to date. What kind of decisions does she need to have experience making? What skills must she possess? How does she acquire these skills?

What kinds of experiences (read: mistakes) are necessary to learn all this? After you've reflected on this, move backward to the present. Your reflections will guide you in developing appropriate structures and limits. (See chapter 7 for more on this.)

> I learned the lesson between overparenting and helping to prepare my oldest for the adult world in a rather shocking manner. I definitely overparented. When he went off to college, he couldn't do laundry, had never balanced a checkbook or made a budget, and didn't know how to clean a bathroom! Never mind the more personal skills of budgeting time, setting priorities, and making compromises such as negotiating with roommates. Believe me, his younger brother is getting plenty of opportunities for experience in these areas before he gets out of this house!

Without the gradual exposure to these types of experiences, adolescents must face them all at once, which is often overwhelming.

> I'm in charge of the freshmen dormitories at "X" University. Believe me, it's easy to see which students were overprotected by their parents. They're typically the ones who get lost in confusion or self-destruct with all the freedom. They party, stay up late, skip classes, and generally dig themselves into a deep hole in the first semester. The freedom is too much for them; they seem to drown in all the choices. During our Resident Adviser training, we even do a session on how to spot these students and intervene in a useful manner. Most get it together by second semester. The ones that don't usually take a semester off or sometimes leave for good.

The ideas of limits and structure are at least as important during adolescence as they are during any other stage of childhood. By nature, human beings are curious limit testers. It is our nature to explore the outer edges of our existence. Teenagers are no different. Before they can relax and settle into something, they need to understand and experience the exact parameters of the environment. Their testing is a means of exploring the limits. Expect the testing; in fact, be wary when it isn't there. And as difficult as it may be, don't take it personally.

Every year it's exactly the same. At the beginning of the year, I pass out
a syllabus along with my rules for the class. We go over each one of them
during our first meeting. The one that really gets them is "Be on time
or not at all." Basically, I close the door as the bell rings at the beginning of class; if they are late without a written excuse, they don't get in
and they get a zero for the day. A simple, no-nonsense rule. Everyone
understands it and is on time, at least for the first few weeks. Then I get
the Test. They show up thirty seconds late without the required written excuse, but with a bag full of "legitimate reasons." Needless to say,
after I send them away, to the shock of their classmates, there is seldom
another incident for the rest of the semester. And if there is, the consequences are taken with minimal grumbling.

When teenagers begin testing limits, parents tend to head in one of two
directions. The first is to become overly rigid, with the structure becoming
symbolic of the battle of wills between you and your teenager. In this extreme,
the trash must go out when you say so, without the least amount of hesitation.
The second tendency is overflexibility, with the structure as an implied reality, but with no real limits. In this extreme, you never mention the trash to
your teenager; rather, you take it out yourself because you can't ever imagine
it happening any other way, and besides, it isn't worth arguing over. Both are
equally disastrous to the adolescent's development. That is, as alluded to earlier, the way in which they negotiate and compromise around these limits and
rules is quite reflective of their level of maturity and responsibility. When kids
are able to negotiate and take stands responsibly, the whole parent-adolescent
relationship shifts. Parents need to be on the lookout for these changes.

You won't believe what happened the other night with me and my
parents! It was totally cool. I've been sick and tired of them treating me
like a twelve-year-old all the time: telling me when to do my homework,
telling me to pick up my room, telling me to get off the phone, telling
me what to eat and what not to eat, and so on. Well, finally I couldn't
take it anymore. So last night I told them that I was sixteen years old
and if they wanted me to act sixteen then they needed to stop treating
me like a twelve-year-old and start treating me like a sixteen-year-old.
I didn't give them any examples; instead I said that I was sick of them

running my life, and that I wanted my life back in my own hands. I was really pissed, so I figured all hell would break loose after I finished, but to my shock they both smiled and said that it was about time! They had been waiting for me to say something for the past six months! I couldn't believe it! It's funny, that happened last week and things have been much better between them and me, and it's not that they are doing things all that different. It is just that they see me differently and, as a result, I understand them better. Pretty weird, huh?

Again, the way your teenager negotiates limits and structure is a great way to measure her current level of maturity.

One final point on the difficulty of limits and structure. Because your kid is an adolescent, you have much less direct control over her, and she knows it. If she decided to go against your guidelines and to skip class, go to an unchaperoned party, stay out past curfew, and so on, there is not much you can do—short of physical intervention (not usually recommended) or calling the police. But over the long run, don't discount the importance and influence of your opinions and ideals. They matter a great deal, which is why they are so important to articulate—though they are equally important not to belabor.

My parents tell me exactly where they stand on all sorts of issues, but they leave me free to make my own decisions, though not necessarily with their approval. They're even willing to discuss things with me— real discussion. It wasn't always this way, though. During ninth and tenth grades I didn't tell them anything. I lied all over the place, and they never caught on. But after a while, it got to where we couldn't talk anymore—at least about anything beyond the local news or weather. I had told so many lies that I was scared that I might tip them off. You know, like asking them about a movie they saw that I was supposed to have seen. Anyway, I got tired of it all one night. I was miserable with my friends and had nowhere to turn. So I sat them down and told them that I lied most of the time. I even told them some of the lies, but they didn't want to hear too many. We stayed up most of that night talking and things, but in the end it was like this giant brick wall had been taken down. It's much easier this way.

5

Natural Consequences

What are fair punishments when teenagers break the rules? For instance, how effective is "grounding"?

When it comes to punishments, the principle of natural consequences really comes into play. As a consultant parent, you work to establish punishments that are natural consequences of the offenses.[1] For example, if the transgression involves a misuse of, deceitful use of, or irresponsible use of the car, then the natural consequences focus on some type of consequence involving the car. In an ideal world, this natural-consequences principle of handling periodic slipups is spelled out with your child in a variety of settings and throughout his preadolescent years, so that he has somewhat internalized the principle by the time the car is a discussion point. (Of course, don't expect him to thank you for helping him to learn responsibility and the consequences of his actions when he comes in late on Friday night and loses the privilege of using the car before a big Saturday date.)

By focusing on the natural—or as natural as possible—consequences of an act, you become the enforcer of consequences in a consistent world, rather than the all-powerful (and resented) judge and jury in an unpredictable world. How would you like it if you appeared in traffic court to argue your

$150 speeding ticket and found the arresting officer acting as judge and jury, not only deciding against your innocence but tripling the fine too! This is exactly how it feels to teenagers when consequences are chosen arbitrarily or when they aren't privy to the logic of the consequences.

The focus on natural consequences allows you to at least reduce and often sidestep many of the power issues of the adult-adolescent relationship, which are often the source of extended rifts between parents and their teenagers. As a colleague of mine, Ray Greenleaf, is fond of saying, "The fight is hardly ever about who takes out the trash. The underlying struggle is more typically about power, more specifically, about who is in charge."[2] The beauty of natural consequences is that they skirt the power issue; the adolescent is in charge, because the consequences are a natural outcome of his actions or nonactions. You simply support the law of cause and effect.

A month or so after an evening meeting with a group of parents of eleventh graders, a mother called with this story about natural consequences.

> It was Halloween night, a Friday to boot. Mark [sixteen years old], was going out with two of his buddies. He said they didn't have any particular plans; there were a few parties and things to check out, but anyway he would be home by 1 a.m. Nothing was unusual except that I realized, after he had left, that he was dressed in really beat-up clothes and they were all riding in one kid's pickup, something I hadn't known them to do before. I didn't know what to make of it, so I filed it away to ask Mark when he got home. Well, as things turned out, I didn't have to ask.
>
> Around midnight, I got a call from the local police. They had Mark and a couple of his buddies down at the station for throwing eggs at cars from the back of the pickup! It seems they hit a pretty fast sports car that managed to get their license plate number. No charges were made; the owner simply wanted to teach the kids a lesson and to get reimbursed for the necessary wash-and-wax job. I was stunned, and for some reason I apologized to the officer. I also told him I would be there in ten minutes to get Mark. But something didn't feel right, so I called the officer back with a few questions of my own. Basically, I learned that Mark didn't yet know that the officer had gotten in touch with me and, furthermore, that the station was pretty busy that night with a usual weekend assortment of crimes and criminals, but that Mark was safely sequestered away in a waiting room. To make a long story short, I told the officer to

tell Mark that he couldn't reach me and that he would try again later. I also told him that I would come and get Mark in a couple of hours, after he had a few hours to himself in the station without his friends. The officer chuckled and said he understood, as he had two teenagers himself. He even added that he would "entertain" Mark until then.

To say the least, when I got Mark he was real pleased to see me. Basically, I didn't have to say much, and, not so surprisingly, he was more than willing to suffer just about any consequence I had in mind!

Let's examine this more closely. If the mom had picked up her son right away, what might have been lost? First, she wouldn't have had time to reflect on what had actually happened. That is, without time, the natural parental response is to overreact to your son getting picked up by the police, but with time she came to see the incident for what it was—her son was facing the societal consequences of his actions and, thankfully, nobody had been hurt. Second, with this time, she was able to separate herself personally from Mark's actions. Remember how she apologized to the officer when he called? Third, because she took this time (after assuring herself of his health and safety), it allowed Mark to sit uncomfortably with his consequences. And really, this is the only way he is going to learn the idea of natural consequences, and subsequently personal responsibility. Fourth, this separation allowed her to calm down, so that when she picked up Mark she didn't verbally lay into him. If she had bawled him out, she probably would have ruined a wonderful learning opportunity. That is, he would have projected his discomfort onto her in the form of anger and indignation. "What do you expect me to say? I screwed up, that's all! It's not like I robbed a bank or something. Look, just ground me or something, but don't preach to me like I'm some five-year-old!" By shaking her head in wonderment and not chastising him too harshly she forced him to stay responsible for what he had done.[3]

After your teenager has committed an infraction, it's essential to communicate explicitly how, when, and for how long the consequence is in place. Both of you need to know at what point trust is restored to its previous level and the breach is relegated to its proper place in history. For instance, it's unfair to tell teenagers that they can't use the car until you decide that they are ready, and then, when pressed, to say vaguely that somehow you'll know when they are once again ready. This will drive them crazy and usually pushes them over the brink of irresponsibility to previously unimagined levels. Concrete steps and timelines help to contain their anxiety and invite them to stay active on their own behalf, in positive ways. Without this, most teenagers get overwhelmed and become passive—or worse, they act out in negative ways. Once the miscue takes place, sit down within twenty-four hours (or when everybody can think rationally once again) and negotiate the consequences. It is perfectly acceptable and wise not to have this discussion in the heat of the moment—a "we'll discuss where to go with this at lunch tomorrow" is often most appropriate. Also, as mentioned above, once a consequence is played out, it is unfair to resurrect it or the feelings associated with it in the future. The idea of the consequence is that it restores trust and allows everyone to move on. Holding history against one another is a prescription for a tumultuous relationship.

> I got in trouble for skipping class today and the vice principal called home already. So I'm sure my mom and dad are talking right now. By the time I get home, they'll be so worked up that I'll have to stand trial for every single thing I've done wrong in the last ten years! You laugh, but it's true! Last time I got in trouble they relectured me about the time in fourth grade when I didn't lock my bike and it was stolen! That was when I blew up and fireworks began. What's a kid to do?

Ideally, before a consequence is decided upon and enforced there is input from both parties. As a parent, you need to briefly state what the problem is and the general direction of the consequence.

> Just to quickly reiterate, we agreed that you would be in by midnight and that, in the event you would be late, you would give us a call so we wouldn't worry needlessly. But you didn't call and you came home an hour late. As I see it, you broke your agreement with us and cost each of us an hour's sleep—actually more, because we stayed up another hour after you got home, discussing what happened—but we won't pass that on to you as we accepted that possibility when we decided to become parents. So, any suggestions as to where we go from here?

The first few times you use this approach your kids probably won't have any suggestions, but over time they'll catch up and offer ideas of their own. Either way, you need to have thought through, without having attached yourself to, a plausible course of action.

Well, let's deal with the lost time first, as that's the easier of the two issues. I was going to do laundry today and your father was going to mow the lawn, and since each task takes about an hour to complete, we suggest that you assume those responsibilities today so that we can have the time either to relax or to take a nap. Now, the broken agreement is a trickier matter. We suggest that for the next weekend your curfew gets moved back by one hour. At the end of next weekend, we'll have a brief discussion and hopefully all will go back to normal. If, however, something else happens, we'll sit down and start all over again. So, what do you say? Any questions or changes you want to suggest? Okay, then let's let this be the end of it.

Note that the consequences discussion is definitely not the time to lecture or explain how the transgression affected you. The pull to have the guilt-inducing conversation is powerful at this point. Resist. Guilt-inducement only sabotages any potential lesson. Naturally occurring guilt is powerful, but when you attempt to up the ante, it usually backfires. That is, without you having to say it, your teenager already knows how her actions affected you. In fact, your explanation will probably only make things worse from her perspective: she now feels talked down to in a way that, for her, simply rubs it in. As for the lesson, well, she'll connect the dots in private, away from you. This is part of her developing sense of independence and personal responsibility.

A few more points about natural consequences. Obviously, understanding the law of cause and effect is the purpose behind using natural consequences. But be careful that an understanding of these laws doesn't let the adolescent off the hook; make sure he has to deal with the consequences in the action of his life. Otherwise, you inadvertently encourage the notion that understanding and remorse are enough and therefore sidestep the learning that will positively change behavior.

Whenever I get in any trouble, I hardly ever get punished. At first, my parents take turns yelling at me, which really pisses me off, but I sit there and take it for the most part. Then, just before the punishment part of the conversation, I take over with some sort of apology, a few tears, and a promise to never do anything like that again. After a while, once they see that I truly understand and that I'm sorry, they just forget about it. And it's not like I do this stuff to just get off the hook. I actually do feel bad and sorry for what I did. I guess I'm just really good at being sorry.

In addition to natural consequences, I like to keep kids as active as possi
ble in their consequences—something that requires your teenager to do something to earn his forgiveness. He rakes the leaves, cleans the kitchen, washes
the car—something that allows him to reclaim his place in the family. Unlike
adults, few teenagers seek out solitude in order to reflect on their actions and
decisions. Instead, this reflection happens while they are physically doing
something—typically some mundane, routine chore. An added advantage is
that when teenagers are active in working through their consequences—they
are outside or scrubbing away at the dishes—there is much less chance that we
as their parents will slip back into a history of all their misdeeds.

It is also important to take your time in determining consequences;
otherwise you'll overreact and then have to go back on what you said. For
instance, to ground your teenager for coming home late is one thing, but in
the heat of the moment to extend the punishment to six months is another.
This is something you will not, should not, or cannot follow through on. Still,
when it does happen and you do overreact, apologize, maybe even taking back
some of what you said. That kind of honesty is more useful than any lecture,
as long as it is sincere.

Personal influence is also quite important throughout. Over time, teenagers will learn that, while they must face the consequences of their actions,
they can also influence the course and creativity of the consequences. Thus,
the door is opened to realistic negotiation and compromise on the front end
of parent-adolescent agreements. Most parents would be amazed at how
many times kids make an agreement knowing that they won't stick to it and
knowing that they'll get caught breaking the agreement. They do this because
they don't feel they have any influence on the front end. If there is no room for
sincere negotiation, they discover that the best course of action is to agree to
anything and get on with their business.

> Half the reason I lie is because my mother doesn't really give me any
> choice. She keeps herself so naive and idealistic that I can't be honest
> with her. If I were honest, she wouldn't let me do anything; I would
> spend every weekend night watching movies with my parents! I wish
> she could handle my honesty without freaking out and let me run my
> life. If she trusted me more, I would trust her more. Like the parties
> I go to. Her rule is that I can't go to any party where there is alcohol,
> even though I don't drink. That rules out most of the parties. So I usu-
> ally lie about the alcohol or where I'm going. But like the other night,

somebody got really drunk and it was scary. Normally, I would talk to my mom about something like that, but because I have to lie to her, I can't talk to her about what happened. And that's too bad for both of us.

This brings us to the topic of grounding, a consequence that is rife with difficulties. If thought through and followed through responsibly and reasonably, it is an excellent consequence. But grounding is seldom done this way. Typically, grounding is the consequence of choice in the heat of the moment, when a parent wants to witness the effects of the punishment on their teenager. Unfortunately, all this does is escalate the tension, anxiety, and general bad feeling. Moreover, the grounding consequence is seldom fully enforced, and teenagers know this. When pressed about getting grounded, most adolescents say they know their parents are acting in the heat of the moment. For one teenager, a one-month grounding typically translates into one week. For another, getting grounded for three weeks translates into being good for a few days with the certainty that her parents will forget about the grounding by the weekend. When pressed even further, kids acknowledge the dance aspect to the whole grounding ritual. This is where they get upset, angry, apologetic, or sullen in order to let their parents know the punishment got to them, but these emotions often mean the loss of the battle (showing the effects of the supposed grounding) in favor of the victory of the war (being able to go out again by the next weekend).

One reason grounding is often ineffective is because too many parents forget that, when they ground their teenager, they also ground themselves. At least that is how it should be. When kids break some sort of rule or agreement, they are guilty of at least a momentary inability to monitor their own behavior; they need assistance in self-monitoring (structure) so they are able to reflect and learn from their error; otherwise it will just happen again. Parents must provide the temporarily increased structure (supervision) for their teenager, which is why grounding also grounds the parent. For example, when a child is learning to ride a bike and he continually falls down, responsible parents provide both the training wheels (the grounding) and the sensitive supervision (their presence). The same must hold true when grounding a teenager.

One more point on grounding. Unexpectedly, grounding can present a rare opportunity for the family to reconnect with one another. Because of the nature of the teenage world, often the only way to ask for something is to do the opposite. The following is a story that I have heard many, many times over the years.

A father came up to me after a presentation to support the idea of multiple meanings of some behaviors. In this instance, his son had clearly violated their curfew agreement, which was unusual for this child. The parents ended up grounding him for the next night, which was Saturday. To be responsible, they also canceled their Saturday evening plans. The early part of the evening was awkward, as they all hadn't been home on a Saturday night in a long time. After dinner they dispersed into their usual evening patterns until about 9:00 p.m., when the son suggested they rent a movie. Since he was grounded, one of his parents made the trip and the movie selection. Well, to make a long story short, they ended up watching the movie, eating popcorn, and then talking for quite a while after the movie—about nothing important, just talking. At the end of the night, the dad told his son that he better be careful, as he liked the way this grounding had turned out, and that he might have to use it more often!

Grounding is an effective consequence when it is thought through and when used for a short duration. However, it is not meant to substitute for responsible parenting; in fact, it demands more parental attention than other consequences.

You learn how to become a better parent through the natural consequences of your actions, nonactions, words, and periods of silence with your teenager. If you are open to your kids and can discriminate between useful and unproductive feedback, they will teach you quite a bit about parenting, and about yourself.

> It's embarrassing to admit, but there are certainly times when my daughter is right about some of the inappropriate stances I take in some of our disagreements. In particular, she is adept at catching me in the "power trip," where I demand her to do or not do something simply because I am the parent. Usually it has her best interests at heart, but other times it is simply to assert my authority. When she is on, she is the clearest mirror around—one that's sometimes difficult to look into.

Notes

1. *Children: The Challenge* by Rudolf Dreikurs offers an excellent commentary on the role of natural consequences in the disciplining of children.

2. Ask yourself these two useful questions after a seemingly ridiculous argument with your adolescent. First, "What in our relationship is this fight really about?" It may take a while and a few different circumstances to get to the answer, but when you do get an

answer, it is well worth the effort. Then ask yourself, "And how can I respond in a different way so we can have a new outcome?"

3. Just a note about this incident: It occurred in a small town and the mom had made sure that nothing serious would happen to her son at the police station. Over the years, I've heard some parents express shock at the idea of leaving a teenager in police custody for a moment longer than necessary. Trust me, this mom had done her homework.

6

The Hidden Benefits of Arguing with Your Teenager

Why is my teenager arguing with me at every possible turn and is there any way to stop this craziness?

Teenagers argue for the same reasons that adults do: out of frustration, to make a point, to force agreement, out of a felt injustice. There is, however, a difference in that they also argue to develop their authentic adult voice and to show off to you their ability to think analytically and critically. Finally, they argue to distract us from subjects they prefer not to discuss, which is part of the hyperdefensiveness of adolescence. We will explore all of this in this chapter, beginning with an overview of the adolescent brain and ending with a much more nuanced view of adolescent arguing.

The Adolescent Brain

The human brain develops in major ways during adolescence. These neurological changes have behavioral responses—that is to say, a lot of your teenager's behavior is the direct result of his brain changing. During adolescence, brain activity expands from the back of the brain (which controls the most basic functions) to the frontal lobe (which controls complicated reasoning and decision making). Your adolescent is only beginning to make use of the frontal lobe, though—in fact, he won't be capable of the most complicated level of thinking until he is in his early twenties. These changes in physiology—specifically, the brain transitioning from basic functionality to complex reasoning—explains many of the distinct characteristics of teenagers. That is, they are often more impulsive than analytical.

This back-to-front brain development and tendency to think more impulsively than analytically partly explains why teenagers can be hyperdefensive. As they develop self-consciousness, they are simultaneously striving to always look and sound their best, but since brain research shows that the complicated reasoning necessary to meet this unrealistic standard is not yet in place, the only recourse they seem to have is defensiveness. In the extreme, this is the exaggerated dismissal of the other (storm off to their room with heightened indignation) or the outright attack of the other (read: Mom or Dad). For parents, this means the slightest raising of your voice or sideways look may send teenagers into an argumentative and defensive posture. When this happens, your only useful response is to back away slowly—in many ways they will act like a cornered animal.

Another common source of conflict between parents and teenagers has to do with the misconception among adults that teenagers always seek out risk. Understanding how the adolescent brain develops can help clarify why this stereotype isn't quite right. Research has shown that teenagers don't exactly *seek out* risk. Rather, they overestimate reward compared to adults. When she tries that double-back flip off the high dive, all she is focused on is the reward of nailing the dive and the praise she will earn from onlookers. When he punches the gas pedal to pass his buddy on the right, all he imagines are the shouts of adulation from friends and the satisfaction that will come from each retelling of the story. In fact, the researchers now understand that the love of thrill peaks around age fifteen.

So, what is the easiest way to get them to engage in less risky behavior? Diminish their inflated sense of reward. For example, simply pointing out the short lifespan of the reward can diminish your teenager's desire to engage in risky behaviors. But this is more difficult than it seems; for many teenagers, the conversation and attention that ensue in the week after driving too fast is a pretty significant reward, especially if they are struggling socially. Still though, it's a better approach than just pointing out all the risks.

The Benefits of Good Arguing

The typical arguing between parent and teenager, at least as portrayed in the media, includes lots of raised voices, lost tempers, sarcastic cheap shots, and manipulative tears. Every family also has its own version of this arguing pattern. And as any of us can intuitively recognize, this type of arguing is not good for teenagers, parents, and families. Everyone loses. There is, however, a type of arguing that is actually healthy for teenagers, parents, and families. This is good news. The harsh reality, however, is that it requires a great deal of emotional intelligence and maturity on the part of parents. Specifically, this type of arguing requires three different behaviors from parents: calmness, courage, and listening.

First, we need to learn to stay calm no matter how upset or emotional our teenagers get. If we respond in kind, then the anger and emotion will only escalate, and we will end up grounding our teenagers for years and they will tell us they hate us. On the other hand, if we learn to stay calm, then at the minimum they will not feel compelled to escalate the argument, and ideally they may even become calm too.

Second, we have to have the courage to doubt some of our assumptions and decisions and to give our teenagers the opportunity to state their case. This means we can't be dismissive of their ideas or insulted by their questions (and questioning). Rather, it means having the courage to sit and listen— essentially an attitude that conveys, "Okay, I can see this bothers you, so let's take some time to talk about this. Tell me what you think and I'll do my best to listen." This courage, and nondefensiveness, encourages our teenagers to gather their thoughts and make their case in a clear and nondramatic manner.

Third, and maybe most difficult for parents, it means really listening to what our teenagers are saying. Deeper still, it means acknowledging some of our own miscues and missteps. None of us are perfect, and nobody sees this as clearly as your teenager!

Indeed, psychologist Joseph P. Allen confirmed all of the above in his research at the University of Virginia. He found that teenagers learned how to argue (for better or worse) in their interactions with their parents. And their style and effectiveness of arguing and standing up for themselves with their parents directly correlated to how they did the same with peers. In a 2012 radio interview, Allen said, "The teens who learned to be calm and confident and persuasive with their parents acted the same way when they were with their peers."[1]

This translates into teenagers that are able to hold their ground with peers around a myriad of issues, including drugs and alcohol. Indeed, they were 40 percent more likely to say "no" than kids who did not argue well with their parents.

When parents and teenagers learn to argue well, they also open the door to *failure analysis*. This is when a teenager is able to talk with his parents about a poor decision or negative outcome in a manner that invites reflection and feedback such that the teenager can learn from experience. In short, it's every parent's dream, and it happens.

> Mitch [a tenth grader] was devastated by the grade he received on this big Spanish test—a C minus. In his mind, he had studied hard. We probed about how he studied and learned that he had reread all his notes several times and reviewed all the vocabulary quizzes. We also learned that he felt the test was unfair, that things were included that were not covered in the class. As he talked, we realized that the teacher was asking the students to think during the test, not simply to regurgitate items that they had memorized. When we pointed this out to Mitch, he was defensive, but we all hung in there. Eventually, he realized that the issue was in how he prepared for the test, and by the end of the conversation, he had some ideas about how to better prepare and how to better understand from the teacher's perspective what would be included on big tests like the one he had just completed.

This kind of failure analysis—where they make the most of us as consultants—will happen if we argue well with our teenagers and, in essence, teach them to argue well through our example.

Using Beneficial Arguing to Develop Your and Your Teenager's Mind

Arguing is often seen as a negative, but there are ways to use it constructively and positively. One of my favorite techniques for "beneficial arguing" comes from social psychology, and it is particularly useful when you're in an active disagreement with your teenager: argue *for* your child and *against* yourself. In other words, switch sides midargument. This concept will be familiar to those of you who have experience in the field of mediation. Having each party describe the situation from the other party's perspective will slow down the argument and encourage *real* listening .

The idea we are about to explore is based on experiments that point out how one's beliefs change when asked to argue the opposing side of an issue. That is, if you are a diehard Democrat, for the purposes of this research you are asked to engage in debate where you take the Republican perspective and argue on behalf of Republicans and against Democrats. The results are consistent and surprising. When participants argue for the "other" side, their core beliefs soften—which means they are more tolerant of the opposing viewpoint. It seems that just defending the other position causes us to shift our internal belief system, and this holds true across a range of issues from political parties to the death penalty to the legalization of marijuana.

Social psychologists explain this phenomenon in terms of "cognitive dissonance"—our brains have trouble holding onto two beliefs that seem mutually exclusive. "I'm a Democrat and I'm arguing for a Republican candidate" is a cognitively dissonant stance, and our brains can't handle it for long. So, to reduce cognitive dissonance, we must modify and soften our beliefs, basically convincing ourselves that the Republican candidate is a more reasonable choice.

The approach of arguing for the opposing side is astonishingly simple and surprisingly fun, especially when used in the parent-teenager relationship. Basically, you take whatever issue is at the heart of your disagreement—staying out late at night, teenage drinking, better grades, "friends with benefits," video games, curfew, cell phones—and switch sides of the issues. That is, we ask our teenager to argue on behalf of the position they do not hold: an earlier curfew, absolutely no alcohol use until age twenty-one, or the harmfulness of friends with benefits. Trust me, when it arises you will have no difficulty identifying the issue and making use of this approach.

One big warning before we continue though, this technique requires your active participation in debating on behalf of a belief you do not hold. This means that in the end your beliefs will soften. And, truthfully, this is the ultimate power of this approach: when engaged earnestly in this process, both parties shift beliefs to come closer together, and this happens through the debate, which encourages outside-the-box thinking as well as empathy and compassion for a different viewpoint.

Let's look at an example of this, say, with your second-semester sophomore, just on the brink of getting her driver's license. She is defending teenage parties where alcohol is served. Remember, in this exercise she will be making the case for why teenagers should not have alcohol at their parties. You will be making the argument for underage drinking and designated drivers.

> SARA: Let's see. Well, to start with it's against the law to drink until you are twenty-one, so you could get in lots of trouble—even lose your license if you are driving.
>
> YOU: That's just silly. Sure, it's against the law, but what are the chances of getting caught? Besides, even if I get busted, I'll never get arrested— they'll just call you to come get me.
>
> SARA: You may be right, but the law is there for a reason.
>
> YOU: It's a silly law! I hear you say that all the time about all sorts of other laws, especially anything to do with two-second stops at stop signs!
>
> SARA: Cheap shot, Dad!
>
> YOU: Stay in role.
>
> SARA: Well, besides the law, drinking is bad for you. It hurts your brain development, so not drinking will make you smarter.
>
> YOU: C'mon! I'm not talking about nonstop drinking, I'm talking about one or two glasses of wine over the course of the whole party. It's probably no worse than having a blueberry muffin everyday for breakfast.
>
> SARA: Then there's the fact that the earlier you start drinking, the more likely you are to become an alcoholic later in life.
>
> YOU: You've been watching too many public service ads. I'm talking about a couple of drinks at one party, not a few drinks every day.
>
> SARA: That's what everyone says, but without even realizing it, a couple of drinks on Saturday night turns into three or four drinks, soon followed by the same thing on Friday night. It's a slippery slope, and nobody notices as they are going down it.

YOU: Why do you turn one night of a couple of drinks into an addiction? That's crazy!

SARA: Ask Mom's sister about that. She started with a few drinks on Saturday nights too and look where she ended up—two times through alcohol rehab and still three sheets to the wind by the time the sun sets.

YOU: I knew you would pull her name out of your hat. But what about the rest of the family? Nobody else has a problem, so why should I? The odds are against it.

SARA: But is that a chance you really want to take for a couple of drinks on Saturday night?

YOU: I just don't want to be the dork with a Diet Coke in my hand all night!

SARA: That's just lame.

YOU: Maybe to you, but not to me. My friends, while I love them, can be so superficial and I can't imagine life without them.

And so it goes for a few more rounds. By the end of this interchange, you will both have softened your views. Having to articulate the other side of the argument forces you to really consider the different viewpoint—it creates a deeper understanding than active listening. In the end, she'll understand more where you are coming from and why, and you'll have a greater appreciation for the complexities of her life. It's a win-win situation.

And I can hear some of you saying, "Yeah, but what's the call in the end? Does she get to go to the party and have a couple of drinks or not?" In all honesty, that's a bad question because you have little control over the outcome. If she wants to take a couple of drinks, that's what she is going to do—maybe not at this party, but down the road for sure. No, what's happened in this interchange is much more valuable than what happens on the next Saturday night—you are both beginning to empathize with each other's situation, even bordering on compassion for one another. Deeper still, you are taking in another perspective.

This is parenting at a high level and can happen only after you have established norms based on consistency, fairness, and clear structure. Skipping to this kind of conversation without these qualities in place will not be productive, and when they are in place, this type of interaction can be monumental in terms of insight, empathy, and compassion.

Note

1. "Why A Teen Who Talks Back May Have A Bright Fugure," *All Things Considered*, NPR, January 3, 2012.

7

Alcohol, Drugs, and Parties

I'm concerned about my tenth grader going to weekend parties where alcohol and drugs are available. What can or should I do about it?

As they should, many parents worry about the influence of alcohol and drugs on their teenager's development, and specifically about the risky complications of "normal" teenage behavior with drug and alcohol use: a drunk-driving arrest, an accident while under the influence, or a sexual compromise—just to name a few possible disasters. These fears are legitimate, especially considering the risk-taking nature of adolescents.

Some parents will find this a frightening chapter to read because the reality is harsh and difficult to face. But try to make the leap of empathy necessary to grasp the following information, which is vital to understanding your teenager's world and helping her successfully navigate this world.

To begin with, take some time to respond to the following questions. Answer them honestly and separate from your role as parent. Then keep your reflections in mind for the rest of this discussion.

Think back to your high school and post–high school years.[1]

- What kind of kid were you?
- Who were your friends?
- What was your family like?
- What did you do for fun? In school? On weekends?
- Did you do things behind your parents' backs? Like what? Why?
- How did these activities affect your development as a person? What was harmful? Helpful?
- Would your parents have been upset to catch you doing these things?
- How did they respond if they did catch you? Was it a helpful response? Why or why not?
- From an adult perspective, were you ever at risk or truly in danger? Did you feel the same back then?
- Is there anything anyone in particular could have said or done to influence your behaviors, even in some minor way?

In part, teenagers experiment with alcohol and drugs because they can. That is, these substances are readily available in their day-to-day lives, and parents can do virtually nothing about this. As frightening as it sounds, alcohol and drugs are accessible to kids beginning in middle school. By the time teenagers reach high school, accessibility isn't the issue—only desire. What parents can do is educate themselves; model a healthy relationship with alcohol; provide clear guidelines, expectations, and consequences; and always emphasize safety as the bottom line. These are the directions we explore in this chapter.

Let's begin by looking at what draws teenagers toward drug and alcohol experimentation. Much of the attraction proceeds naturally from the issues examined in chapter 2, and three horizons identified in chapter 2 play an integral role: social, friendship, and personal identity.

Socially, experimenting with drinking or drugs creates an immediate niche for any teenager. At a time when fitting in is crucial, drugs and alcohol temporarily resolve questions of acceptance. That is, by using drugs or alcohol they often experience an easy acceptance into a group of peers (usually desirable peers in their eyes) and, consequently, slip into a ready-made social life. Teenagers have choices of what to do on weekends, and "friends" are calling and including them in on their plans. Also, teenagers' defenses are lowered under the influence of alcohol or drugs—they are less self-conscious and more spontaneous, two highly desirable traits for any teenager.

I was never all that sure of myself with friends. It seemed like I really wasn't close to anybody, at least not in the way I wanted. But when I started partying a little bit, I loosened up. I was more confident and liked myself more. And most important, people seemed to really like me. They said I was funny and lively. And soon I had a full social life. Lots of phone calls during the week and invitations to parties on the weekends. It was terrific!

Most adolescents long to feel the sense of intimacy that comes when one is accepted into a social group. Under the influence of alcohol or drugs, however, they feel a pseudo-intimacy that many mistake for the real thing. That is, in this new social group and while under the influence, they probably experience their most open conversations, which are often felt as real intimacy. Their defenses are down and they revel in sharing their "true self" and having others do the same. In a sense, they briefly escape their singular identity and somewhat merge with another. The hitch is that while the closeness feels real, the means are artificial (which, of course, is an idea that most parents understand and that most teenagers are unable to comprehend). They haven't yet developed the necessary skills or addressed their fundamental aloneness to achieve true intimacy. They haven't earned it; instead, they have artificially made the leap, which in too many instances leaves them dependent on the artificial means. Or as veterans of the 1960s recall:

When I took drugs I saw God!
What did God say to you?
Don't take drugs.

When teenagers partially define themselves through alcohol and drug use, they also distance themselves from their parents, since few parents encourage the use of alcohol or drugs in their adolescents' lives. In this sense, the choice to go against parental guidelines is an assertion of their independence and autonomy by testing the limits at home. In a strange way, when they do this they feel more in charge of their lives, and we've seen that asserting independence and developing a stable personal identity are crucial for eventual transition into the adult world. However, when alcohol and drugs are the central means to independence and an identity, there is cause for concern, besides the obvious health and safety issues.

Some teenagers use drugs and alcohol as a way to avoid deeper traumas and grief. For them, alcohol and drugs are a means of covering up or keeping unconscious certain pains that are only resolvable on a conscious level. They relegate these conflicts to the unconscious realm where they are routinely "acted out," without ever consciously addressing them. Unfortunately, we have all seen adults stuck in this pattern when they abuse alcohol and drugs. Such people often exhibit significant personality changes while under the influence, such as withdrawal, depression, outrageously extroverted behavior, or aggression. Alcohol or drug abuse, like any kind of addiction, relieves the internal stress and pressure brought on by unconscious conflicts without ever addressing the ongoing source of stress. An extreme example:

> I began getting high daily just as my parents started fighting more (they eventually got divorced). It was really crazy in my house at that time, so I would come home, go up to my room, and get high pretty much every day. Sometimes I even got stoned in the morning while walking to school. It was all just too crazy. But it was the only way I could cope.

And a not-so-extreme example:

> Yeah, I pretty much party every weekend, but it's no big deal. I mean it's the only time I get to relax and kick back. The rest of the time there is so much pressure to get good grades, succeed, practice hard, and be a good person. This [partying] is my time, when I can just forget about all the expectations, goals, and guilt, and just let go and be myself.

Many parents think that alcohol and drug experimentation is a terrible thing. However, in real life it is not that cut-and-dried. Many teenagers are able to experiment with drugs and alcohol without becoming dependent and in a way that doesn't impede their ability to grow and mature. Research by Jonathan Shedler and Jack Block showed that adolescents who experimented moderately with drugs (no more than one time per month and usually just marijuana) were psychologically healthier than those who abused drugs (more than one time per month) *and* than those who abstained from drugs altogether.[2] This is not to say that drug experimentation is either good or recommended; rather, it indicates that drug abuses are the symptoms of deeper problems (or, as we'll discuss later, sometimes the result of a biological or genetic predisposition).

In the Shedler-Block study, which followed the same 101 boys and girls over fifteen years, those who were psychologically the healthiest as children were the same ones who just moderately experimented with drugs as teenagers. This, I believe, puts drug experimentation into a more differentiated framework. While moderate experimentation is not necessarily good, it is also not necessarily a sign of a deep psychological crisis. On the other hand, more than casual experimentation is cause for deep concern, not only as a problem in itself, but also as a sign of deeper problems. This research clearly shows that drug or alcohol use can itself be the cover of deeper issues.

In summary, the initial acceptance into a social group that comes with using alcohol and drugs is provisional, as many teenagers (and adults) discover when they try to drop the use and keep the same social group. Adolescents—and, again, adults—crave intimate discussions and need to learn how to have these interactions without being under the influence of drugs or alcohol. And, as the reliance on alcohol or drugs in the search for intimacy grows, the skills for true intimacy atrophy. Differentiating yourself from those around you in a way that is true to yourself is a necessarily long and at times arduous process—there are no shortcuts, especially through alcohol and drug use.

Before we discuss what parents can do, let's go over some basic information on alcohol and a variety of available drugs. Alcohol is familiar: Most of us go to parties and functions where alcohol is served regularly. We have all developed our own personal relationships with alcohol—possibly punctuated by a few painful lessons along the way. Alcohol is part of the adult world in this country; adolescents using alcohol are prematurely acting like adults.

Drugs are a slightly different matter. They are illegal, and fewer adults have experienced them. To many, they are a frightening mystery. At this point, a piece of advice: If you don't know the differences between various drugs (and you probably won't because they are changeable and cyclical to a very high degree), then educate yourself. Try your local library or bookstore (also see the bibliography in this book). It is both naive and blinding to place all drugs in the same category. In this regard, what follows is a very brief description of a few of the more available drugs.[3]

> **Marijuana (Cannabis):** A plant that is typically smoked. The psychoactive ingredient is tetrahydrocannabinol (THC), which has dramatically increased in concentration from the 1960s and 1970s to the present and is at least five to seven times more potent. "Marijuana can act as a stimulant or depressant depending on the variety and amount of chemical that is absorbed in the brain, but most often, it acts as a relaxant, making users sleepy, drowsy, and more inner focused." The

effects last from four to six hours and begin to affect the user within twenty minutes of smoking.

Cocaine: Comes from the coca plant. In its powder form, this drug is most often snorted and is absorbed into the brain within three to five minutes. The subjective effect of cocaine is very pleasurable: "increased confidence, a willingness to work (sometimes endlessly), a diminishing of life's problems, and a euphoric rush." The drug is metabolized quickly by the body, typically within forty minutes, so the effects are relatively short-lived. Physically, there is a significant increase in the release of epinephrine [adrenalin] that "raises the blood pressure, increases the heart rate, causes rapid breathing, tenses muscles, and causes the jitters."

Crack Cocaine: A chemically altered form of cocaine that is smokeable. It is cheaper than cocaine, with the same effects, except that it is much more intense and is absorbed much more quickly into the brain, generally five to eight seconds.

Amphetamines (speed): A stimulant that is usually ingested orally but that can be snorted, smoked, or injected. Amphetamines have cocaine-like effects but of longer duration and at a significantly lower cost. Amphetamines come in a variety of forms and strengths.

LSD: A drug that "can cause mental changes and psychedelic effects," depending on the dose, the size of which is seldom known by the typical street purchaser. LSD directly affects the emotional center of the brain and thus opens the user to euphoria or panic. Thus, the user's mental state and the setting of the experience contribute significantly to the effects of the drug. Discernible effects from the drug last eight to twelve hours. Typical doses of LSD are smaller than those taken during the 1960s, thus making the effect similar to amphetamines.

"Designer Drugs" (MDA, MMDA, MDM, MDE): Synthetic drugs that create feelings of euphoria, intimacy, and well-being. They derive from the amphetamine molecule and thus also induce stimulatory effects. Each varies in duration but in general lasts eight to twelve hours.

Heroin: Part of the opiate family that, when injected directly into the bloodstream, takes fifteen to thirty seconds to affect the central nervous system. Subjectively, the user experiences intense and extreme euphoria.

Alcohol: The oldest psychoactive drug known to man that, when used in moderation, reduces inhibitions and lessens tension. "The more alcohol that is drunk the freer the user feels, but the blood pressure is lowered, motor reflexes are slowed, digestion becomes poor, body heat is lost, and sexual excitement is diminished." Different types of alcohol vary in strength depending on the "proof" (100 percent alcohol = 200 proof). Generally, beer is 4 percent to 8 percent, wine is 12 percent, and liquors are 40 percent to 43 percent.

Prescription drugs: To go along with all these illegal drugs is the increasing recreational use of prescription drugs by teenagers. Drugs are typically pilfered from parents' medicine cabinets and shared (or sometimes sold) to friends. The most commonly misused prescription drugs are Vicodin, OxyContin, Ritalin, Adderall, and cough medicine (DXM.)

Behind every parent's anxiety over alcohol and drugs, besides the short-term concern over safety, is the long-term question: will my teenager get addicted? If someone had a crystal ball and could tell you for sure that your child would never form an addiction to any of these substances, it wouldn't diminish many of your concerns over these substances, at least in the long run. So the big question is, How do people go from occasional use to addiction? The most common theory of addiction includes components of biology, psychology, and sociology. Some of these statistics are frightening:[4]

- If one parent is an alcoholic or addict, the child is 34 percent more likely to suffer from some sort of addiction.
- If both parents are alcoholics or addicts, their child is 400 percent more likely to suffer from some sort of addiction.
- If a child is male and both his father and grandfather are alcoholics or addicts, he is 900 percent more likely to suffer from some sort of addiction.

The graph below illustrates the path that addiction follows along the compulsion curve in an individual. Two points are important to keep in mind. First, biological predisposition determines how quickly one moves along this curve. That is, a highly sensitive person moves from experimental use to abuse after only several exposures. (Abuse, as used here, is defined as the continued use of drugs or alcohol in spite of the negative consequences it causes in one's life.) A person not predisposed to addiction may take years to move along this same compulsion curve to abuse. Second, once a person goes past habituation, there is no turning back; abstinence is what's needed to stay sober. Prior to that point, an individual can move back along the curve to social or experimental use.

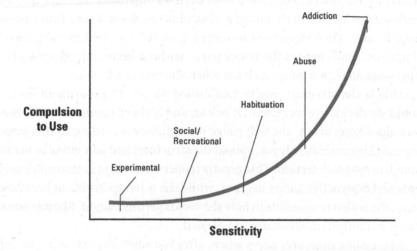

Now to the question of who becomes an alcoholic or addict. As Dr. Inaba is fond of saying, "Contrary to popular belief, it is not exclusively the bad, stupid, amoral, or disenfranchised. It is actually quite the opposite; most addicts or alcoholics fall into the categories of educated, intelligent, skilled, and sensitive." For instance, physicians are eight times more likely to become addicts than members of the general population, and six times more likely to become alcoholics. Also, those with the highest rate of addiction and alcoholism belong to the group MENSA, whose members must have an IQ of at least 140 just to qualify to take the MENSA exam. Ironically, adolescents that are bright, motivated, and ambitious are actually in the highest-risk category.

Back to the initial question of what parents can do. The answer is both a lot and not much. Short of keeping your teenager in the house every night, there is nothing you can do to guarantee that she will not drink or use drugs. Not very practical. Checking her breath at night (or in extreme circumstances, urine samples) also doesn't do much to prevent the behavior. Neither parents nor anyone else can prevent drinking or drug use, but it does not mean that all is hopeless. Far from it.

Perhaps the most crucial factors are the conversations you have with your adolescent before usage ever becomes an issue and the example you set in your relationship to alcohol and drugs. Adolescents look and test for congruency. In your conversations on this topic, clearly outline your position on alcohol and drugs, acknowledge the reality of the adolescent world, and discuss possible consequences of broken agreements, like time-limited grounding, car restrictions, and earlier curfews. Again, let the consequences speak for themselves so that drug and alcohol use doesn't turn into a power struggle later. Then expect her to mess up, or at least don't be surprised if it happens. And—here is the tricky part—without becoming adversarial or hypersuspicious, you must catch her when she breaks the rules.

This is the structure you've established for her to experiment within, should she decide to experiment. It's clear, and it's been communicated. Now, if she does experiment, she will gauge her behavior according to this structure (and how consistently you uphold the structure) and will monitor herself enough to escape detection. This greatly reduces the risk of catastrophic accidents and destructive habits because, while she is irresponsible in her choice to use, she is also responsible in how she avoids getting caught. She has somewhat internalized the structure you created.

At the same time, stay savvy when, after you smell alcohol on her breath, she swears it was the first time she used. Give her ample time to reconsider and stay very suspicious if she sticks to the "first time" story. From the adolescent side of experimentation, believe it or not, it's fairly simple to escape detection if one is very careful and conscientious, so if you catch her, she is getting sloppy in her precautions (a bad sign). If, however, you keep your eyes closed, you essentially relax the structure and create room for more out-of-control and potentially catastrophic behavior.

> At first when I began to party, I was real careful not to get caught. I always stopped [partying] a couple of hours before going home, ate some smelly food, and sometimes even changed my clothes if there had been a lot of smoking going on. It was a hassle and all, but at least I was pretty sure I wouldn't get caught. But after a while, I began to realize

that my parents didn't have a clue! It got to the point where I began to wonder what it would take to get caught. I remember once even finishing a beer on the back porch before heading into bed. I even said good night to my dad! Another time I was so wasted that I never got past the living room sofa, where I passed out for the night. In the morning, they [his parents] asked me why I slept on the sofa. I told them I wasn't tired when I got home so I watched some TV and must have fallen asleep. They believed me without a second thought, even though the TV was off and I was facing the wrong direction on the sofa!

On the other hand, when you pay attention and follow through, it's much easier for your teenager to be honest.

I swear my dad has a bloodhound's nose. If I even have a sip of beer or [have] one smoke, he smells it on me from ten feet away! And since I have to wake my parents when I get home to say goodnight, there is no way I can get away with it. It isn't worth lying about, so I usually cop to it and deal with the consequences. At least it's all on the table that way.

Now, let's turn our attention to the parties. Make your expectations clear to your teenager, as well as your own role. For instance, if the rule is no unchaperoned parties and you insist that your son provide you with the parents' address and phone number, you must be consistent in acquiring this information. (Expect him to test you, and if you forget once, expect him to express shock and indignation the next time you ask for the information.) Then, by all means, get through your own discomfort and shyness and call the parents, if that was the agreement. Otherwise, you'll make it too seductive for him to lie at a future date. If he must follow the agreed-upon rules, then you must enforce them.

Part of the problem is that it is really, really easy to lie to my parents. Too easy. They set all these standards and agreements, but they never follow through, so I just tell them what they want to hear and go about my business.

Also, you might be the only parent who phones the chaperones, which may delight them if they had planned on being out of town that night! Which leads to a very important point on the whole topic of raising adolescents. High school students live in a very tight community. For the most part, they all know or know of one another in their school. They understand the norms of their high school culture, including the various social scenes. On the other hand, parents often live in relative ignorance about their kids' lives, and, frankly, most kids like it this way. So if you want to stay informed, you need to make it happen. Don't be afraid to call the chaperones of any party your teenager wants to attend. And go to school events, even if just to meet other parents. As long as your presence isn't too conspicuous, your teenager may act one way and silently feel somewhat differently.

> I used to be embarrassed that my dad came to every soccer game I played. He was there from start to finish; always wished me good luck before-hand and said "good game" after each game. It was sort of a pain, even if it was sort of cute too. Anyway, he unexpectedly missed a game this year. What was surprising was that I missed having him there. When I got home I asked him where he was, and he said that he had forgotten! I couldn't believe it. I was so mad even though I didn't say anything.

Back to the parties. As in other areas of the parent-adolescent relationship, a useful perspective from which to develop party-going guidelines is the future. Imagine when your teenager is leaving home for college or about to move into his first apartment. At this point, he is essentially on his own with no direct supervision or guidelines other than the law—and the experience he's had with your structure during high school. So, when he leaves home, with what continuum of experiences and decisions must he be familiar in order to successfully handle this level of freedom?

> We talked with Karen regularly between ninth and twelfth grades about party guidelines. Essentially, we had a system of increased freedom and responsibility that developed out of negotiation and her behavior relative to the guidelines. It started in the ninth grade, when she couldn't go to any unchaperoned parties, and increased in freedom until second-semester senior year, when she made decisions on which parties to attend and was responsible for being home at a reasonable time without any explicit curfew. Overall, it worked quite well. Sure, there were a few rough and doubtful moments along the way, but oddly enough there were no problems during the end of the senior year, when

we most expected difficulties. In fact, by then she was talking to us more openly than ever.

Be willing, too, to periodically play the "bad guy" for your teenager. Even if it's a stretch of the truth, you can do things that allow your adolescent to gracefully say no.

> I had gotten drunk a few times at parties with my friends, but I didn't like it too much. At the same time, though, I wanted to fit in. Finally, one night, I couldn't take it anymore, so I blurted it all out to my dad. After he got over the initial shock, he kind of smiled to himself and asked if I wanted some help.
>
> A couple of weeks later, I went to a party and had a couple of beers (as my dad and I had planned). When my friends dropped me off, he was waiting up for me. Needless to say, everyone knew I was in big trouble! And, as prearranged, he yelled a little (just loud enough for them to hear) and I got "grounded" for a week. Of course, I complained bitterly to my friends, but from then on they completely understood when I didn't want to drink anymore.

Finally, health and safety are the bottom line. No matter what poor decisions have been made, what rules have been violated, or what lies have been told, teenagers must know deep in the marrow of their bones that their safety far outweighs all other concerns.

> At the very beginning of high school, my parents sat me down for our "alcohol talk." Nothing unusual there, except at the end. My father leaned forward and said, "Now, no matter what happens, understand that your safety is more important to us than any of these rules. So, in the unlikely but possible event that you are in a position where you are unable to safely get home—you've been drinking, the driver has been drinking, or whatever comes up—you must promise to call us, anytime, day or night. We'll come get you, and we won't ask any questions or ever report your friends. In the morning, we will talk about it, but understand that, when you show that level of responsibility, the consequences will be minimal. No matter what else we've said tonight, this is by far the most important. Do you understand?" Since then, I have had to call a few times, and each time it has worked out fairly well.

In this same health-and-safety discussion (and in the driver's-license discussion in chapter 15), it's a good idea to talk about the role of the designated driver. Fortunately, more and more teenagers are taking this role seriously. It's also a great way for adolescents to be a part of the group without having to get into drug or alcohol use.

> More teenagers use designated drivers than most people think. I know most of my friends do. At most parties, there are actually two parties going on—the larger one with alcohol and a smaller one for the designated drivers who are drinking soda.

As I'm sure you've noticed, as with the earlier chapter on structure and limits, there is no ideal, no right set of rules and guidelines for alcohol and drug experimentation. Each family is different and must develop its own guidelines. What is essential is that they are consistent with other family values and beliefs and that everyone follows through on the agreements they make. This is how trust is developed.

One final thought on this subject that I would be remiss to neglect: parents who allow their high school teenagers to throw parties where alcohol and drugs are served. It is as if they see these substances as a rite of passage that they can't fight and as a result opt instead to keep in good stead with their kids by hosting the parties. They frequently do so under the misguided notion that teenagers are going to drink and use drugs anyway, so it's better that it happen under their roof where they can monitor it. This is bad logic, for a few reasons.

First, the nature of adolescents is that they test limits. When we move the limits back (by allowing them to host an alcohol party), we don't satisfy their need to test limits; we just create a greater distance before they get to the limit they need to test. This means more alcohol and drug use, not less.

> I knew in my gut that it wasn't right, but for some reason I went along with Steven's insistence on having a party where we served alcohol. My husband and I were there the entire time and made sure everyone was safe to drive or go home by the end of the party, but still it was nerve-racking. Thankfully it went fine.
>
> But then, the next weekend, I was horrified on Saturday night when Steven got home from a night out with his friends; he walked into the house, said hello, opened the refrigerator, grabbed a beer, and popped it open before I could say a word! He didn't get that the party the week

before was an exception to the rule; he thought it was the new rule.
I gasped in fear wondering how and where else he was bringing this
"new rule" to bear on his life.

Second, many parents who serve alcohol at their kids' parties never
inform the other parents of what they are doing. So when their Johnny or
Suzy goes to the party, the other parents have no idea that, unlike other parties, drinking is being sanctioned by the adults at this one. The lack of this
information limits their ability to stay active as parents. And, unfortunately,
the results of the lack of these facts are often tragic.

On one of my appearances on *Oprah*, I met a mom whose fifteen-year-old
daughter had gone to one of these parties. (The mom was unaware that alcohol was being served by the parents.) Her daughter went to the party with two
friends and drank, and when they were getting ready to leave, the host dad
refused to let them drive, saying he would call their parents to come get them
or help them find a ride with someone he deemed able to drive. Well, as teenagers are wont to do under these circumstances, the girl and her two friends
declined both options and came up with a third: it was a beautiful night so
they would walk home. And they did. But tragically, while crossing one of the
busier streets in town, the girls were hit by a car, and this woman's daughter
was killed.

Third, when parents allow their kids to host parties with alcohol, they
have abandoned the role as consultant parents. Instead, through their behavior, they are trying to stay friends with their teenagers, which is a recipe for
disaster. Teenagers have plenty of friends, but they only have two parents.
They need you more as a mom or a dad than as a friend, especially during
adolescence. The bottom line is that, if they respect you during adolescence,
you will have strong components for friendship with them as they get older.
But if you lose their respect during adolescence, then getting that respect and
a quality relationship later on is an uphill battle.

Fourth, whether they ever voice it or not, there is a part of every teenager
that wants you to set and hold limits.

> My son is a ninth grader and a couple of days ago came to us saying
> he was going to try marijuana. He said all the other kids are doing it
> so he wanted to try it. We, of course, said absolutely not. As you might
> imagine, we had a terrible argument that ended with him saying: "Well,
> there is nothing you can do to stop me!" That got my husband and me

to thinking—he was right, there was nothing we could do to stop him.
A couple of days later we talked with our son and told him that, because
his wanting to try marijuana scared us so much (and because he was
right, there was nothing we could do to stop him), we were going to get
him some marijuana to try in the safety of our home, where we could
take care of him if something went wrong. He was stunned. But then he
blew up at us: "What kind of parents are you? How can you buy drugs
for me and encourage me to use them? This is nuts! Don't you love me?"
And again, he was right. We did not get him the marijuana and we
learned a great deal about our role with our son that day.

Self-Assessment Tool

Over the years many parents (and teenagers) have asked how to tell if you are
in over your head with alcohol or drug use. The simplest and most elegant tool
I know is the CAGE assessment, referred to me by Dr. Inaba. It's an empiri-
cally validated instrument and is comprised of four, simple questions.

C = Cut down. Have you ever tried to decrease or mitigate your use of
alcohol or drugs?

A = Anger. Have you ever been irritated or angry when discussing your
own use of alcohol or drugs with someone else?

G = Guilt. Have you experienced guilt or shame over your use of alcohol or
drugs, including anything you have done while under their influence?

E = Eye-opener. Have you ever felt the need to drink alcohol or take drugs
in order to function or interact better?

Yes to any one of these questions means there is a potential for alcohol or
drug abuse and probably the need for a more rigorous assessment. Yes to two
or more indicates a problem and calls for more assessment. Sharing this system with your teenagers can help them self-identify their level of use.

Notes

1. The post–high school years are included here for adults, because with the increasing pace of social change, your kids are facing certain issues and decisions much earlier than you did.

2. Jonathan Shedler and Jack Block, "Adolescent Drug Use and Psychological Health: A Longitudinal Inquiry" *American Psychology* 45, no. 5 (May 1990): 612–30.

3. The information that follows is excerpted from a book that I highly recommend by Darryl S. Inaba and William E. Cohen, *Uppers, Downers, and All Arounders*. As drugs and drug potencies are constantly changing, the information is almost or is already somewhat out-of-date. Use this data as background information only.

4. These statistics are quoted from a talk given by Dr. Darryl Inaba to the parents and faculty of University High School in February 1994.

8

Technology and Social Networking

How do I understand and monitor my teenager's use of social media sites like Facebook and Twitter and the Internet in general? Should I be worried about her constant texting and cell phone use?

This is inevitably a huge part of your teenager's life, and the subject of new sites and new technologies raises parents' blood pressure quickly, so let's take our time. Let's start by taking a more global look at this generation and how they have grown up in the context of technology. The list of new technologies and what they are capable of is lengthy and continually growing: texting, Twitter, Skype, Facebook, laptops, tablets, smartphones, email, social networking, and more.

All this technology shares one thing in common: it allows users to stay almost constantly connected. For a moment, think back to chapter 2 when we explored the adolescent world and the importance of friendship and social acceptance. Suddenly, our teenagers' obsession with technology (especially technology that makes peers more accessible) makes sense. Being able to stay constantly connected to their social group makes the generation a more peer-oriented group than we were as kids. Quite simply, they *can* connect more so they do connect more. The relentless need to stay connected often leads to compulsive and obsessive checking of various devices.

> It's like I just can't help myself—every chance I get I pull out my phone
> to check my texts and Facebook. I don't even think about it anymore,
> I just do it. So do all my friends. It's just cool to see a text waiting or a
> comment on my Facebook page—not sure how to describe it. Plus, it's
> not like it's just teenagers. My dad is the worst—he's constantly check-
> ing his "Crackberry"!

In this regard, our teenagers aren't alone in feeling the seductive pull
of connectivity and the cyber world. In fact, just the other day I read a story
that described a new way to figure out who picks up the tab at a restaurant. At
the start of the meal, everyone puts their phone on the table. The first one to
check or respond to their phone pays. There is always a "winner."

We know that this increased connectivity has effects beyond the social
lives of teenagers. Take education, for example. In the complicated world of
unintended consequences, Duke professor and author Cathy Davidson made
a surprising insight about her students and college term papers:

> Given that I was teaching a class based on learning and the Internet,
> having my students blog was a no-brainer. I supplemented this with
> more traditionally structured academic writing, and when I had both
> samples in front of me, I discovered something curious. Their writing
> online, at least in their blogs, was incomparably better than in the tra-
> ditional term papers they wrote for the class. In fact, given all the tripe
> one hears from pundits about how the Internet dumbs down our kids,
> I was shocked that elegant bloggers often turned out to be the clunkiest
> and most pretentious of research paper writers.[1]

Educators throughout the country are wrestling with these types of
observations without any solid conclusions.

> For the most part, I talk to people on three different levels. The first is
> a pretty casual level that I do with all my friends and acquaintances at
> school. The second is the much deeper level of my true thoughts and
> feelings. Usually, these are pretty confusing at first, so I need some
> time to figure them out. This is what I do online, with my friends from
> school. I really got into texting and Skype when my boyfriend graduated
> and went to college a thousand miles away. It's been great for us.

Because technology is ubiquitous, we need to guide our kids on etiquette and safety, and this often means we have some catching up to do ourselves. Fortunately, there are lots of good books and websites out there to help parents.

> I've been computer phobic for years, but once my son started get-
> ting into it in middle school, I knew I had to do something. First, I got
> someone to help me learn the basics of email and getting on the Web,
> and then I spent the greater part of two nights surfing all around the
> Internet: the good, the bad, and all the in-between. I set up a Facebook
> account—even a Twitter account too. It was a crash course, but that's
> the nature of technology. With just a few basic tools, I could explore and
> learn on my own with complete freedom. And I got to experience first-
> hand what a powerful draw web surfing and constant communication
> can become—I wouldn't have picked that up from the books.

As with just about everything, your presence and attention are the best deterrent to your teenager getting in over his head on the Internet. Stay inter-ested in what he is doing and where he is going on the Internet, whether he's using a desktop, laptop, or smartphone. Also, right from the beginning, set up some basic guidelines. Here are some good ones to start you off.

- If your family has a desktop, put it in a public place in your home (definitely not in your teenager's room). This way you can walk by whenever you choose and peer over her shoulder to see what she is doing. (You also might catch her keying in "pos," which means "parent over shoulder"!) According to the experts, this is probably the single most important thing you can do in terms of overall Internet safety. Knowing that you can come by at any moment will help your teenager stay within the agreed-upon parameters of cyberspace. If, however, your family is already overrun with portable devices—laptops, tablets, smartphones—then you have to modify this guideline. This might include a shared account on these devices or periodically reviewing the device and how your teenager is spending her time.
- To be sure, when younger teenagers get an email account, insist that they tell you the password. (With Facebook, get the password *and* require them to "friend" you.) Then tell your teenager that, from time to time, you will check his emails, not to read the details of his life but to make sure there aren't any inappropriate emails in the account.

Tell him this before you get the account. If it's not part of the initial agreement, it's tough to do retroactively unless the teenager has already gotten in trouble online. But checking your teenager's online presence will help him keep himself in line. And as he gets older and proves himself responsible online, you can withdraw the need to know passwords.

- If your teenager surfs the Net, insist that she not erase the history in the web browser. This allows you to periodically check where she is visiting, which is something you should tell her you will be doing.
- The Parent over the Shoulder Rule: When he is in doubt about what he is doing online, tell your teenager to imagine you are standing behind him watching. If your presence would deter him in any way, then he probably should stop what he is doing.
- Make sure your kids understand that they should never give out personal information to people they don't know from face-to-face interactions. Sadly, there are perpetrators out there trolling for sad and confused kids. And it's remarkable how much they can learn about your child with just a little information.

Many parents want to know when they should give their kids access to technologies like smartphones and laptops. This is a tricky question to answer, since the landscape of this technology is changing so quickly. As a general rule, the best time to start is in middle school—and exactly when depends on your teenager's maturity level. The "right time" is almost always a compromise between when your teenager thinks he is ready and when you imagine he'll be ready. Meet him halfway.

For the next bit, we are going to discuss how teenagers get themselves in trouble online, but one significant caveat first. The research shows that the teenagers getting in trouble online are the same ones getting into trouble at school. This does not mean we should fall asleep at the wheel, but rather we should not necessarily make ourselves unduly anxious by thinking our otherwise successful kids are at undue risk.

> Yeah, there are some kids that bully on Facebook and that surf all these crazy sites, but it's not most kids. Of course, they get all the attention, but they're not typical.

When teenagers get in over their heads, boys and girls tend to do it differently, not always, but more often than not, and it fits with how they are developmentally different. Girls are focused on relationships and boys more on outcomes, so let's look at how this plays out.

Facebook and other social networks are more the province of teenage girls than boys. Sure, both use them in equal measure, but for girls it is a continuation of interpersonal power that they are testing out in their face-to-face relationships. Unfortunately, they have to learn this the hard way, and often it happens in middle school by watching a peer get her reputation burned. It is brutal.

> It was awful. These two popular girls, for no reason at all, started picking on this other girl at school—I don't even think this other girl knew it was happening, at least at first. They wrote all sorts of terrible things that weren't true, but how could she defend herself? Finally, her parents went to the school, and, while the two girls got in trouble, the damage was done. She actually transferred to another school later in the year, and I don't blame her.

This is why it's important as a parent to periodically check in on your teenager's various postings. As most teenagers are getting their social networking lives going in late middle school or early high school, you want to get them off to a good start and make the most of your influence on the front end. Should they go off the rails later, on you simply pull back on their freedom for a bit—the world of natural consequences. That is, the best response to misbehaviors in this arena, in addition to making amends with the aggrieved party, is limiting access for a couple of weeks and then watching closely after the consequence has played itself out.

Gaming

Boys certainly stay on top of their social networks, but unlike most girls, the majority of their online energy goes into gaming, and, unfortunately, pornography. The gaming world offers endless challenges with lots of rewards along the way for outcome-based boys.

These games are a wonderful source of enjoyment, diversion, and relaxation for many teenagers—and adults—but like everything else, you need to pay attention to what your teenager plays and how much he plays. Start by examining the rating that comes on all the games. (CommonSenseMedia .org is a great resource for what is appropriate at various ages.) You might not make a final decision based on a rating, but it is a place to start the conversation with your teenager. Then watch or play the game alongside your teenager. That should be enough for you to know.

> The game seemed fine when I read the description on the box, but when
> I sat down with Tommy while he played, I was horrified! It was violent,
> sexist, and racist. I think he was even a little embarrassed by the content, especially with me sitting next to him.

Not all games are bad, though; some of these games are teaching our kids worthwhile lessons (even if they are habit-forming).

> I play *World of Warcraft* [a multiplayer online game that has more than
> ten million subscribers]. Right from the beginning, I got hooked. It's
> another world. I spend as much time on it as my parents allow. There is
> nothing bad about the game either. You learn leadership, strategy, and
> how to work together.

The downside of games like this is that they can easily get in the way of other developmental tasks these kids need to be involved in, as we will see a bit later. The upside is that the games foster and deepen the process of learning. How many places are there in a teenager's life where he will consistently compete until the point of failure, learn from his mistakes, and eagerly start all over again? If we could get kids to focus on math like this, we would have the most and best mathematicians in the world, which is exactly why educators are trying to better understand how to make use of this technology in the classroom.

The dark side of the Internet for teenage boys is pornography and its unprecedented availability in the online world. The pornography online is nothing like the *Playboy* magazines of your adolescence. Easily accessible pornography and adolescent hormones are a bad combination.

I've got an iPad with fast wireless access, so my friends like to hang out at my house a lot. A while ago, Casey went surfing for porn while Terry and I watched. It was wild what he could find in just a few minutes. We all joked and laughed, and after they left I went back to some of those sites. And now, whenever I'm near the computer, it's all I think about. I even get up late at night to surf the porn sites. I'm scared, but I don't want to tell my parents because they would be so shocked and upset.

Stanford professor and author Philip Zimbardo describes what happens to boys on the Internet—between porn and gaming—as an arousal addiction. Unlike a drug or alcohol addiction where someone wants more of the same, in an arousal addiction they want something different and unpredictable, which they get from gaming and surfing the Web. Worse, Zimbardo postulates that this type of addiction leaves boys ill-prepared for two essential areas in their lives: school and romance. In school, students must be able to pay extended attention to mostly unarousing subjects. In romance, it leaves boys without the social skills necessary to build healthy romantic relationships that require time and subtlety.

With both boys and girls, one of the keys in helping them modulate their own use—be it of a gaming console or a cell phone or Facebook—is to make sure they are getting enough of the other experiences essential to a healthy adolescence: face time with friends, exercise and athletics, outdoor time, making art, playing an instrument.

Many parents purchase filter programs that block out many pornographic and other inappropriate websites. This is a good idea, but it is not enough. None of these programs are 100 percent effective, or even close for that matter. They are a good start, but not a substitute for ongoing conversations with your teenager or your presence and supervision as they explore the online world. In general, there is a developmental progression toward freedom for your teenager: more supervision and attention in middle school and less in high school, unless they get themselves in over their heads.

Regardless of content, however, you should worry when teenagers are playing video games to the exclusion of just about everything else. If your teenager has friends and other interests, then video games can be healthy. But if he comes home after school and does nothing other than play, you need to wonder about a lack of social life and a group of friends. (See chapters 2 and 12 or more on these topics.) However, this does not mean that solitary video games and a group of friends are mutually exclusive. Just make sure there is a balance.

> After school, we [three friends] pretty much pick a house and go there until dinner. It may sound odd, but all we do is play video games. All we do is take turns playing games and watching each other. We really don't talk all that much. I know it sounds weird, but it's much better than playing alone.

Along similar lines, texting is another area where parents are playing catch-up to their teenagers. If done with people they know and in moderation, texting is usually fine, but you need to keep your eyes peeled.

> I couldn't believe it. My son sat next to me for the entire ride to the mall and back—we even talked to each other for a bit. I knew he was texting some friends, but I just imagined it was checking in with buddies—that kind of blather that teenagers do just to be in contact with one another. It was only when I got home and asked to see his phone—part of my right as a parent to a surprise inspection—that I discovered all his texts were really sexting [sending explicitly sexual messages, usually from mobile device to mobile device, and at times even photos] with a girl from school. Right in front of me!

For most teenagers, texting is a way to connect with friends when they get home after school or practice, before they start their homework, and, for some, before they go to sleep. Again, thinking about them developmentally, teenagers need the security of knowing their friendships are in alignment before they can settle in to deal with tasks like homework, and texting is an easy way to check in with lots of friends in a hurry. (When we were teenagers, it was the phone—texting has largely replaced the phone in this regard.)

> The weird part is that when we text each other it's not like we have anything new to tell each other. It's usually only been an hour or two since we've seen each other. It's more that we just check in with each other. I don't know, but it's like my body gets home but my mind isn't home until I check in with my friends. I wish my mom would understand this and not act like a hurt puppy when I don't feel like talking when I get home after school.

In this regard, a big question on parents' minds is at what age kids should get a cell phone, which realistically includes texting at the least and possibly even Internet access. Just understand right from the start that it's about communication and status. For some kids, it's conspicuous consumption, which is why they always want the latest phone with the latest gadgets. But when the cell phone has realistic structure and limits in place, it is a great means of communication. It's a wonderful way for your son to give you a heads up when he's going to be late for curfew, for your daughter to let you know that she is leaving the movie theater and heading to a friend's house.

> My cell phone is the greatest thing for my mom and me. Sometimes, after a fight or for no particular reason, we'll leave each other messages where we say things we probably would never say face-to-face, or at least I wouldn't say in person! "I love you. Sorry for what I said this morning. It's tough now because we're so alike, but just think how wonderful it'll be when we get through this phase." And what was really cool is when I found out that, just like me, she saves all these messages on her voice mail and replays them when she gets down. That's so cool!

Bottom line, like any other privilege, make sure you sort through the guidelines before you allow your teenager to have a cell phone. Then make sure the agreements are upheld.

Television and Music

To many parents, music and TV seem like variations of the same thing, but they are quite different. Teenagers are more active in how they listen to and imagine along with music than they are when they sit and passively take in what is on the screen—regardless of whether it is a television or computer screen.

One aspect of television that, I believe, is harmful to adolescents' psychological development is the overly contrived and simplified emotional aspects of the shows and characters. Even in the most poorly written and badly acted shows, a producer can, through the use of camera angles, clichéd lines, and music, manipulate the emotions of an unsuspecting viewer. The illusion created says that I (the viewer) am articulate about my emotions; after all, I'm fully capable of experiencing and handling a full range of emotions when I watch these shows. Not only is this false, but it is also poor modeling for what an articulate emotional life is all about.

Remember that a teenager's worldview is inherently ambiguous. She needs to learn to function and thrive within this anxious ambiguity, to create clarity within herself. So, when plots of action are presented so clearly on TV, it enhances the ambiguity of her day-to-day life ("my life is a mess compared to [insert wildly unrealistic TV character here]!") and makes her more self-critical. As an example, think of a book that you read and enjoyed and that was later made into a movie. How much shallower were the characters in the movie compared to the book? How was the meaning of the book altered to fit into the dominant plot of action necessary for the screen?

The best habit you can get into in terms of your teenager's screen time around television shows is to plop yourself down on the sofa next to him and watch the show together. This gives you time together though, granted, not with much interchange. It also gives you some common story lines and reference points, and these are more helpful than you can imagine.

> My daughter loves *Modern Family*—thankfully, it's a show I also enjoy. Laughing together is fun, but more enjoyable is recalling particularly funny moments together. Last year she even made me a Christmas card that riffed off one of the characters—we both laughed until we teared up.

And as with every other technology in his life, your teenager may at some point need your assistance in how much television he watches.

> Paul was watching TV nonstop: after school, through dinner, and while he was on the phone with his friends. It was terrible. Finally, we had had enough. First, we warned him that he could watch all the TV he wanted if his grades didn't go down but that, if his grades went down, we would take it as a sign that we needed to step in to assist him in breaking his TV habit. In typical form, he showed no reaction and nothing changed. Then his grades came. We quickly reminded him of the earlier conversation and pulled the plug on the TV, for all of us! The first few weeks were hell. He wouldn't even talk to us. But slowly, things got better. Then the next set of grades came out; not surprisingly, he did much better. So now we negotiate TV watching and limit it to specific events, for all of us, which is a big change for our family. But anything less would have seemed hypocritical from his viewpoint.

Finally, for health reasons, your teenager should not have regular access to television in his room. As we shall see, in the upcoming chapters on sports and diet, a television in a teenager's room is one of the highest predictors there is of adolescent obesity. It can be that powerful.

Now let's turn our attention to music, which is a different matter (see chapter 2, in particular Nick's article on page 13). Music is an escape that most teenagers use to reflect on the day's activities and mute their anxieties. The positive feelings associated with the music give them needed distance and perspective. So believe it or not, they are usually being productive when the headphones are in place and they are sitting on their bed.

> The first thing I do after school is put on my iPod. At first, I just sort of space out, but after a while I start to think back on the day and all that happened. Somehow it's easier to sort those kinds of things out with music.

A useful aspect of music is how it helps adolescents articulate what they are feeling. At times, the lyrics help them make sense of their feelings. (To fully appreciate this aspect of music, think back to a couple of your favorite and "deepest" songs from adolescence. How profound are the lyrics to your ears now?) Recently, a student came into my office with his iPod in hand. (A few months ago he had been struggling to articulate how he was feeling about his parents.) As he came in and queued up a song, he excitedly said that what he was about to play summed up precisely how he was feeling. Furthermore, he felt it was important to hear the music with the words—the words alone didn't capture the full meaning. After the song, he told me that understanding exactly what was bothering him had allowed him to figure out what to do. He was quite proud of himself, as he should have been.

Finally, there is the question of content. Historically, it seems that whatever music teenagers are into is at least one step beyond their parents' comfort level; for proof of this, remind yourself about your parents' response to the music you listened to as a teenager. Remember also how you felt about their response. Of course, ultimately, it is your house and this is your child, so you have the right to insist on certain things; but remember, pick your battles. As in other areas, consider your teenagers' stage of development—sixth, seventh, eighth, ninth, tenth, eleventh, or twelfth grade—and their ability to compromise. If some of the content is sexist, racist, violent, and the like, draw the line, at least when it comes to your home. Remember, you never want to make a rule that you can't enforce. In this case, you can't enforce that he never listen to certain music, but you can enforce that he never listen to it at home. You encourage him not to listen at friends' houses, but you can't enforce it. Sure, this is less than perfect. But the good news is that it's often enough for your teenager to come to his own decision about the music, maybe not right away, but probably down the road just a bit.

Teach Them to Wait

At first glance, this next section seems not to fit into the bigger topic of technology. I am including it here because I think it provides a wonderful antidote to the relentless pace of technology and the endless connectivity our teenagers experience.

In 1972, Stanford psychologist Walter Mischel conducted the now infamous marshmallow experiment with a group of four-year-olds. Each child came into a room and was met by a researcher who told him or her that they could have the marshmallow sitting on the table in the middle of the room whenever they wanted to eat it, but if they could wait until the researcher got back from an errand—about fifteen minutes—they could have the marshmallow on the table plus another. A two-for-one deal if they could just wait a short while.

This experiment was designed to test for the ability to delay gratification and was using the extra marshmallow as the incentive. That is, delay gratification and get two marshmallows, give in to immediate gratification and get one marshmallow. It was a straightforward experiment with dramatic repercussions for parents and educators alike.

But first, how do you think your teenager would have responded to such an experiment? Would she devour that first marshmallow before the door was even closed or could she hold off? If she tried to hold off, what strategies would she use? And most important, what would it tell you, if anything, about your four-year-old's (and now teenager's) well-being if she could delay gratification or not? Hold this in the background as we take a look at what Mischel learned.

In the study, one-third of the children immediately ate the marshmallow; one-third tried to wait but were unsuccessful; one-third were successful and waited until the researcher returned. What did this mean? In general, researchers postulated that the children who could delay gratification would do better at school, both academically and socially, but this was mere speculation.

Fourteen years later, the researchers followed up on these same pre-schoolers, who were now seniors about to graduate from high school, to see how they were doing. What they learned was astonishing. There were marked and significant differences at age eighteen between the kids who at four years old were able to delay gratification compared to both other groups—those that tried but failed to delay gratification and those that didn't even bother trying.

Fourteen years later, kids who were able to wait for the researcher to return before eating the marshmallow:[2]

- Were better adjusted emotionally
- Achieved higher scores on the SATs
- Were more positive
- Were more able to stay focused on their goals

These essential differences stemmed from the ability to delay gratification. Fortunately, within limits, the ability to delay gratification is not strictly in the realm of nature, parents and educators can and should nurture that ability.

With age, children naturally get better and better in their ability to delay gratification, and over time the majority of children come to recognize the benefits of learning how to delay gratification. In this regard, I find it useful to think of the ability to delay gratification as a muscle that with exercise gets stronger and stronger. That is, it is a somewhat learned skill that gets better when taught and practiced. The good news is that parents can play a huge role in teaching kids the value of, as well as learning the skills needed, to better delay gratification.

Think of yourself as a personal coach for your teenager by recognizing the opportunities in day-to-day life for delayed gratification training. You should share this with your teenager, because despite his eye-rolling he will get what you are talking about.

- Instead of having dessert right after dinner, insist on some task or activity first—cleaning the table and filling the dishwasher, taking out the trash, going for a family walk around the block. And, when you do sit down again for dessert, you take your time, savoring the treat and increasing your joy.

- On gift-giving holidays like Christmas, ritualize the opening of presents. One or two the night before. A few more first thing in the morning. A few more after breakfast. A few more when you get together with relatives. This allows your kids to take in the joy of each present and from each gift giver.
- Do a project together that spreads out over a few weekends and is something of import to them—making a dress, building something. Then, during the week check in on the project, basking in what you've accomplished so far and looking forward to all that is yet to come.
- Learn to play an instrument together—go to lessons and practice with each other. This teaches them delayed gratification through the process of diligent practice and has the added benefit of serving as a great means for the two of you to connect.

There are lots of opportunities—natural and designed—for teenagers to learn to delay gratification. And given this chapter is all about technology, practice this by delaying your use of technology. Think about ways to creatively replicate the example from the beginning of the chapter about determining who pays for dinner. Do whatever works.

> My daughter and I simply love pistachio nuts. Together we're like partners in crime. We each grab a handful of nuts, excitedly shell them while reminding ourselves how good they taste, and then, after they are all shelled, we decide where we are going to go to eat our heavenly treat—the back deck, the living room, the kitchen table, the park nearby. Once we arrive at our destination of choice, we commence to the eating, though it feels almost like a spiritual exercise as we eat them one at a time, enjoying each pistachio nut to its fullest.

Notes

1. Cathy N Davidson, *Now You See It: How the Brain Science of Attention Will Transform the Way We Live, Work, and Learn* (New York: Penguin Group, 2011).

2. Yuichi Shoda, Walter Mischel, and Philip K. Peake, "Predicting Adolescent Cognitive and Self-Regulatory Competencies from Preschool Delay of Gratification: Identifying Diagnostic Conditions," *Developmental Psychology* 26, no. 6 (November 1990) 978–86.

9

Sex, Romance, and Sexuality

My daughter has had the same boyfriend for more than a month now. What do I need to know about her sex life? Is there anything I should say or do?

Romance

Let's start with the less-anxious topic of romance, since, ideally, sex develops out of romantic relationships. First love is an unparalleled phenomenon. Nothing can match it in terms of excitement, energy, and positive feelings. Also, if this significant relationship occurs when your teenager is in high school, it is all the more exciting for him or her because it seems to resolve other issues of adolescence (see chapter 2).

Romantic relationships expand adolescents' social lives (they now spend time with their boyfriend's or girlfriend's social group as well as their own), and they gain an intimate best friend, which meets their increasing friendship and intimacy demands. This is crucial. Teenagers now have somebody they are open with and who is reciprocally open with them. They share things they've never shared before. Additionally, they are deeply concerned with one another's well-being, which simultaneously feels good and somewhat cracks through their necessarily egocentric world. Trust and compassion build up through their relationship. From their perspective, there is somebody who they feel truly understands them. On the personal identity side, dramatic changes happen: "Here is someone I admire, and not only do they spend time with me, but they admire me too. Therefore, I must be an admirable and good person!" Talk about a confidence builder at the right time.

Take a moment to reflect on your first experience of being in love:

- How did it make you feel about yourself to be in love and to be loved?
- How did this first love affect problems or concerns in other areas of your life?
- How did it affect your relationships with your parents? Your friends?

When a teenager experiences that first love, it makes sense that he will organize his life around that person. In the presence of this person, he feels cared for, listened to, desirable, and admired, all at a time when this kind of feedback is not readily available (see chapter 2). It is no wonder that the couple will spend hours talking on the phone and will see each other whenever possible during the school day.

> I love being in love. It's wonderful! We wait for each other between
> classes, have lunch together, and generally spend as much time as
> possible together. It's not that we're always talking, either; sometimes
> we're pretty quiet—even on the phone. Sometimes, when we talk late at
> night, we even fall asleep on the phone with each other. It just feels so
> secure and relaxed to be together. And she feels the same way, which is
> what's so great.

Of course, most of these first loves are not everlasting, no matter what most teenagers think at the time. However, if you state this directly, it is felt as demeaning and is met with the most venomous of reactions. Remember, this is his first love, not his third or fourth, so he doesn't have a backdrop of experience to draw from. In fact, this first love is so novel and intoxicating in part because it is all uncharted territory.

> Watching my daughter go through the pain and ecstasy of first love
> has been such an experience for me. I feel like I'm going through it all
> again, except this time I'm buffered from the pain by experience, but
> unfortunately, I'm also buffered from the joy by experience. It makes

me envious and thankful at the same time. I'm envious of first experiences and all the firsts she still has before her, and thankful to not have
to live through all that anxiety again!

When this first love comes to an end, it is a very traumatic event in any
adolescent's life, especially if she doesn't want the relationship to end. (What
was it like when your first romantic relationship came to an end?) For most,
the ending of the relationship means short-term crisis and definitely dominates her life for a while. Fortunately, this is usually not too long or too severe.
Just hang in there with her, and things will usually improve significantly
within a month or two. However, in some cases, the ending of the relationship precipitates a full-blown crisis, which is typically tied to some other
traumatic event in her life—such as the death of a loved one, divorce, or real
or felt abandonment by parents. In these cases, professional help is often necessary (see chapter 22 for more on this topic).

> When she broke up with me, it was like my world collapsed. I was so
> depressed it was scary. Half the time I couldn't even get out of bed to go
> to school. My friends tried to help, but after a while they got discour-
> aged by my misery. They just couldn't understand why I couldn't get
> over it. Neither could I. It isn't like I'm the only one to get dumped by a
> girlfriend! The weird part was that, while I knew that I loved her, I also
> knew it was more than that. Finally, my mom dragged me to a coun-
> selor. It took a while, but the doctor really helped me understand and
> get through all that was going on. It was like her breaking up with me
> triggered something much deeper in me.

In the more typical scenario after the breakup (especially if one wasn't
the initiator of the breakup), teenagers experience a fairly thorough reorga-
nization of their worlds. Their social life shifts because they now go back to
spending more time with friends and more time with themselves, which is
tricky if they have lost touch with friends because of the intensity of the relationship. Teenagers tend to structure their lives around their romantic interests, often excluding others.

> After he broke up with me, I felt like I had nobody. We had gone out for
> almost a year, and in that time I had pretty much lost close contact with
> my friends. And I know that they [friends] were pretty pissed about

that. On top of that, they had changed quite a bit over that year, so not only did I have to get them to forgive me, I also had to get to know them all over again. That was actually the hardest part about breaking up: getting my friends back.

Moreover, a teenager's personal identity, which has become fused with his significant other, undergoes a crisis of sorts. He must rethink who he is. Also, he has to rebuild confidence in himself, on his own.

> Carrie was so good for me. She knew just what to say to get me to feel good about myself. I was so confident when I was going out with her. I did better in baseball, in my grades, and in my relationship with my parents. I even took more risks when we were going out. Now I just feel shitty about myself, and I don't know how to get out of it. That's what I miss most, my self-confidence.

Clearly, the teenager who initiates the breakup has an easier time of it, but still it is no bed of roses. Many desperately work at maintaining the friendship even though the romance is gone, but this is no easy task. Some do this out of a genuine desire to maintain the friendship and some to alleviate their guilt; usually it is a combination of both.

> All during the time we were going out, we promised each other that if we ever broke up we would still stay friends, no matter what. I mean all that time we were definitely each other's best friend. And after we split up, we tried to stay friends, but there was no way it could work. I just wanted to be friends, but he still wanted more. So, as a result, I couldn't tell him about the parts of my life that would hurt him [interests in other guys]. It was really weird and tense all the time between us. Finally, we had a big argument, I mean really big. We haven't spoken for over a month now. I hope we can be friends sometime down the road, but I'm not sure. I think we tried to be good friends too soon after we broke up. I think we needed some time apart before trying to be friends, but it's too late now.

After the breakup of a serious romance, your teenager needs gentle and quiet support from you and your family. She may not need or want to discuss the relationship, but be assured she needs your quiet understanding.

My parents were real cool about it [her breakup with her boyfriend].
They didn't ask me a million questions or anything, but it isn't like they
didn't want to. They were there for me, but they weren't pushy. And
they did all sorts of nice little things for me: made me my favorite foods,
bought me flowers a couple of times, and generally hung around the
house more than they usually do. They even looked the other way when I
was texting way after midnight.

Sex

Now to the topic that dominates much of the adolescent landscape: sex. It was
confusing enough prior to AIDS, but now it is even more frightening and anxiety producing. In modern times, teenage sex is often, to say the least, problem-
atic: teenagers' bodies are fully capable and desirous of sex, but they are not
yet adults by society's standards. Sexual feelings and sexual urges are powerful
forces in teenagers' lives. Few are prepared for the complications and disrup-
tions from these emergent sexual drives. For many, it is like their bodies and
their minds are on entirely different wavelengths (take a moment to remember
your own experience as a teenager). Sex is also potentially dangerous and often
carries with it a variety of moral injunctions, further complicated by effective
but less-than-perfect birth control that makes it possible to have sex without
having children—but also possible to take precautions and still get pregnant.

According to recent research, 80 percent of girls and 70 percent of boys
have not had intercourse by age fifteen.[1] By age seventeen just over half of teenagers have had intercourse.[2] Remember, adolescents typically turn thirteen in
the seventh grade, fifteen in the ninth grade, and seventeen in eleventh grade.

Reasons for the increase in sexual activity between the ages of fifteen and
seventeen include the following:

- Adolescents are reaching puberty earlier than ever. In girls, the onset
  of menstruation moves up approximately three months every decade.
- Another reason, according to research is the amount of media that
  teenagers are watching that includes sexual content. "This is the first
  study to demonstrate a prospective link between exposure to sexual
  content on television and the experience of a pregnancy before the age
  of 20."[3] Worse yet, the majority of these encounters are seen through

the idealized lens of the television camera. In the fantasy world of television, most sexual encounters are glamorized and adequately resolved by the end of the hour (or by the end of the minute in commercials). In most cases, sex is elevated above relationships, a subject that receives little attention or education in comparison. Also, each of these sexual encounters explicitly communicates a black-and-white image of beauty, with the implicit message that if you fit this description, life is endless bliss. They represent a standard against which to measure oneself, but which no one can ever match. Adolescent girls are most susceptible here.

- For teenagers, sex is a short-term means of bolstering low self-esteem. Former Surgeon General Jocelyn Elders commented on this pointedly: "Kids can't say no if they don't first learn how to feel good about themselves." With the excitement of the sexual encounter comes the message that you are attractive, valued, and desired by another—a powerful, irresistible message to most teenagers who don't feel good about themselves on a daily basis. From this perspective, sex is an oasis of self-esteem for both males and females—at least in the short term.

> It's exciting to really like somebody. And part of the fun is getting them to like you back. It's a real turn-on. And the physical part is a real trip. The fact that this person not only lets you touch them but enjoys it is totally cool. In fact, once the physical stuff heats up, it can take a while to figure out if you really even like this person or not. It all gets tied together—sometimes in a big old knot!

In an ideal world, the road to sex is paved with lots of information and conversation about its mechanical and emotional aspects. Parents play important roles in many of these conversations. If you are too shy or embarrassed to talk about it yourself, you still need to make sure these conversations take place. Don't let your personal discomfort cost you your adolescent's life, and don't assume the schools handle these issues. Face it, most schools don't do better with this subject than most parents. And given the number of teenagers engaged in sex, this is a major gap in adolescents' education.

So, what is a parent to do? Talk with your kids; hopefully, the awkwardness will go away, but then again it may not. At the same time, talk with your teenager's school, just to discover the gaps that you need to make sure get shored up.

The first time I talked with my daughter about sex, sexually transmitted diseases, and AIDS, we were all very uncomfortable. And while it did get better over time, it didn't get a whole lot better. Now she's a senior in college and we laugh about those conversations, but not without acknowledging their importance.

To bring this point home you need to understand that one-quarter of sexually active teenagers have a sexually transmitted disease, and by age twenty-five, roughly half will have a sexually transmitted disease. In other words, start talking with them now and keep on talking and listening.

Awkward or not, these conversations must take place. You also have to provide other avenues for these conversations, perhaps through older siblings, his or her physician, a friend who is comfortable with the topic and friendly with your teenager, or a prearranged series of visits to Planned Parenthood. The options are limited only by your creativity—just don't let your creativity be paralyzed by your anxiety. Studies by the National Campaign to Prevent Teen Pregnancy report that 45 percent of teenagers said their parents are their biggest influence in deciding whether to have sex or not. Don't miss out on making use of your influence here.

After I watched a TV special on AIDS, I was scared and guilty because I've never talked with Sid [son] about any of this. I'm just too embarrassed. So I called his physician the next day and asked if he would talk to Sid at his next checkup. He chuckled a bit and said that it wouldn't be the first time he had responded to such a request. So we set up a routine physical for Sid later that month. I feel much better knowing that he has had the conversation at least once.

When evaluating your adolescent's sex life, don't assume anything and don't rule out anything either. The bottom line is that you have little control over what she actually does or doesn't do, but you do have a certain amount of influence, especially in the areas of health and safety. You can at least have a conversation with her on the topic (without asking directly what she is or isn't doing, which would be too intrusive for any adolescent to tolerate gracefully). Express your values as well as your pragmatic concerns. Speaking in the "what if" realm, you can let her know that while you don't approve of sexual intercourse at this age (if you don't), you are much more concerned about her overall well-being. Thus, talk about birth control options and how to go about obtaining them, go to Planned Parenthood, make an appointment with a physician, have your daughter see a gynecologist, and so on.

> I'm not sure that it is the right thing to do, but I bought a box of condoms and put them in my son's room. And I told him that if he ever wants more just to leave me a note. While I don't approve of teenage sex, I'm not naive either. And my attitude definitely isn't worth my son's life!

Be graceful about this topic, without necessarily approving. Also, don't assume your adolescent is one of the 50 percent of teenagers who have had sex, because he could just as likely be part of the other 50 percent. Or as Dr. Ruth Westheimer exhorts, "Teach kids everything, and then encourage them to wait."

> Since her father died several years ago, my daughter [a senior] and I have been very close. We even talk about sex sometimes. Recently she said, without my prompting her, that she and her boyfriend [of ten months] wanted to have sex but were waiting for the right time and place. (She knows I don't approve of sex at her age.) They wanted a time when they could be comfortable and a place where they could snuggle and hold each other afterward. They both want their first time to be special, and therefore are willing to wait for the right circumstances.

A number of years ago the idea of virginity pacts between teenagers took hold, and as you might imagine, many anxious parents latched onto this idea with a vengeance. The premise was straightforward: teenagers who signed these pacts were saying they would wait until they were married before having intercourse and they would support other signers in doing the same. The idea is noble, but the reality is a bit more complicated.

Research shows that kids who took the pledge had intercourse about as much as kids who didn't take the pledge. The good news was that kids who took the pledge had intercourse for the first time roughly a year later than those teenagers who didn't take the pledge. The bad news was that the kids who took the pledge were less likely to use contraception and just as likely to catch a sexually transmitted disease. Worse yet for the kids who took the pledge, had intercourse, and caught a sexually transmitted disease is that they were much less likely to know that they had an STD compared to the kids who didn't take the pledge.

But for me, the bottom line is that, even if your son or daughter has signed such a pledge, it doesn't absolve us of doing our job in educating them about sex, sexuality, and decision making. Nobody said raising a teenager would be straightforward or easy.

One of the most crucial aspects of all our conversations with our teenagers on sex is to make sure we tie it to relationships, as sexual experimentation ideally grows out of intimacy. That is, as teenagers get closer and more intimate with one another, it is only natural to experiment sexually, and within the confines of an intimate and caring relationship, this is usually done safely. However, too often our teenagers seek out intimacy through sex.

> I just really wanted a boyfriend, like all my best friends had. I was lonely and wanted someone that I could depend on. I know it was stupid and all, but I just ended up hopping into bed with a few different guys in the hopes that it would lead to a real boyfriend-girlfriend relationship. I was pretty naive.

This is why, at an early age, we should talk with our children about intimacy and friendship—how we behave differently with close friends, how we risk more and trust more with close friends, and so on. This gives them the experience and understanding of intimacy before puberty and sexual feelings are added to the mix.

Tying sex to intimacy is also a great way to explain why you do not approve of "friends with benefits." That is, any sexual act—intercourse, oral sex—should grow from intimacy, not convenience. And no matter what your teenager says, he is not ready for sex without intimacy—nor are adults for that matter.

Some closing thoughts on this topic. First, most teenagers report that they wish they had waited longer before having sex—this is something to share with your teenager and to take to heart yourself. This is why, after a talk I gave to high school students, three girls came up to me and shared what happens with them and their group of friends when someone has sex before they are ready. (Something they can only realize after the fact.) They accept this insight and begin to define themselves as Born Again Virgins! (Only a creative adolescent mind could come up with something like this.) In this way, they act on their insight and refrain from having sex until they are more sure they are ready.

Second, sex is not a value-free topic, nor should it ever be. Teenagers need to know where you stand on this subject. The most obvious reason for this is that they need a clear opinion (structure) to ground them and guide them in their internal decision-making process.

Third, adolescents need to have significant information that is value-free on basic anatomy, birth control, safe sex, and sexually transmitted diseases. Along with this, they need discussions about relationships and their emotional and interpersonal ramifications, all of which need to be addressed in a variety of settings over time.

Fourth, parents have little direct control over what happens. The best you can do is make sure your teenager has the information, knows your values on the subject, and is experienced in learning from consequences.

Fifth, no matter what happens, you need to make sure that your love for your teenager is communicated above and beyond everyone's anxiety and judgment about sexual relations and behavior.

Gay Teenagers

My son is in his junior year, and I'm worried because he seems to have no interest in girls. Could he be gay? And if he is, what should I do?

To begin with, there is no stereotypical manner in which gay people act. An effeminate manner in males or a masculine manner in women is by no means a sign of homosexuality. Nor is an apparent lack of interest in the opposite sex necessarily a sign of homosexuality. With everything else that is happening in the typical adolescent's life, it's no surprise that some teenagers don't pursue an active interest in the opposite sex until after high school. (Somewhat analogous to this situation are the teenagers who aren't interested in obtaining their driver's license, which doesn't mean they aren't interested in obtaining their independence.) There are other reasons besides sexual orientation that may account for this apparent lack of active interest in the opposite sex. (See chapter 2 for more on this.)

But for now, let's suppose that your teenager is gay. Given that between 5 percent and 10 percent of the population is gay,[4] it only makes sense that an equal if not greater percentage of parents have gay teenagers (since many parents have more than one child). Also, if teenagers are aware of their homosexuality, it is probably the single most powerful organizing factor in their lives and dominates over all the horizons described in chapter 2.

Gay adolescents have no one common experience, but some common themes and questions need resolving. After we address these, we'll move to the question of the parents' role. The first step in acknowledging homosexuality is for the teenager to recognize it in himself or herself. This is different for everybody. While some people may know as early as middle school, others won't fully recognize or acknowledge their sexuality until sometime in adulthood. But for now, we'll limit this conversation to adolescents who are aware of their sexuality. Initially, teenagers may attempt to hide their sexuality from themselves or even to change their sexuality. Many gay adolescents date the opposite sex and have heterosexual relationships to try to disprove their gayness. They are acting on this thesis: "If I am sexual with the opposite sex, it will prove that I'm not gay."

> Initially, I was frantic to not be a lesbian. Not only did I date lots of
> guys, but I was also pretty promiscuous with them. Somehow I felt like
> this erased all the strong feelings I was having for women. Needless to
> say, it didn't work, but it sure fooled everybody around me. People just
> couldn't believe it when I finally came out.

Again, as with much adolescent behavior, the signals teenagers send through their sexual behaviors are mixed and complex. Try not to forget this or jump to conclusions.

Actually, according to sexuality researcher Dr. Alfred Kinsey, most of us have varying degrees of homosexual aspects. Gay and straight are not discrete categories; rather, they represent the ends of a sexuality continuum. Combine this with all the other adolescent changes, and it's no wonder that sexual confusion is sometimes a necessary phase in determining sexual identity.

Recognizing gay aspects in oneself and fully acknowledging them to oneself are two very different things. But by the time teenagers acknowledge their gayness, they are usually certain of it; if there has been any hesitancy, it has been dispelled by the strength and persistence of these feelings. But acknowledging gayness is not the biggest or most difficult step; accepting it is. Given that being gay still carries a strong social stigma in society, it is not something that most adolescents welcome with open arms. Typically, they try to fight it as much as possible, in part because of the lack of social acceptance and in part because it may not fit with the long-term image they have of themselves. Many children nurture the dream of growing up and getting a good job, getting married, and raising a family. Few nurture the dream of growing up gay, discovering prejudice in the workplace, fighting the legal system to have your intimate relationship recognized as legitimate, and overqualifying yourself in order to adopt children. In addition, before they can accept their own gayness, teenagers must first undo the stereotypes about homosexuals that they have grown up with. That is, homophobia is not limited to heterosexuals.

> Realizing I was gay was no big deal. I mean, how could I avoid it with the way I felt around attractive men? The difficult part was accepting my homosexuality. I grew up with all sorts of ideas about the kinds of people who were gay: men who dressed in women's clothing, men who molested little boys, men who were promiscuous, and men who were very effeminate. None of these stereotypes fit me, but still I knew that I was gay. I was captain of my football team and wanted desperately to fall in love with a guy my age and have a steady relationship. None of the stereotypes I grew up with fit.

Probably the single greatest fear adolescent gays have is rejection by their family and friends, especially family. It is this deep-seated fear that I believe places these teenagers in the highest risk category of their peers. Imagine, if you can, what it would be like to know something about yourself that you believe could lead to total rejection by your family if they found out—a fact so horrible that they would expel you from the family. This is the reality as many gay teenagers perceive it. They develop this attitude from personal and societal stereotypes of homosexuality as well as from explicit and implicit views about gayness they pick up in their own homes.

> I've known that I'm homosexual for several years now, but I still haven't come out to my family. I'm pretty sure that my mom could handle it, but I doubt that my dad could. And I know that my mom could never keep it from my dad. He's just this sort of macho guy who loves sports and acting like a man's man. On top of that, he is always making gay jokes, which makes me sure he'd freak. I'll probably wait until I'm in college. I think the distance and time apart will make it more bearable. Also, hopefully, I'll meet others who have already come out to their families.

A teenager's secret about being gay can eat away at his developing personal identity and general self-esteem. He believes that, sure, he may be successful in many activities, but still, if his sexuality were found out and the truth were known, all his achievements would be wiped out in one fell swoop. Also, some gay adolescents start to believe that somehow they deserve this fate—that underneath it all they must actually be bad people. Unchecked, this can lead to strong feelings of self-loathing and even self-destructive behaviors.

> For the longest time, I felt that somehow I deserved my homosexuality, that underneath I was a terrible person. During the worst of it, I took some outrageous chances. I felt like if I survived them then maybe I deserved to live after all. I used to get stoned and drive the car really fast; I would get drunk and walk along high ledges in dangerous places; and once I even played Russian roulette with myself—putting one bullet in my dad's gun and pulling the trigger; fortunately, once was enough to feel like I didn't deserve to die.

Avoidance or refusal to accept one's homosexuality can eventually destroy an adolescent. According to research by Mark Hatzenbuehler in the journal *Pediatrics*, 21.5 percent of gay and lesbian adolescents attempt suicide versus 4.2 percent of heterosexual adolescents.[5] These startling statistics don't even take into account other risk-taking behaviors motivated by sexual identity problems, such as drug and alcohol abuse.

> Before I began to accept my homosexuality, I was pretty crazy. I got stoned and drunk all the time. In fact, I managed to become an alcoholic. It was in AA that it became clear that I had to address my sexuality. When I was drinking, I would engage in unsafe homosexual sex and then blame it on the alcohol; that way I never had to believe I was gay. In retrospect, I can see that it was the denial of my sexuality that led to the exaggerated use of alcohol, but nonetheless I managed to become an alcoholic. And ironically, the only way I could get on the wagon was to deal with my sexuality.

Besides family acceptance (addressed later in this chapter), the adolescent needs a group of peers who understand and appreciate the issues faced by gay and lesbian teenagers. They often need access to a supportive community for their developing sense of identity: other gay teenagers. Thankfully, these types of networks are becoming more frequent these days, but they are still not readily accessible to most adolescents.

> The really hard part was finding other gays and lesbians at school to talk with. Because of the stigma attached to homosexuality by peers, family, and society, it isn't easy to find each other. It's kind of crazy. For a long time, I traveled across town to a support group for gay teenagers, which was very helpful at first. I got to hear other people's stories, fears, successes, and failures. Suddenly, I didn't feel quite so alone. And they were very helpful in my coming-out process to my parents, giving me lots of advice and general encouragement. But after a while I realized that, with most of them, the only thing I had in common was my sexuality. They were interested in very different things than I was and attended different schools all over town. All of a sudden, I felt the split of living in two worlds simultaneously and yet never in one completely. My sexuality was set apart from my daily life at school. So I began selectively coming out to friends at school. It was with mixed results, but by the time I graduated, most of my close friends knew. Anyway, it wasn't until college that my two worlds came together. There is a strong Gay and Lesbian Alliance at my college and it helps a lot.

Gay peer groups are important because they represent a place where adolescents' sexuality is accepted as a normal part of them, not some secret to keep hidden. And never forget just how important acceptance is during the teenage years.

When adolescents do come to a conscious realization and acceptance of their gayness, they must make some decisions: Are they going to come out to anybody? If so, who? How and when? Can any family members handle their coming out? Can they deal with others who don't accept their sexuality? Is it worth the risk? Are they going to be active sexually, or are they going to put it on hold until after high school or some later date? If they are going to be active, where is a safe place? Could they handle their classmates learning about their being gay? Do they feel an obligation to speak out? Are there others who feel like they do? How can they find one another? Are there any "safe" adults with whom to talk?

So, what do you do if your teenager is gay and comes out to you?[6] Once you learn of your adolescent's sexuality, you can expect your world to shift dramatically. Parents are seldom prepared for a child's homosexuality and, as a result, have quite a bit of catching up to do. First, when your teenager comes out, don't doubt her. By the time she is telling you, she is quite sure of her sexuality. Sam Thoron, president of Parents, Families, and Friends of Lesbians and Gays (PFLAG), told me about when his daughter came out to him. Like most parents, his first question was along the lines of "Are you sure?" Moments later that was followed by "How do you know?" His daughter responded to this question with a question of her own, a question that gets right to the heart of the matter. "Dad, how do you know you are heterosexual?" He got it right then and there, to his enormous credit.

As mentioned earlier, a gay teenager's main fear is rejection by the family, so you can be sure that she won't risk this rejection unless she is certain. And gay teenagers cannot change who they are; you are the one who must do the changing.

> It was really quite a trip; it was like they [parents] were reading from a script or something. Initially, they were speechless, but once their voices came back their first question was "Are you sure?" I mean, by the time I could even think of telling them, I had to be absolutely sure myself. How could they think I would tell them something like this unless I was sure! After a long while, they finally got that I was quite sure of my sexuality. Then, following this "Parent of a Gay Teenager" script, they took another approach, wondering if it might just be a phase I was going through. At which point, my mom cited a friend who thought he was gay until he met the "right" woman! Dad took it even further, wondering aloud if possibly I couldn't change. It was crazy!

And, here is another story, from the parent's perspective.

> I must admit that when Sarah came out to me, it took me by complete surprise. And I'm afraid I didn't react very well. I was angry and confused. I felt like she was doing this to me. I was so self-absorbed that I couldn't imagine what she was telling me from any perspective other than my own. I was worried about what my family and friends would think, as well as how I would tell them. It was all so confusing to me. And not just her sexuality. Probably the most difficult part was in letting go of all the dreams I had for her: getting married to a man we liked, having children, and most of all for me, becoming a grandmother. While we worked to understand and accept the implications of what Sarah was telling us, it was by no means either smooth or easy. In retrospect,

I can see that we were the ones who had to change and begrudgingly get caught up to our daughter. Thank goodness she was both insistent and patient with us; we had a great deal of growing up to do.

What your gay teenager needs more than anything else is your acceptance and love of him and an honest reaction. You can be confused, angry, and frightened, and still assure him of your continuing love and acceptance. He doesn't expect you to immediately accept what it has taken him so long to come to grips with. But he does expect and need you to work with him toward honest acceptance. And considering how important parental and family acceptance is, he will grant you plenty of patience and openness throughout. Also, genuine acceptance paves the way for new hopes and new joys in your relationship with your teenager.

Finally, for yourself, don't try to do it alone. Make use of organizations like PFLAG[7] for education and support. Hearing other parents' stories, struggles, and victories is a great source of support and inspiration. And, of course, this holds true for most parenting issues: alcohol, drugs, eating disorders, depression, academics.

Notes

1. S. Singh and J. E. Darroch, "Trends in Sexual Activity Among Adolescent American Women: 1982–1995," *Family Planning Perspectives* 31, no. 5 (1999) 211–19; special tabulations by the Alan Guttmacher Institute (AGI) of data from the 1995 National Survey of Family Growth; and F. L. Sonenstein, et al., *Involving Males in Preventing Teen Pregnancy: A Guide for Program Planners* (Washington, DC: The Urban Institute, 1997) 12.

2. Alan Guttmacher Institute, *Sex and America's Teenagers* (New York: AGI, 1994) 19–20.

3. Martino Chandra, et al., "Does Watching Sex on Television Predict Teen Pregnancy? Findings from a National Longitudinal Survey of Youth," *Pediatrics* 122, no. 5 (November 2008) 1047-54.

4. No two groups or studies agree on the exact percentage of gays in this country. From the work of Alfred Kinsey (1948 and 1953) emerged a figure of 10 percent. But in a recent study by researchers at the University of Chicago (Laumann and others, 1993), 5.3 percent of men and 3.5 percent of women acknowledged having sex with a same-sex partner at least once since puberty. In this same study, 2.8 percent of men and 1.4 percent of women identified themselves as homosexual or bisexual. Personally, I don't believe the exact percentages are critical. What is critical is that homosexuality is a fact of life in our society. Even if the percentage were only 1 percent, that would still be a lot of people.

5. Mark Hatzenbuehler, PhD, "The Social Environment and Suicide Attempts in Lesbian, Gay, and Bisexual Youth," *Pediatrics* 127 (April 2011) 896–903.

6. Some adolescents who are unable to come out to you directly will do so in a variety of indirect manners, such as leaving gay literature in your sight. But don't jump to any conclusions, and also don't keep yourself unnecessarily naive.

7. PFLAG. www.pflag.org, 1726 M Street, NW, #400, Washington, DC 20036.

10

Words Make
a Difference

**Sometimes when I talk to my teenager she looks
at me in a confused way, almost like she
doesn't understand what I'm saying—actually,
more like I'm giving her a mixed message.
I try to speak clearly, but is there a chance that
this is not what she is hearing?**

Communication experts use the term "congruency" to describe messages that are consistent in word choice, tone, and body language. In any context, congruency is essential if you want your message to be clear. When communicating with your teenager staying congruent is a big deal—and too often we don't do it.

In some ways, what follows are a few key concepts from Communications 202. If you practice these ideas for a week, you will see a positive difference, in that your teenager will reflect some of these behaviors back to you. That is, they will be more agreeable, less defensive, and generally more open to what you think.

Yes, and . . .

In his book *Blink*, Malcolm Gladwell describes a fundamental rule of improvisational comedy that I think applies equally well in the parent-teenager relationship. Specifically, he refers to the rule of "agreement": good improvisers accept and *agree* with everything that happens to them, so as not to "block" the action of the scene. One of the founders of improv theater, Keith Johnstone, puts it this way: "Bad improvisers block action, often with a high degree of skill. Good improvisers develop action." This idea of developing—not blocking—action is a cornerstone to effective communications with your teenager.

One of the simplest ways to put this principle into action is to use the "Yes, and" approach. Basically, "Yes, and" is the opposite of the all-too-common "Yes, but" response we usually give our teenagers—a response that shuts down or "blocks" conversation. At the heart of "Yes, and" is the notion that every idea is a good idea.

As we all know from personal experience, when you say "Yes, but," all the other person hears is what comes after the *but*. Even worse, the *but* puts them in a defensive mode before hearing what you have to say.

- Yes, you want to watch television, but first you need to do your homework.
- Yes, I like the idea, but I don't think it will work in this case.
- Yes, I heard you, but no, you can't stay out past curfew tonight.

Compare the above to the *Yes, and* approach.

- Yes, you want to watch television, and first please figure out when you are going to do your homework.
- Yes, I like the idea, and I think we need to explore it more to see how it might work in this case.
- Yes, I heard you, and I need to hear more of your thinking and planning before I can answer your request about staying out past curfew.

In the first set of statements, communication has come to an end—and the wrong kind of arguing is teed up. In the second set, there is an explicit invitation and expectation that rational discussion will ensue, which is what generally happens.

Acknowledge Reality

In the section above, we looked at how the word *but* blocks continued action and conversation. There is another way that parents often inadvertently block conversation: when they deny the reality of what is happening right in front of them. In these instances, we continue to talk even though it is clear our teenager isn't listening, or we pretend everything is fine between us when in fact our teenager is quite angry with us. Teenagers, more than any other population, pick up and relentlessly zero in on this incongruence.

When you feel communication breaking down between you and your teenager, don't ignore this reality. Just plowing ahead to get your message through not only is ineffective, it makes matters worse, as it leaves teenagers feeling disrespected and, on some level, doubting their perceptive abilities. Just be willing to stop: "Seems like this is not a good time to talk, so let's put it on hold for now." Or, "I feel like we're both getting defensive, so let's come back to this later."

> I have really worked at this *Yes, and* concept—it's really hard. And when I can do this, I see the expression on my son's face. He is on the verge of dismissing me. When I keep the energy moving, he seems at first surprised, and then always leans into the conversation with more energy and confidence. And he has no idea I am doing this!

Moderate Your Voice

Next time you are in a public place—park, airport, museum, ballpark—where children and parents are present, play the observer for a few minutes. Specifically, whenever a child is on the verge of acting out or ignoring a parental statement, watch and listen to what ensues. Here's a rough description of the process I've observed many times over.

- The child ventures too far from the parent or dallies over something that has caught her attention.
- The parent gently calls out to the child: "Sara, please wait for us."

- Sara does not hear or pretends not to hear.
- The parent adds more intentionality to her request, with specific emphasis on the first and third words: "**Sara,** please **wait** for us."
- Sara does not hear or pretends not to hear.
- The parent's voice becomes louder and the sentence shorter: "**Sara! Wait!** "
- Sara looks at her parent, smiles, and continues doing what she was doing.
- The parent marches over to Sara, firmly grasps (or grabs) her hand: "**Sara, you need to listen to me. Do you hear? Now stay close to us and don't make me yell at you again.** "
- At this point, Sara either acquiesces (though she is sure to act out again in the next bit of time) or breaks into tears.

We've all been there. Worse, we know that in these cases, while in public view, we are actually on our best behavior. At home, without the scrutiny of the public eye, we are typically quicker to yell and grasp.

Research on brain use and development points out that, when children or teenagers are feeling a strong emotion, they lose access to rational thought. This is huge. As parents of teenagers, you need to understand that once you raise your voice teenagers essentially stop hearing your words. Their brains process the voice tone over the word content, and as a result they are flooded with emotion. For them, it is an experience of panic, or shame, or indignant anger, or overt hostility. Worse, they are stuck, emotionally paralyzed, while you drone on.

(Bart listens to his teacher, Mrs. Krabappel, lecture him about his failing grades.)

MRS. KRABAPPEL: Your grades have gotten steadily worse since the beginning of the term. Are you aware of that?

BART: Yes, ma'am.

MRS. KRABAPPEL: Are you aware that there is a major exam tomorrow on colonial America?

BART: Yes, ma'am.

MRS. KRABAPPEL: Blah, blah, blah-blah. Blah, blah, blah?

BART: Yes, ma'am.

MRS. KRABAPPEL: Blah-blah, blah-blah-blah, blah-blah-blah-blah.

BART: Yes, ma'am.

MRS. KRABAPPEL: Bart! You haven't been paying attention to a word I said, have you?

BART: Yes, ma'am.

MRS. KRABAPPEL: Well, then what did I say?

BART: Uhhh, "Straighten up and fly right?"

MRS. KRABAPPEL (Blows raspberry): That was a lucky guess.

Just keeping this scene in mind will improve your communication behaviors with your teenager.

I Know

This next one is a bit more subtle and just as much a conversation stopper as the others.

DAUGHTER: Dad, did you know that talking on the cell phone is as dangerous as drunk driving?

DAD: I know.

Where can she go from here? A child might state more facts that her father already knows simply to hear herself talk or to impress her dad. A teenager will go silent. Most of the time the *I know* response is a conversation blocker.

Now imagine that Dad responds with a something that encourages more, especially more curiosity.

DAUGHTER: Dad, did you know that talking on the cell phone is as dangerous as drunk driving?

DAD: That's right. Do you know why?

These responses encourage your teenager to dig deeper into the topic at hand, and to do so in a way that is engaged with her dad.

One final note about the power of *that's right* kind of statements. When your teenager gets used to this response from you, and is thus encouraged to keep digging into a topic or exploring her feelings, she learns that with you it is safe, even cool, to trust herself and follow her curiosity.

Okay?

I am shocked at how often I hear parents give a teenager a nice, clear directive in the appropriate context only to undermine themselves and confuse their teenager by adding a Valley Girl *okay?* at the end of the sentence.

- Jason, a few more minutes until dinner, so please turn off the television at the next commercial, okay?
- Stephanie, please pick up your backpack from the living room and put it in your room, okay?
- Rickie, how many times have I told you not to throw things in the car! If something hits or distracts me while I am driving, we could get in an accident. Plus I told you not to do it before, okay?

I can already feel people lining up to challenge me on this one; after all, the use of *okay* in these instances is to seek clarity, not to ask for permission. I beg to differ. And my proof is in the confused face of the teenager who is asked *okay?* at the conclusion of an otherwise clear statement. We may intend *okay?* as clarifying, but it comes off as a question to most teenagers. This is especially so because, when used, it generally comes with the inflection of a question, with our voices rising at the end of the word, which leads the listener to recast what he heard as a statement into a question, right? And this just opens up the possibility of your teenager disagreeing with you—No, it's not okay—and starting an argument that never needed to happen.

Keep it Positive

Do not think of a pink elephant with wings. Go ahead, give it a try.

My hunch is that to not think about a pink elephant with wings you first imagined a pink elephant with wings and then had to erase, cross out, or expunge the image in some way. This is the nature of our minds; we are inclined to action and doing. To *not* do something, we need to first imagine doing it. Therefore, paying homage to the old cliché *Be careful what you wish for*, we need to be careful how we phrase the behaviors we are looking for in our kids.

Research has shown again and again that when we tell people how we want them to behave, they behave that way more often. This is what I mean by *positive*—it doesn't have to do with *good* or *bad*—rather, it describes the way we frame what we are looking for or desire. Since we know our teenager's mind is going to automatically imagine the words we say, do your best to frame your statements so they describe the behavior you want—not what you *don't* want.

This can be simple, as in:

- "Time to get up and get ready for school," as opposed to "Stop hitting the alarm and procrastinating."
- "Please finish your milk before you are excused from the table—it helps strengthen your bones," as opposed to "Don't get up from the table with any milk left in your glass. What do you want, brittle bones?"
- "Please help your sister get in the car and put your backpacks on the floor," as opposed to "Don't lock your sister out and don't put your backpack on the seat."

In the next few days, pay attention to how you phrase your directing statements to your children. You might be surprised by the words you use. And once you get better at stating more of want you want, as opposed to what you do not want, you will see a difference in how your teenagers behave.

The effect of positive statements can go much further than simple behavior interventions when we apply this idea to attitudes as well as behaviors. By focusing on the positive—and remember that by positive I mean what you are looking for in terms of behaviors and attitudes—we help our teenagers create and imagine desirable images of what we want them to aim for over the course of their lives. Here are some examples of statements that can shape your teenager's attitudes:

- "People are basically good if you give them the chance to earn your trust," as opposed to "Everybody wants something from you, so trust nobody."
- "Nobody in our family has ever wanted it as much as you, so I imagine you will do better than anyone in our family has ever done," as opposed to "You're a McGillicutty, so you will never be an athlete; it's not in our genes."
- "It is never too late to learn something new," as opposed to "You can't teach an old dog new tricks."

You can also use positive thinking to anticipate tough situations and come up with a healthy resolution:

> I can imagine you in a situation where a friend who has been drinking insists that he is fine to drive home. This will be tough. At the same time, I see you having the courage and the wherewithal to convince him to let someone else drive or to get a ride with someone else.

What is key when having these kinds of conversations is that you enter them with a sense of positive expectancy. That is, your voice, tone, and pacing all convey that you expect your teenagers to figure out these difficult situations. You are confident in them. Or, as a well-known basketball coach once told me:

> I just know in the marrow of my bones that when one of my players is stepping to the line for a pressure free throw, and the other team calls a time-out to try and make her doubt herself, I must design the next play for after she makes the shot. I never entertain the idea of a miss. Then at the end I look at the player who is taking the shot and say something like "After you make the shot, make sure you get back on defense quickly." It's the best I can do, and while I can prove nothing, I do know that my players go to the line with confidence for that pressure shot.

11

Academics, Grades, Motivation, and Learning Differences

What can I do to keep my kids motivated in school and working toward good grades?

First, a few general comments about grades. For many parents and teenagers, grades are a source of conflict. This conflict is far from simple, because grades take on so many different meanings in the typical adolescent's life.

Melinda, a high school student, is an example of how complicated the issue gets when her dad asks how she did on a recent history test. For now, assume that Melinda is doing fairly well with her grades. When her dad asks about the history test, the following thoughts go through her head, but at such a rapid rate that few are articulate even to her:

- Cool, great that he remembered, what a great dad!
- I'm glad he asked because now I can tell him how well I'm doing and maybe he'll give me some more space or extra allowance, but if I tell him how well I did, I know I'll get that smug "I told you so" look! He'll think it was because he told me to get off the phone early last night,

140

even though it wasn't (and I can't tell him that I sneaked the phone into the bathroom and talked for two more hours!).

- If I tell him now, he'll always expect an answer; then when I do poorly, he'll know because I won't answer. So maybe I shouldn't answer at all.
- Amazing that he remembers to ask about my history test, but he never remembers what time I have to be picked up after practice.
- History test, what history test? Oh God, was that today? It seems so long ago; I mean, so much has happened today. How can he expect me to talk about that history test compared to everything else that has happened?
- Can't he just trust me a little bit? I mean, why does he have to check up on me all the time?

Whatever mix of thoughts goes through Melinda's head, a minimal response is often the result: "Uh, okay, I guess. What's for dinner tonight?" Any other response, from Melinda's point of view, is too complicated, risky, and cumbersome to get into.

Unfortunately, our current education system takes grades as a literal indicator of a student's success. Most students study for the grade first and for the knowledge and education second. This gets the entire educational process off on the wrong foot. Grades reflect only an aspect of a student's intellectual development, and an even smaller portion of their development as people. Kids ought to be in school for the sake of learning, not simply for getting grades; and parents play an essential role here. Over the long run, parents pay dearly for driving their kids to study solely for the sake of grades. But what are the alternatives?

When most parents ask their teenager how she is doing in geometry, they are really asking about the grade (at least, that is what it feels like to the adolescent, regardless of the parent's intent). And when parents ask how their teenager did on a history test, they are really asking about the grade (again, this is what it sounds like from the adolescent's perspective). From the parents' point of view, they make such inquiries because, one, they grew up with and understand this system, and two, asking about grades is often the only way they know to show interest in and monitor their adolescent's studies. But if you wish to instill learning and education as a lifelong and enjoyable process for your teenager, consider these new lines of inquiry:

- Ask Melinda what she is finding challenging as well as boring in her history class.
- Ask Melinda if she has had any particularly difficult math problems lately that she has surprised herself by being able to figure out.
- Ask her how she managed to hang in there long enough to figure out the problem rather than giving up on herself.
- Ask her what kind of questions she is asking about *Jane Eyre* in her English class.
- Ask her where she is getting her ideas for painting.
- Ask if the history test was a good test: did it help her to understand the material at a deeper level, or was it simply a check to make sure she was doing the reading?

These questions inquire about the process of learning—the actual fabric of learning in all its nuances and subtleties—without ever focusing on grades. I call these questions that linger. Your teenager can't answer them right away, and they tend to think about them for much longer than the moment you ask them.

This type of questioning is the only type that makes sense if you want to turn your child on to learning. Once kids get excited and curious about learning, everything else will more or less fall into place, even motivation and grades. However, if grades are the focus for you, then you are inadvertently supporting certain undesirable behaviors, including cheating. That is, with an overemphasis on grades, it makes a great deal of sense to a teenager to figure out ways to cheat—read: to get the best possible grades.

Recall an academic experience of which you are fond. What comes to mind first: the grade or something about the process of how you got through the experience? The fact that I completed a dissertation and that my committee liked it takes a distant second place to the satisfaction I had in knowing I had hung in there when things were ambiguous and seemingly at a dead end. Nor could the passing grade I got hold a candle to how I knew the process had changed my way of thinking and my perspective of the topic as well as of my own person. Yet very few people know how to ask about this stuff. Go ahead, learn and practice on your teenagers. They might be confused at first, but they'll catch on quickly. And who knows, with time they might even come to enjoy it. Further, this kind of dialogue feels much less judgmental to adolescents than talking about grades.

In this same regard, what makes these kinds of educational experiences so memorable is how we dealt with our confusion throughout the assignment. Rather than get defeated by confusion, we bore down and worked harder. This is something you need to explain directly to your kids: don't be afraid of confusion! Teenagers often equate confusion with not being smart.

> I was riding in the car with Nick and a couple of his friends the other day when I mentioned one of the girls in his class who had just won an academic award at the school. I commented on how smart she was, but they quickly corrected me by saying that she wasn't all that smart. She just worked harder than everybody else. That's when I got it: they think if you have to work hard then you must not be smart. I corrected that line of thinking in a hurry!

That's it in a nutshell, and it makes the parental role crystal clear. We need to point out that confusion is a sign of growth. It's more about their ability to tolerate confusion, not confusion itself. Teenagers need to know that the most successful and knowledgeable people get confused the most. That is, they have a higher tolerance for confusion than their less successful peers. Bottom line for kids: Confusion is a sign of imminent learning if one can learn to hang in there despite the uncomfortable feeling of confusion. Or to put it another way, no confusion, no learning.

Mel Levine, the great pediatrician and expert on different learning styles, put this idea to me another way in a radio conversation. He declared that it is the school's job to educate kids on facts, formulas, writing, reading, and the like, and it's the parents' job to teach kids how to work. This is why we sit by them from time to time when they are doing their homework: To make sure they know how to work hard. To make sure they know how to get through confusion.

Finally, the single most influential thing you can do to support learning is to practice what you preach. Set aside family time in the evening for study and reading. Kids do homework and parents read or work quietly. Sure, some parents say that they've worked all day, so they need to relax at home—but kids have worked all day too.

If you sit down in front of the television for a few hours and yell at your kids to go study, you're sending a mixed message: "I say that learning is important, but I don't act that way."

Questions about Teenagers and Schoolwork

What can I do to help my teenager improve his poor grades?

In my mind, the best way to improve a teenager's grades is to demonstrate that grades are a result of natural consequences (anything else is probably at least inefficient and uncomfortable). Nagging your adolescent about homework is an unenviable task, and it usually doesn't work. I have had the following conversation countless times with teenagers (and their success as students is an irrelevant variable):

ME: So, what exactly happens when you sit down to do your homework?

STUDENT: Well, after texting with my friends for a while and checking Facebook, I finally sit down and begin working. And I usually can get into it and get a lot done if I'm left alone! But that hardly ever happens. My brother wants to show me something in his room, or the TV is on loud and gets my attention. But even these aren't too bad; I mean I can get it back together after that.

ME: Then what's the problem?

STUDENT: The problem is when my parents constantly check in on me and treat me like a little kid! I'll be reading or something and my mom will stick her head in (without knocking!), look at me, and say, "Oh, I just wanted to see if you were still working." By the time she closes the door behind her, I've lost it. I mean, what am I, ten or something? At that point I throw the book down in disgust and usually never open it again that night.

ME: Have you ever talked to her about this?

STUDENT: I've tried, but all that happens is that she gets more slippery in how she checks in.

ME: What do you mean?

STUDENT: Well, instead of directly asking about my homework she finds some excuse to talk to me: "Any dirty dishes in here?" or "Do you have a game tomorrow?" or "Do you want me to wake you in the morning?"

But like the whole time she is staring at what book I'm reading and what is on my desk. It's just too obvious!

ME: Hmm, any chance she really is legitimate in what she is asking?

STUDENT: Sure, but it's the way she does it and when she does it that gets to me. It's so transparent.

Essentially, school is your teenager's job, a job that has clear parameters and expectations. Have a conversation with your adolescent about school and studying—usually sometime during freshman or sophomore year. Include what is important to you, and ask what he thinks needs modification. Then ask him what role he wants you to play; expect a surprised look followed by, "Uh, what do you mean?" Then have a few options laid out to appeal to his creativity: "Well, we could agree to a specific homework time, and we (Mom and Dad) could remind you of it when you forget and periodically check up on you so you don't get distracted. Or we could go over each homework assignment with you to see how well you've done on each one. Or we could . . ." Eventually, you want him to assume honest responsibility for his homework and ask for your help periodically, though you might have regular, agreed-upon check-ins (once every week or two) to see how things are going. Build a means of support that allows you to feel active and that actually does support your adolescent. This is easier to say than do, but it can be done with some patience and persistence.

My husband I recently realized just how much we nag our daughter Karen about her homework. But to not do or say anything feels terrible. So finally we talked with her about our dilemma. We wanted her to help us with a solution. After just a few minutes (once she understood that we were sincere and how much she stood to gain), she came up with a great idea. At around 9:30 each night, one of us would knock on her door and get her "order" for the night. We would then make her the tea of her choice and bring it to her in her room, along with three cups. We would then drink tea together and chat lightly, sometimes about homework and sometimes not. We would let her lead the conversation. After about ten minutes, we would leave, wishing her a good night's work on the way out. And, of course, we built flexibility into the plan. If her grades ever took a nosedive, we would take it as a sign that she was inviting us into her homework worries, to which we would respond accordingly. Well, that was two months ago, and we haven't had to nag her once in that time. And most important, we still feel like good parents. In fact, my husband and I both genuinely look forward to our family tea time each evening.

A strategy that some parents use to encourage motivation is good old-fashioned bribery. That is, money (or things) for grades. Bribes seldom work, though, mainly because the teenager doesn't internalize the good feelings that come from working hard; in fact, the material reward typically obfuscates these feelings. The only time I've heard of this bribery approach working was when it was used as a one-time intervention.

> We were very frustrated with Sheila's academic performance during her first two years of high school, but then, prior to her junior year, we did what had been previously unimaginable to us. We bribed her! But we did it with a long-range purpose in mind. Before the beginning of the semester, we sat down and expressed our disappointment at her not doing better in school. We felt that she wasn't turned on to learning, and, worst of all, she was afraid to really push herself 100 percent. It was as if she were afraid of discovering that maybe she wasn't actually all that intelligent; it seemed safer for her to be lazy. Anyway, we came up with a bribe that everyone agreed to (I'm still too embarrassed to admit what it was). The motivation (bribe) was sufficient enough to outweigh her hesitation and fear at giving 100 percent academically. So we set high standards and got out of the way. She knew this was a one-time offer and that we were doing it so she could feel the success that comes from giving her all.
>
> Well, it worked. She got terrific grades and written reports (along with the promised reward), and she broke through her fear. In fact, for the duration of high school she maintained her high academic standards. At one point, she even thanked us, saying that in the long run it was much more satisfying, fun, and easier to go all out than to flake off!

This brings up another important point: the experience of giving 100 percent. With all that is happening in the adolescent world, it is far too easy for teenagers to become afraid of total effort. As parents, you want to encourage your adolescents to find a place where they can give their all—in classes, sports, clubs, music, the arts—regardless of the results. They need to experience how success is less about talent than persistence. Or, as Thomas Edison once said,

"Genius is 1 percent inspiration and 99 percent perspiration. Accordingly, a 'genius' is often merely a talented person who has done all of his or her homework." This experience of all-out effort becomes an important reference point to them as they grow and mature into adulthood; and with the proper nudging, this experience will transfer to other aspects of their life.

I once talked with a sophomore girl about her poor, and getting worse, academic performance. She was very concerned but didn't seem motivated to change anything. She was quite passive. Fortunately, I remembered that she was a terrific basketball player, so I began to ask her about her approach to big games. All of a sudden, she became very animated and passionate; not a trace of passivity remained! After a bit, I reflected aloud that she sure seemed to play to win. She nodded quite assuredly. And then I added, "So it is kind of odd to see you playing the academic game so passively; it's like you're playing not to lose rather than playing to win." Her face went from assuredness to confusion to conviction in the space of a few seconds. Academics and 100 percent effort were now in a framework that she understood. As you can imagine, the conversation took a dramatic turn after that, and it was without much surprise to both of us that she turned her academic spin around in the ensuing months.

Whatever transpires, the final goal is rather simple when it comes to schoolwork. Realize that, if parents worry too much, it doesn't leave any worrying available to the adolescent. The goal is to give the appropriate amount of worrying back to the teenager so she can begin to take responsibility. And it is essential to find a pace of handing over the worries and responsibility that works for everyone. Go too fast, and she feels abandoned and overwhelmed. Go too slow and she feels belittled.

Finally, your adolescent's ongoing relationship to grades is a baseline for your understanding of her world. Any sudden and dramatic change in her grades usually reflects other changes in her life. Undue stress and anxiety in other areas often reveal themselves most obviously in grades.

> When my parents were getting divorced (and for about a year afterward), I had the hardest time concentrating on schoolwork. My brain was fuzzy and I couldn't stay focused for more than a few minutes before my mind would just sort of take off. It sucked. I remember hours of staring at the same history paragraph without understanding a bit of it. And it wasn't like I was thinking intensely about anything else. I was just drifting all over the place. It was like my concentration was drunk.

In response to this phenomenon, a student and I formulated what we call the "Homework Anti-Worrying Technique." It has been quite useful to a number of students over the years:

1. As you sit down to study, put a pile of blank scraps of paper in the upper-right-hand corner of your desk.
2. Begin studying. Whenever a worry, concern, or vague, drifting thought occurs, take a slip of paper and, as concisely as possible (in four or five words), write down the worry. Then put the paper, face down, in a pile in the upper-left-hand corner of your desk. Continue studying.
3. Whenever you notice yourself drifting, repeat step 2 and then resume studying.
4. End your studying time a half hour early. Remove your books and the blank sheets of paper from your desktop.
5. Take the pile that you've written on and browse through the sheets. Pick one and think about it for a while. When you're done, pick another. Go through the entire pile or think about these concerns for a half hour, whichever comes first.
6. Go do something enjoyable for at least a little while.

This technique is simple and useful to students at times of high stress. Until they learn to put aside their worries internally, it is easier and more efficient to put aside their worries externally.

Use your developing understanding of their world to creatively and gracefully assist them in handling their various pressures. Encourage them to recruit you into their solutions.

> Last year I had terrible grades—so bad, in fact, that I was on the verge of getting expelled. Part of the trouble was that schoolwork seemed to come real easy to my friends, so I was the only one flunking out. Anyway, a big part of the problem was that, while my friends were supportive of me and everything, they still didn't take no for an answer when I said I had to stay in over the weekend to study. I mean, I started out saying no, but always ended up going out with them. I guess I just wasn't strong that way. It finally got so bad that one day the vice principal told me that, if my grades didn't get much better very soon, I had better start looking for another school. So that night I finally broke down in front

of my mom and told her how scared I was. Well, to make a long story short, we decided she would be the "bad mom" from then on, at least with my friends. So that Saturday, when they called me to go out, I said that my mom wouldn't let me (she was standing right next to me when I said it). Then when my friend started giving me a hard time, my mom screamed at me to get off the phone. Then I started screaming back at her, and we had a real vicious argument (all fake, of course) while my friend listened on the phone. It was actually a lot of fun! Maybe it wasn't the most honest way in the world, but at least it worked.

What should I do if I think my teenager might have a learning disability?

This is indeed a tricky issue in schools these days. Many more kids are getting diagnosed with learning disabilities than ever before. In part, this is attributable to greater awareness, but at other times, some of these efforts are simply misguided. Sometimes parents use a diagnosis of a learning disability to get a student more time on tests. Other times, a diagnosis is a simple way to deal with typical teenage angst. This is why, at least in my mind, more medications and psychotropics are given to teenagers than ever before. In some cases, that is the absolute correct path to take, but in many more cases, I fear drugs are not justified.

Obviously, this is not a book on learning disabilities and learning differences, but nonetheless let's take some time to take a quick look at each. Some students have learning disabilities, and some students just learn differently—no disability, just a difference that makes a difference. Let's look at learning differences first. Dr. Mel Levine did as much if not more than any other professional when it comes to appreciating and understanding all the different ways that kids learn. As he pointed out in his wonderful book *A Mind at a Time*,[1] every student has a different learning style, and some students suffer because the way they are taught is not the same as the way they learn. In such cases, these students are often mislabeled as having learning disabilities, bad attitudes, or a lack of motivation. Or, in some cases, all three.

As your child's parent, you understand better than anyone how she learns. All these years, from toddlerhood through adolescence, you've observed how she puts ideas together, where she shines, and how she does it. Part of your job is to help her understand these same things about herself and to help her teachers understand the same. Or, as Dr. Levine would say, to "demystify" how she learns, for her and others.[2]

Here are some simple examples of different learning styles:

- Some kids learn by sitting in their seats and listening to what the teacher has to say. These kids naturally do well in school.
- Some kids learn by asking lots and lots of questions, by intellectually engaging and challenging the material. These kids can do well in school if they are not first labeled as disruptive.
- Some kids learn by doing. They need hands-on experiences to make sense of the material. These kids often struggle when forced to sit still all day.
- Some kids learn visually, so they do well with teachers that support their lessons with lots of visual cues. They don't fare so well, however, with instructors who tend to lecture.

The point is to help kids understand themselves and how they learn. They literally become experts about their own learning styles. And sometimes, as we roll up our shirt sleeves and dig in there, we discover the problem is not how they learn; it's a lack of organizational skills—frequently because they have never been taught these skills. Ninth grade is a time when many students falter academically and, not surprisingly, it's also a time when students need to develop better and more articulate organizational skills.

> I always did well in school, but during the middle of ninth grade I started getting poor grades and I didn't know what to do. I thought I was stupid! It wasn't until my history teacher asked to see my notes that I understood what was going on with me. She looked at my notes, looked at me, smiled, and said, "Well, this explains it." She went on to show me how to take effective notes in high school, which was different than middle school. It was less about memorizing and more about understanding. That hour with her helped me in all my other classes too.

Of course, sometimes there is a real learning disability that is getting in the way. In this case, you need the assistance of a good professional, someone who is experienced in dealing with learning disabilities and learning differences. (The school should have a list of such referrals.) Get a thorough assessment; this will take time and effort in gathering lots of observations from the adults who work with and teach your teenager. In this regard, trust your parental intuition. When an assessment is done well and is on target, it has the effect of an "Aha!" moment with most parents and students. That is, they now understand why there were lots of certain types of difficulties along the way. And if your intuition doesn't jibe with the assessment, don't be shy about getting another opinion.

But most important throughout, whether there is a learning difference or a learning disability or nothing of note, stay optimistic, curious, and hopeful.

> In my sophomore year, I was diagnosed with dyslexia, which made perfect sense because I always had trouble reading. At first, I was relieved to know there was a reason, but scared that it meant I was stupid. And it wasn't fair either. I had to work way harder than my friends for the same or worse grades. But to make a long story short [she was a junior in college when she told me this story], my parents were great throughout. They hung in there with me and wouldn't let me give up on myself, and they kept pointing out my other kinds of smarts. In the end, I did work harder than anybody else for average grades, but in all this I came to really understand myself and how my mind works. And more important, I learned how to work hard, which most of my classmates in college haven't even figured out. Now I don't mean to sound arrogant, but I know I'll do well in the real world knowing these two things—how I learn and how to work hard.

Notes

1. Mel Levine, *A Mind at a Time* (New York: Simon & Schuster, 2002).

2. More and more this is becoming an essential task of teachers: to help kids learn how they learn.

12

Making Friends

My son is having trouble making friends.
I know there is not much that I can do, but
should I be advising him somehow?

Given that loneliness (see chapter 2) is one of the most powerful and painful forces in teenagers' lives, watching your teenager struggle to make friends is heart-wrenching. Unfortunately, parents cannot do much directly. There is very little useful advice you can offer that he will take advantage of, which is not to say that you do not have useful suggestions. Even when he seeks your advice, he'll often resist what you have to offer. In fact, he may resent you for offering what he asked for! Here's why. When adolescents ask for your advice (on just about anything), they are often asking for something else. Basically, they seek your advice because they have momentarily lost belief in themselves, and what they are seeking is not your advice so much as your belief in them. That is, they want to borrow your belief in them until they can restore their own belief in themselves.

> For a long time, whenever Miles asked my advice, I assumed he wanted suggestions. Given the long silences between us, I was more than ready to be helpful, so I gave lots of suggestions. But he inevitably got sharp with me and never followed any of my suggestions. In fact, things usually got worse and he got more passive. But finally one day it clicked. When he offered the bait by asking my advice, I sidestepped the trap

with a different response: "Wow, that's a tough one. What do you think? I mean, what have you tried so far? Well, I'm not really sure, but I know you'll figure it out; you seem to manage pretty well. If you come up with anything else or want me as a sounding board let me know." And the less advice I offer, the more he talks to me!

This simultaneous seeking-and-refusing behavior has to do with the development of a personal identity during adolescence, which includes moving away from (but not becoming disconnected from) family and establishing independence. Suppose you try to help? On the one hand, he welcomes your efforts (after all, he's asking for your assistance), but on the other hand, he resents you for your intervention, as it only spotlights his dependence on you (this moving-away process is about independence and showing that he doesn't need you as much anymore). Since he is in this dilemma, you can expect inconsistency.

Now, back to the issue of friends. Without friends, moving toward independence is difficult, and given the influence of loneliness (especially at this age), lacking friends can become an impediment to healthy development.

In assessing the problem, ask yourself, "Does my teenager have friend-making abilities? Did he have friends in middle and elementary school?" If the answer is yes, then with time he will probably find a niche of friends, and most likely all he needs is some support and borrowed belief in himself. With a history of friend-making abilities behind him, one could view what is happening now as a temporary aberration. What can you do about this, then? What follows is a sample letter I might send or a parent might give to a teenager experiencing such an aberration

Dear Jim,

When we met earlier this week, you expressed concerns over your recent inability to make friends in high school. This has surprised you, given the ease with which you made friends in middle school and continue to make friends in various sports camps during summers. After a bit of discussion, we agreed that the problem seems more situational than personal, but if it doesn't change in the near future, it has the potential to become personal, something you very much want to avoid.

After further discussion, you realized there wasn't much more you could do to secure friends without being untrue to yourself—an approach that neither of us advocates. So we were momentarily stuck, until we came up with the "What the hell!" solution. Once this was on the table, you exploded with ideas—well, after you overcame some initial doubts and hesitations. It was time to experiment; we brainstormed all the things that you could experiment with at school in order to break up your current nonfriendship patterns and simultaneously follow up on some interests while pushing yourself to learn more about your school. Your ideas included go to a swim meet, attend a student council meeting as a visitor, work with the technical crew on the winter play, get involved with the homecoming celebration, find out about the various clubs at school and attend one or two of the meetings that seem interesting, go on an outdoor education trip, volunteer to tutor one day a week at your old middle school, write an article for the paper, check out the peer counseling office, and so on. Your list was much longer than this: these are just a few of the ideas I remember.

From there, you committed to following through on two ideas in the next week. And I must say, Jim, when you left my office you seemed relieved and excited about your new direction. I'm curious as to how it goes. Keep me updated.

The point here is twofold: First, to help your teenagers understand that this is only a nonfriend phase, that is, that their friendship horizon will improve over time and that it's more situational than personal; and second, to break up the pattern they are caught in by helping them understand that, when a person acts out of genuine curiosity and a sense of adventure, they in turn become more interesting to those around them and, ultimately, to themselves too. These latter qualities are prime components of making new friends.

The lack of friends is more worrisome when teenagers don't have experiences of friendship and making friends somewhere in their history. The same process described with Jim can work, but it takes more persistence and presence on the part of the adults involved. Probably the most important thing you can do is be on the lookout for "red flags," signs that loneliness is getting the better of adolescents and involving them in at-risk activities: using alcohol or drugs, skipping school, sleeping all day, and in the worst case, self-cutting or other self-harm. These are clear invitations for professional help. (See chapter 22 for more on this subject.)

So, what can you do to help your teenager through all this? I advocate an indirect approach (which is often very successful in many other areas). First, see if you can get other adults (not your spouse) involved in the situation—ideally a school counselor, teacher, or coach. Talk to them about the problem, but not with the expectation that they will do anything about it other than be aware. If they have a good relationship with your adolescent, perhaps they will feel comfortable bringing up the topic in a future conversation. Chances are that your teenager will more readily take advice from someone other than either you or your spouse, mainly because the relationship is one of the adolescent's choosing. (Nonparent adults who teenagers have chosen to have a relationship with are important resources for both adolescents and parents.)

Also, feel free to communicate on this topic with your teenager through notes or letters. This circumvents a couple of potential problems. First, it allows him to save face and removes him from the independence/dependence power struggle. Second, because this struggle is minimized, it allows him to "hear" what you are saying. That is, in the privacy of his own room and on his own time, he can read the letter. By being in charge of time and setting, there is a much greater chance that he will also feel free to take the suggestions that he deems useful—he's less defensive and more open.

> Jason,
>
> I know that this has been a rough year for you. For some reason, it's been hard to find friends at this new high school. But it'll get better in time. You've had too many good friends for me to think otherwise—Isaac and Phil from summer camp, Tom and Billy from eighth grade, and Lewis from elementary school. Remember how you were elected vice president in seventh grade? Anyway, know that your father and I are very proud of you—both for your accomplishments and for the kind of person you are. We couldn't ask for more. I know you'll have plenty of friends by the end of high school, so just hang in there and never doubt yourself. While I can't help you find friends, I can support you in any way you want, even if it means being quiet. So let me know if there is anything I can do.
>
> I love you,
> Mom

Also, and perhaps most important, a letter is a communication of your love and respect for him. It takes time to write a letter, and he appreciates the effort. It also makes him feel that you're on his side without being intrusive, that you actively believe in him. A letter also lasts; kids tend to hold on to these letters and read them over time, similar to old pictures that are saved.

> The other day my son called and asked if I would do a huge favor for him: bring the history paper that was due next period to him at school (he'd forgotten it at home). Well, when I was getting the paper, I noticed my handwriting on a piece of paper in his top drawer, so I looked more closely. In the drawer were dozens of brief notes I had given him over the past few years. He had saved all of them! What is most incredible is that at the time he barely even acknowledged getting them. I always assumed he read and tossed them without a second thought!

Finally, notes acknowledge teenagers' struggle without either taking it over or abandoning them in their time of need. This is a tricky and essential line to walk, but as with so much a parent must do, walking this line must become a high art.

13

Sports and Extracurricular Activities

What role do sports and extracurricular activities play in kids' lives?

Adolescents invest themselves in sports, drama productions, dance, creative arts, and music for essentially the same reasons, though with some important differences.[1] First, playing on a sports team or participating in a production gives teenagers a sense of belonging to a community that has more in common and is generally closer than the greater community of high school. As we saw in chapter 2, especifically in the "Horizon 2: Social" section, belonging helps the teenager deal with self-consciousness and loneliness.

> I enjoy cross-country a lot, especially the sense of accomplishment after finishing a good run. Also, it's a great way to snap out of a bad mood. But honestly, I enjoy the hanging out before and after practice as much as the actual running. Over the course of a season, I come to feel comfortable around these people; I feel more myself at cross-country practice than at any other time during the school day. Plus, as I get to know my teammates, I have more people to spend time with during

school besides my few close friends. And this lasts beyond the cross-country season. It adds variety to my life.

Second, sports and most extracurricular activities present very clear and concrete challenges. At a time of life when things are less black-and-white and more gray than ever, it is a relief to have these clear challenges. For instance, at the end of a game, it is clear which team has won and which has lost. Or at the end of a concert, the audience has either responded to the music or it has not. Also, your performance generally speaks for itself: you play well and you play a lot; you play poorly and you play a little.

At least in sports, each day is new and the outcome is unpredictable.

> I enjoy playing soccer every day, whether it is practice or a game, although games are better. Each game tells us if we are getting better and also keeps us humble. (The other day we played a team we had beaten seven to one earlier in the season, and they beat us three to two! We were in a daze the entire game.) But when we are all playing well, we are much better than eleven individuals. It's totally cool!

Third, extracurricular activities and athletics present daily opportunities to expand self-confidence. (Remember the discussion in chapter 2 about declining self-esteem in adolescents and girls in particular.) Through daily drills, rehearsals, and intrasquad scrimmages, participants have a means of assessing themselves and their improvements.

They also have an adult who is invested in their improvement, which, given their more typical perspective of adults, is a refreshing change for most teenagers. In fact, it is often through the coach or director-type relationships that teenagers begin to see adults as other than simply authority figures.

> Coach Johnson is a nut about free-throw shooting. Each of us has to take a hundred shots a day and record the results. But it is kind of cool too. I mean, over time I get to see how much I've improved. And even when he yells, I know it's because he wants me to get better and that he has my best interests as a player and our best interests as a team in mind. Also, with all of us doing it together, it becomes kind of a bonding thing for the team. So, I guess it makes sense, even though I still don't really like it.

Fourth, athletics and extracurricular activities help organize adolescents' lives. Most teams and productions practice a few hours each day during the season, which leaves less available time for other teenage activities: schoolwork, family responsibilities, and maintaining a social life. As a result, most teenagers must become much better organized during the season (when they have less time) than out of the season (when they have more time). With the production or sport as a priority, they organize themselves around it. (It is no surprise that most student athletes do better academically in season than out of season.) Adolescents do well with lots of activities, provided that most of what they do is structured through consistent practice times and game and production schedules. This is why musicians practice better when performing with a group or taking regularly scheduled lessons than trying to learn on their own. The lesson or group organizes them and their practice.

A common error adults make about teenagers is that they try to understand what is best for their teenager through a strictly rational framework. For instance, if students are slipping in their grades, it is not uncommon for parents to insist that the students drop their involvement in, say, the basketball team. But, given the loss of this organizing factor in their lives (not to mention their loss of autonomy), their grades slip even further. The parents' intervention works in the opposite direction from what logic would indicate is correct. Does this mean that parents should always intervene in the least logical manner? No. It does mean that you must talk with and listen to your teenager to understand what the slipping grades mean and what participation on the team means.

Sophia was doing poorly in school when she came home and told us that she made lead in the spring play at school. Obviously, we were quite happy for her, yet we were disturbed at how we imagined this would affect her grades. When we brought this up, she broke into tears and became very fearful that we would insist that she drop the play (which we had planned to suggest!). We listened as she explained how important the play was to her. She promised that, if we would support her in this, she would do better in school. In fact, she suggested that we call her teachers after the first month of rehearsals to make sure that she was improving. Since she had never shown this kind of initiative or responsibility before, we grudgingly went along with her proposal.

Well, she stayed involved in the play, did wonderfully in her role, and even improved her grades. It was quite an eye-opener for us.

Finally, these long-term commitments to activities (especially to a group of people) are important in teaching adolescents how to get through their egocentricity and personal doubt in order to accomplish something of their choosing. Much of what it takes to become successful in life depends on how one handles doubt and adversity while working to achieve a goal. If doubt and adversity get the better of people, then they seldom accomplish their goals and even more seldom delve into anything in depth. Extracurricular activities are ongoing workshops in addressing doubt and challenge, and the lessons learned here transfer to the classroom and to life.

A major difference between good students and poor students lies in how they view a difficult problem on a test. Poor students see the problem and panic, often talking to themselves in a manner that supports doubt: "I knew I didn't study enough for this test. I can't believe I don't know this; I don't even know where to start! I'm sure the rest of the test is even more difficult. I'm going to flunk for sure. Look at everyone else, they're just cruising right along. I'm so stupid I can't believe it!" Good students, however, see the problem, and with self-confidence, begin to dissect it: "This is difficult, but if I stay with it long enough, I know I can figure out where to begin. And from there, all I have to do is stay calm and patient and it'll begin to come together, just like a puzzle. Ahh, there is something I know. Not much, but at least a beginning." This same thought process is experienced and lived through in extracurricular activities. The more committed one is to the activity, the more directly these issues are confronted.

Obviously, a great deal is happening when your teenager gets involved with an extracurricular program or a sport—at least as much as has been discussed so far, and probably much more. Your best bet is to support these activities even though you may not fully understand them. Also, especially if your teenager is particularly talented at one activity or another, be careful not to make that activity the core of his identity. Your esteem, and his too, is much safer when it's focused on supporting him as a full person, rather than when it's dependent on him succeeding at some event or achieving some specific goal.

The Lost Playground

A number of years ago, while hosting a radio show, I spoke with NPR commentator and author Ralph Schoenstein, who wrote *My Kid's an Honor Student, Your Kid's a Loser: The Pushy Parent's Guide to Raising a Perfect Child*, and he was making the point about how few kids play pick-up sports these days. Gone are the days when kids show up at the baseball diamond or the basketball court, choose teams, and play. Instead, kids are driven from school to practice. Gone are the days of skins vs. shirts or blue vs. green. Instead, they have uniforms, gym bags, and often two or three different pairs of the latest turf shoes. And these days, if the sport is at all organized, everyone gets a trophy.

Ralph's main point was that much is lost when kids no longer participate in pick-up games at the park and in the cul-de-sacs. A pick-up game is rich in teaching and learning. You develop empathy for the last couple of kids selected when sides are chosen. If it's a game at a new-to-you playground, you read the social nuances to learn the unwritten rules: If you call your own foul is that okay? How about if you call the other guy on a slight rule violation? More than what we learn from these games is how we learn it. Nobody guides us, we figure it out on our own. (Oddly enough, this is the exact way kids learn the rules of the latest video games.) This information is hard-won and precious. So, naturally, we feel satisfaction with each glimmer we get. It's difficult if not impossible to create this same sense of accomplishment that is subtle when kids' activities are too organized and too neatly packaged.

The point here is to make sure your teenagers' lives are not too organized. They need time that is unscheduled not only for relaxation, but also for casual interactions with other teenagers, whether it is pick-up games on the field, dramas performed in the backyard, concerts staged in the garage, or videos made at the skate park.

Practice

In his insightful book, *Talent Is Overrated: What Really Separates World-Class Performers from Everybody Else*,[2] Geoff Colvin reviews with a critical eye the research on what it takes for someone to achieve mastery. In accord with popular wisdom, he does conclude that it takes ten thousand hours of practice, and he adds an essential caveat: it has as much to do with the hours of practice as with the quality of practice. He calls the practice that leads to mastery "deliberate practice."

In deliberate practice, people focus on their areas of weakness—the basketball player dribbles with her nondominant hand, the musician works on the chord progressions that give him the most trouble—as well as areas where they have achieved proficiency.

> When I practice on my own, I like to imagine I'm playing for both teams and always end it with me making the game winner for my team. It just makes the time go by faster. Actually, I use it as reward time because I start by spending some time on the fundamentals that give me the most trouble, and when I get frustrated I go into my own imaginary game, and then come back to the fundamentals after a few minutes. I know it's a little strange, but it works for me.

The above is the reason we all hope our teenagers find a healthy passion during their adolescence, because passion is what will keep them motivated to learn how to engage with deliberate practice. Sometimes, however, you just have to set something in motion and hope it catches fire. In my mind, learning to play a musical instrument is one of the best means possible to invite kids into learning about deliberate practice.

> My guitar teacher gives me practice assignments each week, and in every twenty or thirty minutes of practice he gives me three minutes of something that is really hard. He tells me to give it my all for just three minutes. I hate this part of the practice, but he is right, whenever I stick to it I get much better, probably more from this than the rest of the practice . . . but don't tell him that!

Notes

1. The following discussion, while most directly about sports, is also true for drama, student government, creative arts, music, and similar activities.

2. Geoff Colvin, *Talent Is Overrated: What Really Separates World-Class Performers from Everybody Else* (New York: Portfolio, 2008).

14

Exercise, Nutrition, and Stress

Teenagers seem more stressed out now
than in previous generations. Why is this so
and how can a parent help?

In my experience, this generation of teenagers is more stressed out than ever
before, and there are lots of reasons for this. Primarily though, I think it is
due to increased expectations combined with a prolonged adolescence that
both starts earlier and ends later.

Stress

These days adolescence doesn't end at eighteen or nineteen; it ends at twenty-
two or twenty-three. Think about it. Not too long ago, the big push was for
teenagers to make sure they got their high school diploma. Then, in the 1960s
and 1970s, the bar was raised to get that college degree. Now it's solidly the
college degree and moving quickly upward to the graduate degree. All this

163

leaves adolescents more dependent on their parents for longer and longer. Higher expectations force longer dependence on parents, which equals stress—for you and especially for your teenager. Not only that, many kids feel the pressure not only to go to college and beyond, but to go to the "right" college and beyond. And, of course, the preparation to get into these institutions starts early, at least in high school and sometimes before.

> I've been a college counselor in high school for just over thirty years now, and things sure have changed. I used to start talking with kids and families in their junior year about college, just getting them thinking about it and starting the process of finding three or four colleges that they might apply to. But these days I am besieged by ninth grade parents (and just as often their kids too) right from the beginning of school. They want to know what courses they should be taking to get into such and such college in their senior year. Now, when I reassure parents that most colleges pay little attention to ninth grade grades, especially first semester, they look right past me, not acknowledging a word I've said.

The pressure to get into the "right" college, along with what was discussed in the previous chapter, has led parents to get more involved in the management of teenagers' free time and extracurricular activities. Just think how many parents play driver for their teenagers on any given weekday: taking them from music lesson to game to play practice to home. And the real loss for kids here is downtime. Many of our teenagers are overscheduled and overprogrammed. This is the stress we feel as parents—to give our kids all the opportunities available so they have the most options when they graduate.

> I was totally unprepared for the onslaught of fear-inducing materials from the SAT prep courses once Jenny entered high school. It seems like there is a new one each week. At first, I just tossed them, but of late I've been reading them, as has Jenny, and we're both beginning to wonder if maybe she shouldn't take one of the courses. Neither of us likes the idea, but we're realistic about not wanting to put her at a disadvantage with her peers. It's too much too soon, but I'm not sure what else to do.[1]

This is a variation of adult peer pressure. We have to stay strong enough to do what we think is right with our kids, not what everybody else says we should do. Sure, we need to seek out and listen to different viewpoints, but in the end we need to support the decisions that are best for our families and our kids. And in the above scenario, it doesn't mean disallowing Jenny to take the SAT prep course—that is micromanaging and trying to control. But, instead, it's using our influence to help her come to the best decision.

> My mom and dad always told me not to grow up too fast. They were on me not to sign up for so many activities or to take so many AP courses. It was weird, because most parents are just the opposite. I mean, I'm pretty driven and like doing lots of things, but, at the same time, their support for just being a kid did help me lots to learn not to take on too much. They might be surprised to hear that, but it's true.

Teenagers are more stressed than in previous generations, and it's up to us to help them learn to recognize and address some of the stress in their life, and in particular, to help them develop healthy lifestyles, which is the single best antidote to stress.

Obesity and Nutrition

With all the research coming out on the huge increases in child and adolescent obesity, what can parents do to make sure their teenager is healthy?

According to the Centers for Disease Control, from 1980 to 2008 the percentage of obese children rose from 6.5 percent to 19.6 percent and in adolescents from 5.0 percent to 18.1 percent. A direct cause of this is the combination of a more sedentary lifestyle for teenagers and eating habits that have taken a dramatic turn for the worse—more fast food and in larger proportions.

Adding to this sad situation is what is happening, and not happening, in most schools across the country. Nutritionally, many schools have resorted to vending machines full of junk food as a way of making money to keep valuable programs that would otherwise get cut. Fortunately, many states and many schools are seeing that the real cost of these deals shows up in our teenagers' expanding waistlines. As a result, states are backing out of these arrangements, which is a good thing.

On the other hand, and again due to budget cuts, physical education classes are suffering like never before. In fact, many elementary schools can't even afford qualified PE teachers. And in high school, PE classes meet less often and are less rigorous than ever before.

In quick summation, teenagers now have worse eating habits than ever before and are less active than previous generations, and this all adds up to big weight gains. Walk around any mall—it's not a pretty picture. Fortunately, this is an area where we as parents can exert a great deal of influence. Let's start with nutrition, which begins at home. Ideally, we've been making meals with our sons and daughters as they were growing up, not only because it's enjoyable, but also as a way to teach them about food and about basic nutrition.

> Ever since I can remember I've helped my mom make dinners at least a couple times a week. And each time she reinforces the same three ideas, which are like burned into my brain: 1) Cook with healthy and fresh ingredients, and you'll seldom make a bad meal. 2) Always serve a vegetable and make sure it's as fresh and in season as possible. 3) Make the meal aesthetically pleasing.

It's through these simple rituals that we have the best opportunities to teach our kids about food and nutrition. It's important to realize, too, that most kids want to know how to make a few decent meals. Not only that, once teenagers cook even a little bit, they become even more discerning eaters, which makes it less likely that they'll fall into the trap of bad eating habits. And there are lots of ways for parents to do this, from cooking together like the parent of the teenager above, to having teenagers pack their own lunches, to having them make their own breakfast. It also means that, as parents, we choose our battles.

> I can't control what he eats at school and at friends' houses, so I don't even pretend. But where I really hold the line is on breakfast. He doesn't get out of the house without eating a nutritious breakfast—I know, because I make it for him every morning. Maybe he should be more self-sufficient in this regard, but I don't care, I just want to make sure he starts the day out on the right foot.

As parents, our bottom line is to make sure our teenagers understand good nutrition. Sure, they won't practice it all the time, but who does? It's not about never eating fast food; it's about having an overall balanced diet, something your teenager stands a better chance of learning while under your roof.

Exercise

When it comes to physical activity, again much of the responsibility falls on parents. You need to help your kids develop the habits of staying active and teach them to appreciate how staying fit can help in all the other areas of their life: less stress, better sleep, healthier body, less sickness. The point is to insist that they find some activities they will do on a regular basis: playing on an athletic team, taking a class at the local YMCA, hiking with friends. They must find some means of staying active that they enjoy. This is when lifelong habits take root, for better and for worse.

Please note that the goal is a long-term internalization of the importance and pleasures of physical fitness, not a short-term commitment to a sport. Research shows that many teenagers, particularly girls, who are actively involved in a sport will stop exercising completely if they quit that sport. (According to the Centers for Disease Control, only one-quarter of girls engage in regular exercise compared to one-half of boys.)

Now, as you're trying to figure out how to get your teenager involved with and interested in physical fitness, let me share what one of the leading nutritional and fitness experts in the country does with her college students at the University of California in Davis. Early in the semester, Dr. Elizabeth Applegate (author of *The Encyclopedia of Sports and Fitness Nutrition*)[2] talks with her students about the health benefits of basic walking, especially if your goal is to take one thousand steps per day. She then has her students get themselves pedometers—which keep track of how many steps and how much distance you cover in a day—and has the students start keeping track of how many steps they take a day. She says that at first most students are around three hundred steps per day, but within a week or two most are up to or above the one thousand steps per day goal. To my mind, this is the perfect adolescent intervention: give them a tool they can use themselves and then back out so they can learn and discover on their own. It works for Liz and her students.

Providing an Example

With both nutrition and physical fitness, talk alone isn't enough to convince our kids. Kids pay attention to what we do, the walk we walk, or not. We need to take a good look at ourselves in the mirror: what message are we sending our kids by our own behavior? Make no mistake about it. If you are a model of healthy eating habits and regular exercise, there is no guarantee that your teenager will follow suit, but there is a much better chance, in part because you follow your own advice and in part because you will feel a different kind of authority and have a more solid authenticity to what you say. Kids pick up on this.

> I'll never forget the look on my mom's face when I yelled back at her for nagging me about eating better. I told her that maybe she should pay more attention to herself than to me. She hit the roof! But then she caught herself, shook her head, and walked away. Later that night, she came into my room and wanted to talk. Basically, she said that I was right, she needed to take better care of herself, but then she added that she was right, too, that I needed to take better care of myself. From there, we talked for an hour and both committed to eating better and getting more exercise. That was a month ago, and both of us are doing pretty good, not perfect, but it's definitely changes for the better.

While we need to get our kids involved with nutrition and fitness, these areas are different than most other areas we have to educate our kids about because they provide us wonderful opportunities to connect with our kids too. Whether by cooking together, walking around the block, going to an exercise class, or shopping at the local farmers' market, these activities are chances to connect with our kids. These are also classic times to take the consultant role, listening more than talking and thinking much more in terms of influence than control.

Say What You Want

In chapter 10, we examined the importance of positive and constructive communication. Here is a positive message on nutrition and exercise that was
developed in 2007 by the Harvard School of Public Health and the Centers
for Disease Control. It is the 5-2-1 Go! Program, developed to counter the rise
in childhood obesity. The program name was meant as a mantra that would
be easy for kids and adults to remember and use. The 5 stands for eating five
servings of vegetables each day; the 2 for limiting television viewing to two
hours a day; and the 1 for getting at least one hour of physical activity each
day. In the program, success is straightforward to gauge and track. It is beautiful in its simplicity and directness. The mantra also focuses on the positive
aspects of the behaviors it endorses. There is nothing in 5-2-1 that is about
what *not* to do—even the "limit television viewing to two hours" statement
has a positive spin, since it is about what *to* do, not what *not to* do.

Notes

1. An insightful and useful guide to the entire college admissions process is *College
Admission: From Application to Acceptance, Step by Step* by Robin Mamlet and Christine
VanDeVelde.

2. Elizabeth Applegate, *The Encyclopedia of Sports and Fitness Nutrition* (New York:
Prima Lifestyles, 2002).

15

The Driver's License

How can we expect our sixteen-year-old daughter to be ready to drive a car when she can't even keep her room clean?

Dr. John Dyckman, a professor and developmental psychologist, believes that there are two events in peoples' lives that change their worldview forever. The first is learning to walk. When infants go from crawling to walking, their perspective of and relationship to the world expands dramatically. The ability to walk enhances adventure, strengthens self-determination, and lends efficient mobility to curiosity. The second irrevocable change to one's worldview is getting a driver's license. If walking and, later, riding a bike represent dramatic changes in mobility, driving a car is an exponentially larger change. For teenagers, it is especially dramatic because they now also have an expanded sense of consciousness to go along with this newly increased mobility. Adolescents who obtain a driver's license have more independence and more say over what they do and where they go. Conversely, you have less say over what they do and where they go. This is no minor change.

Ideally, parents start to consider driving privileges when their child is twelve or thirteen years old. You ask yourself: "What do I need to see from my daughter in terms of responsibility and maturity to feel comfortable with her driving the car in three or four years?" From there, you gradually give her more and more responsibilities so she can mature and gain experience—along the way to the driver's license, not afterward. My own mother was quite familiar with this kind of forward thinking.

As early as grade school, my mother realized that I needed to slowly learn to take care of myself, so that was when my lessons began. Typically, she would meet me after school and fix me a snack, but at times she would not be home (there would be a note) when I arrived home from school. While I was nervous about this, I did learn to fix my own snack and go about my after-school routine. It was only later, as an adult, that I learned that whenever she wasn't home she was across the street at a neighbor's house running from window to window making sure I was all right! In this way, she taught me to manage my anxiety so that later in life—adolescence—when she didn't have such direct control over me, I would be familiar with taking responsibility in the face of anxiety.

Handled this way, turning sixteen and driving aren't such a leap of faith for both parents and teenagers. Otherwise, the possible dangers of driving are justifiably overwhelming for parents. As every parent knows too well, one mistake here can be life changing and even life ending, something no parent wants to have to live with.

> Even though Josh is a junior, I still refuse to let him drive the car any more than a few miles away on a weekend evening. I'm just so fright-ened about drunk drivers, never mind the possibility that he might drink and drive. It's really sad, but I'm almost willing to have my son hate me during the next two years in order to ensure his safety. I would rather have a relationship to work on a few years from now than nothing to work with besides grief and guilt. I know I sound ultra-conservative, and I don't think I am in most areas, but there is just too much to lose on this one.

Before getting to the practicalities of driving, let's think about another inevitable conflict it stirs in the parent-adolescent relationship: time spent with one another. As teenagers get older, most parents see them less and less, which is fine with the kids. In fact, they do need to move away from you and toward their friends as a part of the normal development to adulthood, but as far as most parents are concerned, they don't need to do it with such glee.

> Ever since Tom started high school, we've been progressively seeing
> less of him. It began with him being home but preoccupied with phone
> conversations and homework. Now his friends, who all seem to have
> their licenses and ready access to cars, get him at nights to "go out"
> for a while. We're afraid we'll never see him after he gets his license! It
> almost feels like he is a boarder now; I can't imagine what it will be like
> after he starts driving.

Most states currently have a variation of the graduated license for new adolescent drivers. This is when the new driver is limited for anywhere from the first six to twelve months to driving only when a licensed adult over the age of twenty-five is in the car. This person is most often mom or dad. As hoped for, this legislation has significantly reduced new driver accident rates. But one unanticipated result is the stuff of dreams for parents: this extra six to twelve months of riding in the car, side by side, has improved parent-teenager relationships all over the country. For example, since the graduated license was implemented in North Carolina, just over 40 percent of parents and 40 percent of teenagers have reported that this extra time has considerably improved their communication with one another.

Because the topic of driving brings on significant amounts of anxiety, be as clear as you can on the topic and keep it separate from other issues. Making driving a power issue isn't good for anyone. Rather, make it a process that requires teenagers to behave responsibly (something that is within their control) en route to successfully acquiring the license. Your job is to consult, assess, and possibly help out at appropriate times along the way. In this sense, the driver's license is an invitation to responsibility.

> I know my parents will never let me drive. I'll have to wait until college.
> I'm serious! Every time I bring it up they're like, "Well, we'll have to see
> how things are going when the time comes." But when I ask, they can
> never tell me what these "things" are. Then to cinch the deal, when-
> ever I get in any kind of trouble, they say that these are the kinds of
> "things" they're talking about! Of course, they never point out or seem
> to remember any of the good things I do. They're nuts. I'm probably not
> even going to bug them about it when the time comes; I don't want to
> give them the satisfaction of holding that power over me.

It's unfair to communicate mixed messages to your teenager and then get mad at her when she gets upset at the mixed messages (and then to use her reaction as an example of why she is not ready for her license!). For instance, who is going to teach her to drive and who is she going to practice driving with? Are you necessarily the right person? At times, it makes a great deal of sense to hire a professional if neither parent is honestly up to the task. This is also a good time to put more responsibility back on your teenager. Why should you have to make all the difficult decisions while she gets all the perks? Beat her to the punch: Talk to her about driving on her fifteenth birthday. Tell her what a big deal it is and encourage her to take control of the process and make it impossible for you to refuse her license when she turns sixteen. Invite her to create her own plan for getting her license and your approval.

> At the beginning of tenth grade, my parents had a parents-to-daughter chat with me. I knew it had to do with my upcoming sixteenth birthday. Sure enough—but what they had to say was kind of cool. They were putting me in charge of getting my license. Of course, I had to meet their requirements. After impressing upon me how big a deal it was to drive a car, they talked about how it was also very frightening to them. They understood their fear was natural but nonetheless it was there and, as far as they were concerned, it was part of my job to keep tabs on their fear and keep it to a minimum. Their requirements were I could have no sudden drops in grades before or after the license; I would find, enroll in, and complete a certified driver's education course (they would pay); I would talk to the insurance company and get the required paperwork for us to go over together; I would pay for half the insurance adjustment; and I would drive for ten hours with my dad prior to making the appointment for the driver's test (after I'd completed the driver's ed course).

Act as the health and safety consultant on this issue. Separate actions and consequences ahead of time. For instance, no parents want their teenager to get behind the wheel after drinking or ride in the car of another driver who has been drinking. This is the place for clear structure:

> If I ever discover you driving under the influence, that's it; you'll never drive again until you go off to college. No exceptions. However, if you

take the car and go out drinking, but get a ride home or call me for a
ride, that is a different matter. That, of course, would involve other
consequences—but nothing around the car, as you would have been
quite responsible about the car in that instance. Understand the
difference. Risking your safety unnecessarily is not negotiable.

Along the same lines, a parent recently told me that she leaves twenty
dollars in the drawer by the front door for her daughter's emergency taxi fare.
If her daughter needs a safe ride home from anywhere at any time, she can
call a cab and use the twenty to pay the fare—no questions asked.

Whatever format you agree upon for learning and practicing driving,
make sure you stick to it unless you mutually decide otherwise. Make the time
to come up with a plan. After your daughter gets her license, you will see less
and less of her, but that is the case whether she gets her license or not. Also,
there is a small percentage of adolescents (especially in urban areas that have
accessible mass-transit systems) who are not interested in obtaining their
licenses. There is nothing wrong with them; just give them their space and
independence to choose if and when.

The driver's license is not only a real change in lifestyle, but it is also a
very symbolic change in your relationship. Society recognizes adolescents
as citizens responsible enough to earn the privilege of driving. It won't be
long now before your relationship with your teenager will change even more,
since graduation and future decisions are just around the corner. Finally, as
in all aspects of the parent-adolescent relationship, don't expect perfection
on your part or your teenager's part. It'll never happen. The only thing you
can honestly do is your best. And when you mess up, be forthright about taking responsibility for your behavior. Given the high stakes that accompany
the driver's license, you'll mess up somewhere along the way. As always, your
response is important.

This chapter concludes with an article by D. L. Stewart.[1] It will help
you both appreciate the complexity of the driver's license issue and decide
if you are the right person to teach your teenager how to drive. It will also
make you smile.

A TEEN'S LESSON IN LURCHING

I know it is going to be a tough afternoon when I explain to the
sixteen-year-old that learning to drive a stick-shift car is a simple matter of moving a lever into first, second, third, and fourth gears. And he
replies:

"In any particular order?"

Teaching a sixteen-year-old how to master four-on-the-floor is
simple. All it takes is the patience of Mother Teresa, the courage of Dave
Dravecky, and the neck muscles of Mike Tyson. I don't care how many
times you may have been rear-ended, you don't know what whiplash
is until you've sat in the passenger seat next to a sixteen-year-old who
decides that it would be a good idea to go from third to reverse. Without
using the clutch.

But each time another of our kids turns sixteen, their mother
tosses me a set of car keys and informs me it's a father's job to teach his
child how to operate a stick-shift car.

"Why do I have to do it?" I always whine.

"Because I'm the one who went through labor," she always replies.
There's no sense arguing with a woman who has waited sixteen years
for revenge.

On the first Sunday after our latest kid hits sixteen, she tosses me
the car keys again, and I drive him to an empty parking lot that sur-
rounds a football stadium. It is a place that obviously is frequently used
by parents teaching their kids to drive. The lot is littered with empty
Valium bottles.

I stop in a spot as far away from the stadium as possible. It's not
that I don't have complete faith in his driving ability, but it's not a real
big stadium and there is always that chance that he might not notice it.

The sixteen-year-old and I trade seats, and I start to explain to him
about the clutch and the "rpms" and how the gears are arranged in the
figure H.

"I know, Dad, I know," he says, impatiently, pushing in the clutch
and stepping on the accelerator. He lets out the clutch, the car lurches
forward, bounces twice and shudders to a stop.

"Did I do something wrong?" he asks.

"Don't worry, you'll get the hang of it," I assure him. "Next time give it just a little more gas."

He turns on the ignition, steps on the clutch, shoves the accelerator to the floor and revs the engine. If he pops the clutch now, I realize as the tachometer needle goes through the red zone for the third time, I won't have to worry about us running into the stadium. We'll just catapult over it.

"You might want to ease off on the gas a tiny bit," I suggest, bracing my feet against the dashboard.

He cuts it back to two million rpms and pops the clutch. The car lurches forward, bounces six times and stalls again. When it has finished shuddering, I crawl out of the backseat and rejoin him in the front.

"Sorry about that," he says.

"No big deal," I assure him. "When I was teaching your sister, I wound up in the trunk."

He tries again. This time the car does not lurch. It soars. I'm not sure what kind of mileage this car gets, but it gets great altitude.

"How was it that time?" he asks when we have returned to earth.

"Well, the takeoff wasn't bad, but you need to work on your landings."

After half an hour, we have covered approximately fifty yards. In forty-nine lurches.

On the other hand, I've got to give the kid credit. It's not often you get to drive with someone who can stop a car forty-nine consecutive times without ever using the brakes.

Note

1. D. L. Stewart, On Being a Dad: A Teen's Lesson in Lurching, *San Francisco Chronicle* August 21, 1991.

16

Graduation

What can I expect from graduation?

The end of the high school years is a complex time, whether your teenager chooses to pursue college or not. Issues of dependence and independence intertwine as new graduates get ready to go off on their own. They have reached a significant life marker; for many, the formal entrance into the adult world or, at the very least, a more adult-like world. Also, with graduation comes a variety of inevitable experiences and confusion regarding identity and readiness that parents are unable to (and should not try to) resolve for their kids.

On the one hand, most students are pleased to have completed high school, are more or less satisfied with their performance, and are looking forward to beginning a more independent life. Many are thankful that high school is finally over, as they feel more than ready to move on with their lives. On the other hand, some are reluctant to leave a place that they know well, where they have a known and accepted identity, where they have created many happy and sad memories, and where they grew a great deal. And to complicate this, many are secretly wondering if they are indeed ready to be out there in the "real world," but since they've been talking it up for so long and because they can't leave too much room for self-doubt, they are reluctant to voice any misgivings, especially to parents.

> I've been ready for graduation since the beginning of senior year. I
> mean, by then I had basically done all that I wanted to do in high school.
> I don't mean to sound arrogant, but it's true. I'm really ready to be on

my own. But at the same time, there is this nagging doubt in the back of my head. Sometimes I lie awake at night in fear of going away, making new friends, and doing it all over again. What if I'm not as good as I think I am? And there is no way I can tell my parents about it—they would freak out!

For parents, this is a similarly complex and confusing time. They are proud of their teenager's successful completion of high school and they are excited at the prospect of their adolescent becoming an adult, but they are also apprehensive that maybe their child is not quite ready for the "adult world." They are not sure how they are personally going to handle their teenager moving away from home, if that's the next step. Parents often feel a compulsion toward perfection before their child leaves home—what amounts to a kind of last-minute cramming-in of all the "right lessons." Resist this tendency; it never works.

Some parents also feel the need to regress to behavior and rules they used when they had more control of their teenagers. For instance, curfew may suddenly sweep back several hours to what it was when their daughter was a freshman, with the only justification being "Because I said so! And as long as you live in my house, you'll follow the rules of this house!" Or, as one student said of his parents, "It's as if they're trying to fit in all their parenting in these last few weeks when what I need is room and time to absorb and deal with all that's been happening." And as one parent said of his son, "I'm ready for him to go to college; I'm just not ready for him to leave high school."

With all of this (and the points raised in the "Family and Life Events" section of chapter 2), it's no wonder that many homes undergo a fair share of stress and arguing around graduation time. This conflict is often the result of the excitement and anxiety that come with change; it can also be a way for parents and kids to move away from one another in preparation for the next phase.

During the second semester of my senior year, I was a real jerk to my teachers at school and to my parents at home. I was moody and angry most of the time. I argued with teachers about assignments, skipped school, went to school stoned, and played rude pranks on people. At home, I was even worse. I don't know why. I was just angry at everyone around me. Everyone was relieved by the time I graduated. But a couple of years later I came back to school for a basketball game. It was the first time I had been back since graduation. And I know it sounds corny, but all of a sudden it made sense: I had felt like I was being thrown out of high school (where I had done well before second semester of senior year). So, rather than get tossed out, I unconsciously decided to reject them first. I really loved high school, but I had been too scared about leaving to face up to it. Somehow it was easier to get angry.

This young man's reaction gives an idea of all the changes teenagers try to integrate during and immediately after graduation. This is not to say, however, that they are separating from home. Separation implies a breaking away and disconnection; a better description is that they are extending themselves away from family and friends. This extension allows the room to grow and maintains the vital family connection. The bottom line is that, more than anything, graduation requires a thorough updating of close relationships, especially with parents.

When my parents and sister dropped me off at school, they stayed a few hours and helped me set up my room. It was nice, but still I was itching for them to leave. Anyway, when they did leave, I walked them to the parking lot and gave everyone hugs—we all sniffled a bit too, which kind of surprised me. My dad was last, but before I could turn away to leave, he handed me a cassette and said, "We all love you." When I played the cassette, it was a message from my parents and my sister. Basically, they each said what they were going to miss about me, what they weren't going to miss about me, and how they thought college would affect me. It was mind-blowing! I must have listened to that tape twenty times during that first semester. In fact, I still have it. Oh yeah, my dad also managed to tuck a few twenties into the cassette case, which was cool.

When your teenager goes away to college (or moves far away from home), I suggest you ask her to take lots of photos and send them to you—photos of her room, the cafeteria, the library, friends, classrooms, and whatever strikes her interest. These images will help you accurately imagine your adolescent in her new home. Any activity like this that allows for full extension without disconnection is helpful. And, of course, with the increase in technology this gets easier and easier: texting, email, video chats, and social networks. Just be careful how you use these tools; that is, remember she has the need to extend from you, not simply have your presence replaced with a cyber you.

My first couple of weeks at college were crazy with my mom. She texted
me every hour, sent photos like crazy, wanted to videoconference meals
together, Facebooked me nonstop, and generally intruded more on my
life than when I lived at home. I finally had to tell her to back off. Fortunately, she understood, though it was still hard on her.

This mom had it right in the sense of using technology to keep the connection going, and she had it wrong in the amount and intensity. All of which
goes to say, use the technology wisely and judiciously.

17

Eating Modifications and Eating Disorders

My daughter, who is on the slim side, seems to be eating less and less these days, and I think she is losing weight. What is going on?

There are really three questions here: "Does my daughter have an eating disorder?" and, more specifically, "How do I tell if my daughter has an eating disorder?" and, "If she does have an eating disorder, what can I do about it?" There is no simple answer to any of these questions; it is indeed a tricky area for both parents and educators. On the one hand, many parents think they can let the problem take care of itself:

> It is best not to say anything until I am absolutely sure, as I don't want to offend my daughter and inadvertently alienate her. Maybe it's just a passing thing, and if I ignore it it'll go away—kind of like when she was seeing that awful Bobby G. I held back on that one, and sure enough, she dropped him of her own volition. Besides, she is growing quite a bit, so perhaps I'm overreacting. I'll wait until I'm sure.

But, on the other hand, some parents feel the need to take care of the issue immediately:

> I must confront her on this right now. If I ignore it, it'll only get worse, and I'll be ignoring my responsibilities as her mother. Not only that, but I have to get her to a therapist as soon as possible. Or at least we have to make an agreement on her eating so I can keep track of how she is doing.

The problem is that neither of these two strategies is typically successful. Ignoring the problem and hoping that it'll go away is often worth a short-term attempt, but if an eating disorder is the problem, other strategies are called for. Also, by the time the parent notices the change in behavior, a problem with eating has probably been going on for a while. Parents are often the last to notice, for two reasons: First, you are around your daughter every day, so the gradual loss of weight over time is difficult to notice. Second, since you don't want to see this happen to your child, your natural tendency is to not notice it.

Before we get too far into describing how to respond, let's take a moment to look at where eating disorders come from and what they are all about. Bulimia and anorexia are the two most common disorders. *Bulimia* is characterized by self-induced vomiting or the overuse of diuretics, typically after gorging or bingeing on food. Bingeing comes about after short periods of starvation or extreme dieting, and the teenager often thinks of it as a lack of will, which is "made right" through vomiting. In this misery-go-round, not only do bulimics do themselves harm, but they also feel bad about themselves for having succumbed to the bingeing behavior. Bulimia is therefore crippling psychologically in how it erodes its victim's self-confidence and developing personal identity.

Anorexia is a distortion of a person's self-image that leads to self-starvation. It can, but need not, be accompanied by bulimic behavior. Anorexia is also often accompanied by rigid and extreme exercise, often running and aerobics. Most frightening of all, the most frequent victims of these two eating disorders are bright, creative, talented, and motivated adolescent girls: in short, the kind of kid every parent hopes for.

During high school, a fair number of teenagers flirt with eating modifications of one variety or another—usually during their freshman and sophomore years. At first, such behavior is seductive and gives them a sense of accomplishment and control, a crucial counterpoint to the frequent out-of-control feelings of most teenagers.

> I'm not bulimic or anything, but I've experimented with making myself throw up. I hated it! Still though, every once in a while I'll go a few days where I hardly eat anything, mostly to lose a few pounds (which I know doesn't work!), but also to feel better about myself. It is like I prove to myself that I am in control and that I do have strong willpower. I can see how it could become addictive.

Teenagers with eating disorders often have the notion (supported by media images and cultural values) that "thinner is better" and that by becoming thinner, they become more attractive and popular. This idea is reinforced by the attention they get when they lose weight.

> Lots of people noticed and complimented me, including some people I hardly even knew. Even my father noticed and said something positive, which really threw me! It was kind of funny, though; even though I was getting all this attention, it didn't make any difference in the long run. My standards were so much higher than everyone else's.

Parents need to be thoughtful about the messages they give their adolescents regarding food and weight. "Playfully" teasing girls about getting fat because they are having a piece of cake is harmful 99.9 percent of the time. They are already self-conscious, and your teasing only magnifies those feelings, no matter how benevolent the intention.

> I wish I could tell my mom how much it hurts me when she comments or gives me a raised eyebrow when I eat dessert. I imagine her heart is in the right place, but it sure feels awful.

In the adolescent world of ambiguity and rapid change, weight is something that can be controlled, as it is tangible and measurable. Kids with eating disorders can and do regularly assess themselves with a high degree of accuracy.

> The scale never lies. Every morning when I wake up, I weigh myself to see if my weight has changed. If I've lost even a little bit, I'm in a great mood. If I haven't changed at all, I'm pretty medium. But if I've gained even a little bit, I get real angry with myself and make plans [by exercising and not eating] to lose the weight by the end of the day.

As weight and food become a greater focus in a teenager's life, she may focus all her anxiety on weight rather than on the more ambiguous but necessary issues of adolescence. (See chapters 2 and 3 for examples of these issues.)

> After a while, all I could think about was food: what I had and had not eaten already during the day, what I would or wouldn't eat next, and how I would eat tomorrow. I even began saying yes or no to social engagements based on food. If it was a get-together around dinner, I always said no, but if it was just for coffee, I was fine. I definitely wasn't interested in alcohol or drugs—I was afraid of losing control and bingeing. It pretty much took over my life. Because I was so focused on food, I blocked out all sorts of other concerns and worries that I would otherwise have to face daily—like getting close friends, my sexuality, and most of all, figuring out what I want to do with my life and who I want to be.

If you suspect your teenager has an eating disorder, asking her directly sometimes works, but more often ends with the feeling of having run into a brick wall.

> When I confronted her with her eating habits, she looked at me like I was from another planet. She gave me a look that sent a shiver down my spine and simply dismissed the subject! I haven't brought it up since.

Still though, it is irresponsible to not bring up what you notice. It's important to set the stage before raising the questions. Specifically, you need to understand that this is a disease that is taking or has already taken over; it is not a sign of weakness or a matter of willpower. When you speak with your daughter, she needs to understand and feel that you are not accusing her of any wrongdoing. If you can create this environment, many adolescents will be fairly honest with you, even somewhat relieved. In this regard, some parents have had success with writing letters to their teenager voicing their concern and support. Then, when they have the conversation, the groundwork has already been laid.

> At first, I wanted my not eating to be my own secret, but when it got out of control, I wanted to tell my parents so they could help me. But I just couldn't bring myself to tell them directly. It would have been too

humiliating. So what I did was give them all sorts of hints—telling them all about my exercise, not eating with them because I didn't feel hungry, wearing tight clothes that showed how thin I was, and telling them how some people were commenting on how much weight I had lost—so that they finally had to ask me. Even then I acted angry with them when they asked me about it, but eventually I did tell them.

In fact, by the time the amount of food intake has changed, the disorder is probably comfortably settled in with your teenager. So as she recovers, the last thing to change is usually her eating habits.

Once I told my parents that I was anorexic, they completely panicked and misunderstood what I said. Sure, they were supportive, which was nice, but they were also pretty naive about what I needed. Asking me daily about what I ate, making lunches for me to take to school, and insisting that I eat dinner with them were all counterproductive. The anorexia was so strong in me that when they asked about what I ate, it [the anorexia] got me to lie. I gave the wonderful lunches to street people on my way to school. And eating in front of my parents only made me resort to throwing up afterward.

Think of an eating disorder in the same way you would any other disease that might infect your child. If your daughter were lethargic and sleeping all the time, you wouldn't ask her if she had mononucleosis. You would take her to the doctor. Do the same with eating disorders. Accurate and honest self-diagnosis is rare. Immediately alert your physician to your fears. Then, if this is an area your physician is comfortable addressing, set up an appointment for your daughter to have a physical. The physician should be able to spot signs of anorexia and bulimia and make a reliable diagnosis. From there, if an eating disorder is diagnosed, a treatment plan can be formulated, mainly between the physician and the adolescent. Parents typically play an adjunct role in treatment, which often includes some form of psychotherapy.

The doctor was good with my daughter, and even better with me. It took a while, but she finally convinced my husband and me that it would be best if we didn't bring up the topic of food with Susan. She said to leave that to her and the therapist. We were to be supportive and loving of

Susan as a person and to hold her accountable as we would any other young adult. She also told us that we might be asked to attend her counseling sessions periodically, but that we should wait for the invitation. She was immensely helpful to all of us.

By now you have noticed that I have used the female pronoun in this chapter; this is because the majority of adolescents suffering from eating disorders are female—though the number of boys diagnosed with eating disorders is on the rise. In general, however, boys experience other types of body image issues. The most obvious is extreme weight lifting in combination with steroid use. Steroid use is increasingly common, and adolescents typically turn to their use to either shed unwanted weight or to increase muscle mass. Sometimes the desire for more strength comes from wanting to excel at a sport, such as football, wrestling, baseball. At other times, it is just to improve their physique.

Steroid use is dangerous for teenagers, and over time can cause liver damage and play havoc with hormone production, sometimes manifesting in reduced sperm production and testicular atrophy in boys. There is also a host of behavioral symptoms centered on extreme mood swings that include aggression, irritability, fatigue, depression, and anxiety. If you see these signs in your teenager and suspect steroid abuse, bring your son to his physician for a checkup and before the appointment give the doctor a head's up as to your concern. As you might suspect, most teenagers do not respond well to confrontation on this subject from a parent. They stand a much better chance of hearing it from their doctor, who can then bring you into the conversation.

A useful way to conceptualize eating disorders or other body image disorders comes from New Zealand therapist David Epston and Australian therapist Michael White, who view an eating disorder as a separate entity that is attempting to take over the body and personality of the host.[1] This is also a useful way to discuss this issue with teenagers, as it pits them in a fight against an external agent rather than an internal part of themselves. They can eventually reclaim themselves from the foreign entity without sacrificing a part of themselves. Moreover, this is how the eating disorder is experienced by the victim. The following is a sample of the type of letter I might give to a teenager suffering from anorexia.

Dear _____,

From our conversation, it is clear that you are now making a stand against the tyranny of anorexia in your life. You also understand that this is both a lengthy and arduous process. To this extent, you need all the support you can muster, which also means separating, on a deep level, what supports you as a person and what inadvertently supports the anorexia. You've discovered that this is not so obvious as it seems at first glance.

Clearly, you want your parents' full support, but past efforts have failed to claim that necessary support. You've insisted on nonfat foods, avoided family obligations that have centered on dining, exercised fanatically within their plain view, and still have not gotten the attention you need from them. Further, you visited a physician in an attempt to get the subject out in the open with your parents, but that failed miserably because all he did was focus on the vegetarianism and refer you to a nutritionist—as if you need any outside assistance in monitoring your eating habits!

Even though your skin is slightly jaundiced, your wrists are tiny, your hair is beginning to fall out, and you've lost twenty pounds over the past six months, nobody seems willing to recognize what is going on. They all want to look the other way in the hope that it's "just a phase." Which was probably a suitable strategy in the beginning, but you are now way beyond the beginning. On top of this, what notice your parents have paid to the anorexia has resulted in a lot of mixed messages: Your mom is upset with your exclusively nonfat diet, but she reprimands you for eating a taco with cheese and sour cream! Your dad is worried about the amount you exercise, but compliments you on how good you look. (To this end, you've sadly recognized how "thin beauty" has taken over the typical American mind—especially in men.)

You fear that if you do muster the strength to tell your parents you have anorexia, you'll inadvertently invite them in as "food monitors," a possibility that you understandably dread. You really liked what happened with Karen and her anorexia. Once her disease was recognized, she started seeing a therapist and her physician. The therapist was someone she liked and with whom she simply talked about her life's events and seldom directly discussed food. The physician she met with asked only about the anorexia. He was very firm and had a clear weight in mind, that, if Karen dropped to it, would automatically land her in the hospital for at least a month, and Karen knew he wasn't kidding. Further, you especially liked that he forbade her family, and especially her parents, to ever talk to her about food or the anorexia. In fact, he insisted that Karen eat what, where, and when she liked. Her parents could never insist that she join them for dinner or for any other meal. Only he, the physician, would discuss food and eating with her. And yes, this was the person with whom she was brash, pouty, rude, and outspoken—all without feeling guilty!

Your friends. You need them now more than ever, but you understand how hard you are to access and how paralyzed they feel. The anorexia, gradually taking root in your thinking, has created this fog all around you that literally leaves you a step behind in conversations and misperceiving all that happens around you. In fact, the coldness of the fog encourages you to retreat further into your own world and the world of anorexia, which is compulsive in its focus on food, grams of fat, calories, and future planning for food. However, once your friends had gotten over their shyness about the food and focused on their concern for you, they tried to be supportive. While you didn't like them offering you food and encouraging you to eat, you did appreciate the intentions. And you understood why, with no results, they stopped offering the encouragement. You felt somewhat abandoned, but not able to tell them clearly what you needed: their unconditional love and support throughout this ordeal, even though they wouldn't be able to help directly. If only you could have gotten them to view the anorexia as a kind of long-term pneumonia. Anyway, they've gotten discouraged, and, with the distancing effects of the anorexia, they have drifted away from you.

Your teachers. Oddly, this has been the best support system you've had to date. Unexpectedly, Mrs. Nelson recognized what was going on with you and spoke her concerns and support to you directly. It was a great relief for someone to recognize what was happening without your having to tell them. Further, she was not afraid to talk about it with you and seemed very understanding and nonjudgmental. In fact, it was the relationship with her that encouraged you to squarely address the anorexia by coming to my office to get some ideas and the names of some local therapists. Quite a step.

We left our conversation with the idea of deciding how to alert your parents to the situation without further strengthening the anorexia. We discussed several options: you could write them a letter (as conversation often goes down undesirable and seemingly unavoidable paths); we could invite them into my office so you could tell them here; or we could invite them into my office, without your presence, so I could catch them up. It is now in your hands. While you want all the support you can get, you also fully understand that only you can make this stand against anorexia. You call the shots as to when, where, and how.

That is where we ended yesterday. Since then, however, I've thought of a few more questions I wished I had asked when you were here. I thought to include them, as they might assist you in determining your next step.

How did you manage to overcome the paralyzing effects of anorexia to voluntarily come into my office to enlist my help? You attribute much to Mrs. Nelson, but I suspect there is more. For instance, were you valuing yourself differently in order to make such a dramatic move? And if so, how were you valuing yourself differently? And how did you manage to do this in the presence of the anorexia?

See you soon.

Mike

As with alcohol and drug abuse (discussed earlier), eating disorders require the services of a professional. Without outside and ongoing intervention, these behaviors will turn into a power struggle between you and your teenager. (See chapter 22 for more on this topic.)

Note

1. Michael White and David Epston, *Narrative Means to Therapeutic Ends* (New York: W. W. Norton, 1990).

18

Adolescent Grieving

Is there a normal grieving process for teenagers who have suffered the death of a parent or other loved one?

The death of a loved one is an emotional catastrophe in any teenager's life, and it is something common to many teenagers. How this grief is handled is both an individual matter and also a somewhat known process, much the same as for adults. However, the competing horizons of adolescence, along with the interdependence of family members, make teenagers especially vulnerable to the death of a loved one. The death of a parent, in particular, is the single most traumatic event a teenager can experience. In this case, the adolescent is affected not only by a significant emotional loss, but also by a change in family responsibility and day-to-day life.

> After my father died, my relationship with my mom became much more grown-up. We had to talk about real issues with each other: responsibilities around the house, finances, and the behavior of my little sister in school. Mom was still the mom and I was still the son, but we were also different. We had to trust each other more. She had to work a lot, and as a result, I assumed more responsibility around the house. I began to cook many of the meals and to do some of the shopping. It was kind of weird at first, but I'm glad she turned to me like that, even if it was out of desperation.

There are definitely stages to grief. (Psychiatrist Elisabeth Kübler-Ross identifies five stages: denial, anger, bargaining, depression, and acceptance.)[1] These stages are, however, not experienced in a discrete or linear fashion. People cycle through these stages at various rates, sometimes getting stuck in one or completely skipping over another. There is no orderly process to grief, especially with the volatile nature of adolescence (see chapter 2).

Given the nature of death, ambiguity is a part of the grieving process—it is difficult to know what to think or feel. This ambiguity is often rough on teenagers, who are relatively inexperienced with such concepts, and at the same time it maximizes their coping skills. That is, this loss coupled with the resulting changes in daily life, causes certain behavioral changes that must be acknowledged, especially in mood changes.

> For at least the first few months [after her sister's death], I was all over the map. Sometimes I would go from laughing with friends to suddenly crying. I mean really crying and sobbing uncontrollably. It really freaked us all out at first! Other times I would have this chip on my shoulder, sort of looking for something or someone to get angry at. And sometimes I had so much energy I couldn't sleep, while other times I could hardly get out of bed. But the worst for me was that I couldn't make a decision about anything. I was so indecisive that I drove myself crazy! The worst was one day at a pizza place when I broke down crying because I couldn't decide what toppings I wanted on my pizza. Thank God my friends were with me.

While there is more or less a pattern to the grief process, it is also quite individual. There are no rigid rights or wrongs. Some teenagers will talk and emote a great deal; others get very physical (especially through sports); and others go more or less into seclusion. Some become very focused on one area of their life (academics, sports, music), and some make an abrupt change for the worse in their lifestyle. One observation I've made is that often adolescents react by making their world smaller. That is, they turn their attention and focus to one or two things that suddenly emerge from their usual variety of activities. This shrinking of their world gives them a greater sense of control in the face of an uncontrollable event and is often a healthy and useful response.

> After my mom died, it was pretty strange. Everything was unreal. But shortly afterward I got very focused on my schoolwork. It became a real

priority for me and, as a result, I dropped some of my other interests . . . for all that year I got better grades than ever before. It was the opposite of what everyone expected, including me.

How a teenager reacts to death is attributable to a number of interrelated variables: his relationship to the deceased, his prior experience with death, the type of death (sudden or prolonged), the reactions of those around him, the reactions of his friends to him, and his basic personality. However he deals with his grief, it is a long-term process. It is not something that he simply goes through and beyond in a few weeks or months. It becomes a sedimented part of his past; when other loved ones die, the previous death is recalled as both an experience and as a process of grief. (See diagram 1, "Stress Buffer Zone," in chapter 2.)

So, what is helpful? Time and persistent invitations to conversation. Give him all the time you can, but make yourself available, be it by quietly tagging along on errands, helping with tasks around the house, or going to shows and games together. And while you give him time, don't take offense when he says no. Let it be okay, but don't let it stop you from asking again in the future. Talk to him about what happened, and don't try to take away his anxiety or sadness. Also, don't insist upon anxiety or sadness.

A month or so after my sister [Cheryl] died, I was on a walk with my dad. At one point, his voice got a little high pitched and he said he wanted to talk about talking about Cheryl. He didn't want to force anything on me, but he wanted the subject to always be open between us. He didn't want to turn a deaf ear to me or make me talk about Cheryl. It was kind of scary, because I realized that he was as confused as I was. But at least we had each other, which helped.

It's important to understand that for most people the major effects of the death of a loved one usually begin a couple of months after the death. Prior to that, most people are so overwhelmed by the event and the concern of others that they don't have the time or space to do their own processing. Be sure to check in with your teenager after a few months, when talk and companionship are most helpful and useful.

When my dad died, we [the family] got all this immediate attention and sympathy from friends, neighbors, and family. And the food! Everyone we ever met must have brought us meals during that first month. It was all amazing, so much so that it was hard for anything to sink in. It wasn't until a few months later that my dad's death really hit me. All of a sudden my family and I were developing a routine that didn't include my father. It was like there was this giant empty hole in everything we did. Those months were by far the hardest. And, of course, by then everybody had gone on with their lives and had stopped talking with me about my dad. I didn't see the empty void until all the support was gone, so I had to deal with it alone, which was pretty much a drag.[2]

You should also look out for the periodic appearance of "red flags" that insist upon your intervention in your teenager's grieving process. He may become overwhelmed and self-destructive in some manner, whether blatant or subtle: skipping school (sometimes bordering on dropping out), getting heavily into drugs or alcohol, or becoming violent toward others (fighting) or himself (suicide). (See chapter 22 for more on this topic.) These are signs that health and safety are at issue. You must intervene directly and may have to enlist the support of others, including a professional counselor.

For a while after my mother died, I was pretty crazy. I would get drunk and do anything on a dare: walk on a high ledge, steal booze from a liquor store, drive incredibly fast, or talk back in class (when I went). Finally, a couple of teachers, my soccer coach, and my dad all sat down and confronted me with what I was doing. It was a pretty ugly scene. I didn't cop to anything. But in the end my dad and I both went to a shrink for a while, often together. It also helped my dad, as he wasn't doing much better than me. I think I would be dead otherwise, or at least thrown out of my house.

As odd as it sounds and no matter how difficult the course, most adolescents are resilient and with time they develop strength and resources from having to deal with this type of hardship, as long as they are allowed to move at their own pace. Most people who have endured hardships of one kind or another will say that suffering made them stronger and gave them more depth.

Finally, in discussing the death of a loved one with students, I find it is frequently useful for them to work through this process in their own time (without feeling abandoned), with the implicit message that they are capable of handling this and that you can trust them. They also need to discern how to move on with their lives without forgetting the person who died. I often give a variation of the following letter to teenagers to take home and read at their leisure, and to reread over time. In this example, the letter references the death of this teenager's mother.

Dear _____,

In trying to come to grips with the death of a loved one, people often speak of "letting go" and "moving on," which are all said with the best intentions. People want to see you whole again, happy again, and living your life fully again. However, there is also the underlying message that this person is dead, the relationship is over, and that life is for the living. While this is quite true, it is also not the entire story.

When your mother was alive, you had a relationship with her that was important and vital to you. With her death, it feels like the relationship has died along with her, even though the relationship need not die. To "get on with your life" and "let go of your grief," you may need to first form another relationship with her that replaces the old relationship. Your mother was too important to you to simply forget about her, and many people won't or can't "move on" until they are sure that they won't forget. But the process of creating this new relationship is seldom spoken of, even though it is common sense. You see, the new relationship is one in which you bring your mother into yourself, into your imagination if you wish. You create a small space within yourself for her, a place that you can reference whenever you wish. Believe me, this is not as crazy as it seems at first glance.

You knew your mom quite well, well enough to know how she would respond to certain situations and certain questions. You knew how she acted and felt when you misbehaved. You knew how to please her. You also knew how to tease her, make her laugh, and anger her. There are many more general and idiosyncratic things that you knew about her that occur to you whenever you think of her. And there are many more things you knew about her that perhaps you don't yet remember. That is part of the purpose of this letter: to help you remember some of the aspects of your mom that you knew so well in a manner that allows the essence of her to remain within you. You can have an active and changing memory of her in the present versus a passive and stagnant memory of her in the past.

With the above in mind, take some time to reflect on the following questions. You may want to come back to these questions at various times. You will probably also come up with some of your own questions that help create a living memory of your mom. Do whatever is most helpful to you. (However, if you do come up with some new questions that are useful to you, please pass them on to me so they can be incorporated into this letter for others to use.)

What are some of your favorite mental snapshots of your mom? What do you imagine are some of her favorite mental snapshots of you? How about of the two of you together?

When did she surprise you by something she said or did? How did this increase your understanding and appreciation of her? And how did you surprise her by something you said or did? What did this tell her about you that she didn't know before?

Is there any particular song, book, poem, or art piece that you associate with her? If not, think of one now. What about that represents her to you, and what aspect of her does it represent? What did she see in you that was special? How did she communicate this to you? And how did you let her know that you got it?

I hope these questions help in the building of a new relationship with your mother, one that keeps her alive within you, and you alive within her.

Best wishes,

Mike

Notes

1. Elisabeth Kübler-Ross, *On Death and Dying* (New Haven: Yale University Press, 1968).

2. Because holidays and anniversaries are difficult for many adolescents, I have often led a "holiday blues group" during the major holiday season. By talking, telling stories, and reinventing traditions, participants "sing" themselves and one another through to the other side of the holiday funk.

19

Divorce, Remarriage, and Blended Families

How does divorce affect a teenager? What is a parent's remarriage like for teenagers? Is there anything I can do to ease the transition?

Divorce

Just as there is no one common adult experience of divorce, there is also no universal adolescent experience of divorce. Divorce is one of those phenomena that dominates (as it should) the landscape of the teenager during and intermittently before and after the actual divorce. Before, adolescents usually feel what is coming—I've rarely spoken to a teenager who was genuinely surprised, no matter how discreet the parents were.

> I knew they were going to get divorced before they ever said anything to me. There are lots of signs if you just look: hushed conversations when I walked into the room, tearful phone conversations, late-night

arguments, separate bank accounts and, in general, lots of haggard and exhausted looks.

Teenagers react to this in a variety of ways. Some try to make things better between their parents by being nice and supportive to both of them. They hope that somehow if they are good, their parents will become more peaceful and loving with one another. These teenagers work hard to create the illusion of control, that they can keep the family together if they just are good enough.[1] Others, feeling the lack of consistency and attention at home, begin to act out in a variety of ways: getting heavily into the party scene, slacking off in school, arguing with teachers and coaches, or becoming depressed. Adolescents must face reality: they are essentially powerless to do anything about the impending divorce, and this is stressful, but once they get it, ironically, they are more able to move on.

During the actual divorce, most teenagers are overwhelmed and confused by the combination of divorce and adolescence. How they handle this varies, but their behavior changes are often an extension and escalation of their past behaviors. Some get lost in confusion and act without thinking. Here, one sees an increase in self-destructive and depressive behaviors: appetite changes, partying, sleep problems, and a general lack of motivation.

> When my parents were getting divorced, it was pretty crazy around
> my house. They were arguing so much with each other that they kind
> of forgot about me. You know, nobody checked on my curfew, and they
> pretty much let me do whatever I pleased. It wasn't that they trusted me
> any more than before; I just think they didn't have the energy. Anyway,
> I spent most of that year partying and just hanging out. I did awful in
> school and in sports too. It was a real drag. Actually, I was pretty crazy
> then in some of the things I got into.

Other teenagers make their worlds more manageable by making them smaller (see chapter 18). Here one sees the adolescent get very focused on one area of life: sports, academics, a relationship, a theatrical production at school.

> When my parents split up, I was a junior in high school. Up until that
> point, I had been just a fair guitar player. Well, during the divorce,
> I picked up the guitar again and got into it like I never had before. I

probably spent three to four hours every weeknight, and more on weekends, playing guitar during my junior year. It was a real escape for me, a place where I didn't have to think about anything.

However it is manifested, most divorces, at least in the short run, undo the home foundation that is so necessary for teenagers to cope with all the inevitable changes and decisions of adolescence. As one sophomore who was struggling with her personal identity told me in the midst of her parents' divorce: "How can I find myself when everything around me is going crazy?"

After the divorce, hopefully, things settle down, with both the parents and the teenager coming to conscious grips with the realities of their new worlds. But this doesn't happen overnight; it generally takes at least a year. The analogy I use with students is that the psychic and emotional injuries from the divorce are similar to seriously breaking a leg. If you break your leg badly, you can expect an operation and a short hospitalization. When you get back home, your movements are limited by a cast and crutches for three to six months. Then you can expect several more months of physical therapy. If everything goes exceedingly well, you could be back to normal in a year or so. But during that year of recovery, you would scale back your goals and expectations. You would drop certain activities. You would also expect a short-term drop in grades because of the hospitalization and the subsequent lack of durable concentration. You would be sleeping more—because of both the body's healing process and the extra effort required to get around with a cast and crutches. And you could expect lots of attention and sympathy from your peers and family, who would constantly inquire about your leg—after all, everybody knows how to support someone with a broken leg. There would be lots of "Get Well" cards, books, crossword puzzles, rented movies, and the like to keep your spirits up during your recovery.

When a family goes through a divorce, it is a similar sort of injury, except that the injury is psychic and emotional instead of physical. Further, people don't know about the injury (divorce) unless you tell them, which isn't easy for even the healthiest of teenagers. With the hyper-self-consciousness of adolescence, it is exceedingly difficult to make oneself voluntarily vulnerable to peers, which unfortunately is the only way to get the healing support of friends for the "divorce injury." Also, because of the relative invisibility of the divorce, others (teachers and coaches) may misinterpret behaviors: apathy, disrespect, carelessness, lack of motivation. One of the best things parents can do for their teenager during the divorce is to call the school and confidentially let a trusted teacher, coach, or adviser know enough of what is happening at home so they can make sense of any sudden behavioral shifts. You want someone at the school who can act as translator for some of your adolescent's behaviors.

> As dean of students, I find it helpful to hear from parents when their son or daughter is dealing with a traumatic event like an extended illness in the family, the death of a loved one, or divorce. I can then confidentially let the teachers in the school know that the student is going through a difficult time, without having to divulge any of the details. Unless teachers have a close relationship with the student, I ask them not to mention it until he or she brings it up. This way, teachers won't misinterpret a sudden change in the student's behavior.

So what is helpful in assisting a teenager through a divorce? Clearly, there is no ideal scenario, as divorce is the result of a failed ideal. You must simply do your best with what is at hand. For now, I'll focus on what I believe are some of the essentials.

While all adolescents are familiar with the concept of divorce (through friends and the media), don't overestimate their knowledge of what divorce actually means: the vocabulary, rights, choices, and responsibilities are often foreign to them.[2] It is, therefore, helpful to directly answer questions for your kids as well as to find out what they need to know: a time line for the divorce, details about living arrangements, school changes, financial changes, and the role of their input. Even though you may have this conversation with your adolescent, realize that she'll forget much of it, so expect to repeat it later on—she is on overload too. This information serves as a structure for her; it gives her an idea of how to make sense of what follows, as well as a sense of an official end to the divorce proceedings.

Since divorce is overwhelming for all concerned, it's sometimes wise to acquire a "divorce consultant" whom your teenager can call or see when he has questions. It can be a friend of the family familiar with divorce logistics, an attorney or mediator hired for a couple of hours, a therapist, or perhaps the counselor or health educator at school. Your teenager simply needs a place where he can get reliable information and support from a neutral source. He may or may not make use of it, but the important point is that someone is in place for him should he ever need it. Finally, having someone in place for your teenager gives you some peace of mind as well as the room to take better care of yourself and attend to the divorce in a more responsible manner, which ultimately is in everyone's best interest.

In any divorce, consistency is crucial but virtually impossible. The little things matter a great deal, such as who picks up your daughter after school, where and when you meet, and in which home she spends the night. Even though consistent information is tough to come by, because information is constantly changing, stay consistent in passing the updated information along.

While teenagers can't be protected from the divorce process (nor should they be), they shouldn't be required to play superior roles either. Most kids fear that they'll have to choose between Mom and Dad, a choice they could never live with within themselves. For them, it is a question of divided loyalty; internally they feel compelled to keep the loyalty split at roughly fifty-fifty. At some point, you'll probably encounter what I call the "defensive/empathetic response," which occurs after you have implicitly or explicitly disparaged the other parent:

MOTHER: Your father will pick you up after school today, so don't panic if he isn't waiting for you; you know how he's always late.

DAUGHTER: Mom! Dad is not always late. And when he is, which is less and less these days, he always has a good reason and says he's sorry.

MOTHER: No, he isn't getting better at being on time. I had to wait twenty minutes at the lawyer's for him the other day! He simply forgets.

DAUGHTER: He does not forget! Why don't you give him a break? He is real busy at work, what with everyone making all sorts of ridiculous demands on him. You could relax a little, you know.

MOTHER: I can't believe this. Are you the same girl who insisted that I pick you up after last week's dance because you didn't want to be embarrassed by having to stand on the corner to wait for your late father?

In this vignette, the daughter feels compelled to defend her father in his absence (just as she would feel compelled to defend her mother in her absence). What is unfortunate about this is that the daughter gets so busy defending and watching over the fifty-fifty split that she doesn't have time to discern her own feelings and opinions, which is what she most needs to do to move through and beyond the divorce. Your teenager must determine his own relationship with each parent, and you must let this happen.

Unduly trying to influence the relationship will only come back to haunt you. As your teenager gets older (regardless of when the divorce occurred), he will naturally have more questions about the divorce that need answering. As his thinking changes (see chapter 2), he needs to reconsider the divorce in light of his new cognitive abilities. As with any traumatic event involving family, you can expect these questions and general issues about the divorce to resurface during the holidays.

> Thanksgiving and Christmas really suck since my parents divorced [five years ago]. I know they [holidays] are supposed to be relaxing, fun, peaceful, and all that, but that just isn't the way it is. It all starts about a week before Thanksgiving, when my sister and I have to decide where we're going to spend Thanksgiving and Christmas. Each of our parents gets one day, which is better than a few years ago when we spent half a day at each house. A person can eat only so much turkey in one day! No matter what we decide, someone is upset. And then during dinner it is so phony. Everyone just tries so hard to be one happy family that we're all miserable. I can't wait until college, because there is no way I'm coming back for the holidays!

The structure of the final divorce agreement goes a long way toward establishing consistency. Your teenager, through the formal agreement with the courts and the less formal, logistical agreements between parents (with as much input as he can handle) knows now what to expect. This can be further reinforced with some of the logistical decisions. First, he should at least have his own space, even if it means rearranging the house each time he stays there. Second, while some packing and unpacking of things for visits to either parent is necessary, keep it to a minimum. As much as possible, make sure his room is complete. He shouldn't have to bring the alarm clock from apartment to apartment, or his entire wardrobe, or his piano. Ideally, he packs his favorite clothes, books, and music. It especially helps if you recognize the stress factor of having to pack up several times a week by purchasing him some luggage or overnight bags that he likes. Finally, it is a pain to have to pack up once or twice a week, so expect some ramifications in unpredictable manners from time to time.

> My husband and I divorced when Jackson was seven. For the most part, it was an amicable divorce, with the two of us remaining friendly and supportive of one another. We've had joint custody of Jackson the entire time. In fact, we hadn't discussed the divorce in years until one

day it came out of the blue, staring me right in the face. I was down-
stairs preparing to go to work when I heard this loud thud from my
son's room. I ran upstairs and saw him sitting despondently on his
bed. He looked at me and said through held-back tears, "Sorry, I threw
my shoe at the door." I asked, "Why?" To which he replied, "Because
the other shoe is at Dad's."

Also expect some settling-in and settling-out time on either end of stays
in your home. These transitions are tough on teenagers. While you await your
daughter's arrival and set an extra plate for her, she packs, says good-bye,
checks her bags, and reminds friends to call her at the other house. You both
prepare to make adjustments to different routines, so simple greeting and
good-bye rituals go a long way.

Every time I go to my mom's, the first thing we do is sit down in the
kitchen and have a cup of tea. We each have our regular cups. We catch
each other up on our weeks and check in on any plans during the next
few days. Sometimes it lasts ten minutes, and other times an hour or so.
It's a nice way to get started with each other.

You may as well consciously create these rituals; otherwise, they'll simply
develop on their own and won't be nearly as enjoyable.

Most of the time, on the rides back and forth between Mom's house and
Dad's house, I have a big fight with whoever is driving me. Then I go
into the other's house and can't talk to them for a while because I'm too
upset at the other one, which, of course, gets them upset at the other
one and leaves me having to defend them even though I'm also upset
with them . . . kind of confusing, huh?

One family I knew handled all these logistics in a novel way. When the
parents divorced, they kept the house and the kids stayed in the house. Mom
and Dad each got their own one bedroom apartment and they shuttled back
and forth each week as part of their joint custody arrangement. What is great
about this is that they did their best to create stability for their kids, and they
knew they could handle the back and forth logistics better than the kids.

Leave room for negotiation, especially from the adolescent perspective,
in the divorce settlement. Let your teenager influence the logistics when what

she suggests makes common sense. If she has to take the SATs on Saturday at school and your ex lives next to the school and you live ten miles away, let her negotiate where she stays on Friday night. The same for vacations and other trips. You want the spirit of the agreement to be met, which at times will differ from the letter. Also, as she gets older, she should have more influence over these decisions. And don't use guilt against her when she finally decides to skip a vacation or holiday with you. Support her and her growing decision-making abilities.

> It was so difficult during Karen's junior year when she said she wanted to live with her father during her senior year. [He lives in the next state and she spends summers with him.] Obviously, I was very upset. I felt like somehow he had beaten me. I talked to lots of divorced friends about this. They finally convinced me. So when Karen brought it up to me again, I said I would do whatever she wanted. I said I thought it was a good idea for her to get to know her father better, and, besides, it would give us some practice for college. I just insisted that she spend the summer before college with me. I also told her that I would really miss her. That was four years ago. From this perspective, it's clear that I made the right decision. She and I are very close now, and I can see that, if I had fought her on the idea of living with her father, we would have had a bloody war that would have taken years to recover from.

Finally, for some parents going through the throes of divorce, it is a near-irresistible temptation to use your adolescent as a support and a confidante, at times verging on your personal therapist. Don't! This is unfair to both of you. Keep her apprised of what she needs to know, but there is no reason to air dirty laundry. Know the difference. This only puts her in the middle and forces her into a defensive position, a lose-lose situation. She is grown-up enough to observe and make decisions on her own, but not so grown-up that she can serve as your main support system, especially when it is as a support against her other parent. As much as possible, allow your kid to be a kid. The very nature of divorce forces her to grow up faster than her peers; don't accelerate this process by expecting her to be anything more than a teenager.

> The other day I was at a friend's and his mom reminded him that it was his father's birthday the next day. Of course, he had forgotten. But her reminder saved his butt so he could get his dad a present in time and

not have to feel like a jerk the next day. Neither my mom or dad would ever do this for me. In fact, I think they hope that I forget the other's birthday. It's sad. It's also kind of unfair that I have to be so responsible all on my own.

As the divorce forces kids to grow up faster, it also gives them more things to think and worry about. Often, these worries affect their sleep patterns; this disruption is the last thing they need. In this regard, I often offer the "Putting Your Worries to Bed" technique for teenagers who for one reason or another are unable to fall asleep.

1. Comfortably lie on your back in bed and imagine a small room that contains a large cabinet with lots of small drawers.
2. In your mind's eye, take all your worries and enter the room.
3. Now take your worries, and, one at a time, place each in a drawer and close the drawer.
4. Label the outside of the drawer with a word or phrase that captures the essence of that worry.
5. When all the worries are safely tucked away in their drawers, say "good night," turn the light off, and quietly close the door.
6. Now, back in your bed, get in your favorite sleeping position and fall asleep with the knowledge that your worries are resting safely and securely where they belong for the night.
7. If, for some reason, one of the worries gets out of its drawer and wakes you, be sympathetic yet firm in insisting that it climb back into its drawer for the evening. It can wait until morning, after you've had a restful night's sleep.

In any divorce, there is an overriding sense of family sadness. But staying conscious of this sadness makes it possible to relieve it. Without consciousness, this sadness is transformed into guilt. Or as one student said about her experience of growing up in a painfully and unconsciously divorced family, "One day I'm going to write a book about the experience, the title of which will be *Guilt*."

Remarriage and Blended Families

Parents can actually do quite a bit to ease the creation of a new family, but you should not gauge the success of the blended family by its immediate results. These transitions are usually somewhat awkward, reserved, tense, and messy, no matter how much you intend otherwise. The results of a successful blended family are, however, evident down the road. Time and thought invested on the front end of this transition are well rewarded over the life of the new family.

Remarriage is a confusing concept for adolescents, as it is fraught with built-in conflicts and joys. Let's look at the "simplest" remarriage as an example: a teenage boy's mother marries a man who does not have children. On the one hand, the son is pleased that his mother has found someone who makes her happy. Yet because it also impacts him as a member of this new family, he must thoroughly address his feelings for this new man, which does not occur in a conscious and systematic manner: "Is this someone I could grow to like? Will he try to take over the role of my father? Will he try to push me out of my mother's life? Does he like me? Can I avoid him for the next three years? Do I respect him?" Further, these questions are not asked or answered in a vacuum. The duration of the relationship, the kinds of time the new spouse and teenager have spent together, preceding relationships, and the environment in which the first marriage ended (death, drawn-out illness, amicable divorce, hostile divorce, affair, and so on) all play vital roles in determining how your teenager responds to the new spouse. Also, your teenager's intellectual abilities can easily mislead you: judge his state of acceptance and readiness more by what he does than by what he says.

In a blended family, the location of the other biological parent and the adolescent's relationship to that parent are crucial factors.

> My mom died when I was in fifth grade, which was pretty awful. My dad met Valerie when I was in eighth grade, and they got married last year [tenth grade]. I knew her for a few years before she moved in with us. I was really looking forward to them getting married, so I was a little surprised at how awkward it was at first. I hadn't realized how my dad and I had developed so many routines to keep the house going. Now, all of a sudden, Valerie was living there too, and of course things were bound to change. At first, it was little things, like rearranging the

furniture and buying new dishes, which was fine. But when she tore up Mom's garden to redesign the backyard, I went ballistic! I know it was unfair of me to react that way, but it was just too much for me to handle. Obviously, we all got through it, I think in part because I knew Valerie so well beforehand and I wasn't afraid to tell her what I thought. Still, I would recommend other families to start your new family in a different house or apartment; that way everyone begins on more or less even ground with each other.

Living space (with either the addition of the new person into the current space or a move to another space, possibly even to a new school district), living patterns, and family economics all contribute to make remarriage a complex negotiation with many pushes and pulls on both teenagers and adults. Remember, it isn't the adolescent who is initiating the new family. Adolescents must react (see especially chapters 2 and 3), so it is best to find ways for them to stay as active as possible in the development of new family norms and logistics. They don't want or need to be a full partner in this, as their lives are busy already, but they do need to be consulted regularly for input.

When my mom married Jack, she really wanted me to feel included. In fact, she dragged me to every open house in the area before I finally had to call a stop to it. I mean who has the time or energy to spend every Sunday going in and out of other people's houses? So I just told her what I wanted: to stay in the same school district, to have my own room, and to have a chance to see the place before they bought it. From then on, everything was fine.

From the teenager's perspective, remarriage often implies "taking the place of" and "forgetting," which causes anger. If not consciously discussed, these thoughts fuel all the negatives of remarriage. In divorced families, this happens when the new spouse tries to be or is perceived as trying to be a parent, and in widowed families when the deceased spouse is not discussed from time to time within the new family. When either of these happens, the teenager is in the unenviable position of having to loyally hold on to the family history. To "forget" or "replace" a parent is a frightening proposition to teenagers, or anyone for that matter. It is best if he is encouraged to remember the other parent. Otherwise, a part of him is lost, as well as fueling the often but not always unconscious fear that he too can be "forgotten" or "replaced." In the following story, the son's parents had divorced five years earlier and the father had moved out of the area, only seeing his son during the summer.

> I couldn't believe what happened when my mom got remarried. Bill had been okay until then. But all of a sudden he was trying to be my father: telling me what to do, when to study, when to go to bed, and even coming to my games and cheering me on like I was his son! When we moved into his house, he insisted that I leave my old furniture behind because he had already picked out new stuff for me, stuff that went with the house. Hell, I liked my old bed just fine! Also, before getting married, he used to ask me about my father and the kinds of things we did when I was a kid and over the summer. But afterward he didn't want to hear about it. In fact, when my mom and I would mention something from the past, he would act like a hurt puppy, usually just walking away. Of course, my mom would hurry after him to make everything okay. He even tried to get me to skip a summer with my dad so we could all go away together!

In the above story, the new spouse is clearly both too eager and too sensitive. New spouses need patience and thick skins. A relationship with a teenager takes time to develop. Let things happen as naturally as possible. Also, as difficult as it is, let and even invite teenagers to talk about their childhood and the parent who is not there. This kind of talk isn't a slander against you; rather, it is how adolescents integrate their histories with the present. Let them gracefully hold on to their histories.[3]

Now, rather than going through all the possible permutations of newly formed families, let's look at a few issues that are constants: siblings, parental roles, and living space.

Biological siblings are a natural source of support and constancy for one another in any change to the family structure. In various custody arrangements, it is usually in everyone's best interest to keep the kids together in their movements between households. Especially in cases of joint custody, kids with siblings have a stronger sense of stability and support. In cases where two parents with kids get together and make a new family, there are a host of complications to consider. The parents may be in love, but the kids are not. They will need time to develop their own relationships with one another, and it won't happen overnight. While you hope for deep friendships between them, it is an unrealistic expectation. Perhaps respectful tolerance is all one can honestly hope for. Let it happen naturally; if you push your expectations, you will probably get the opposite of what you want. The kids must have their say in this.

When a new family is formed through remarriage, the spouses must be clear on their parental roles with the kids. With teenagers, it is best if the biological parent assumes most of the direct parenting responsibilities, especially in the areas of structure and the enforcement of natural consequences. It is unfair to expect a new spouse to play that role; it hardly ever works and it creates undue and inevitable resentment.

> When Cherie and my dad got married, I think she was pretty confused about how to treat me. It was especially odd because, when my parents were still married, it was my mom who did most of the discipline and stuff like that. I think my dad must have subconsciously expected Cherie to do the same. But after one or two attempts at that, she and I both knew that it would never work, so she backed off. Then, for a while it was like nobody was watching me, and I went a bit overboard. It was hard for a while, but it got better when my father finally began acting like my father. Now I'm a freshman in college and Cherie and I are pretty good friends. I like talking to her when I call home, and sometimes I even prefer talking to her!

The nonbiological parent has a tough line to walk, and it's different with each child, depending on personality, age, and temperament. What works with a seven-year-old probably won't be effective with a seventeen-year-old. In many respects, the nonbiological parent is like an aunt or uncle to the adolescent. But no matter what, it is essential that they form their own relationship based on their personalities. Don't rest on the assumption that a working relationship will happen. What is most important is that the teenager and new spouse come to genuinely respect one another, and this is something that is earned over time. Also, if the new spouse is not interested in forming a relationship with the adolescent, it is unfair to go ahead; try waiting on the marriage until the adolescent is out of the house. A lack of interest is perceived by teenagers as overwhelming rejection.

My mom's husband seems like a nice guy, but we don't have any sort of relationship. If we're all together and my mom walks out of the room, we have nothing to say to each other and he usually picks up a book or turns on the TV. I'm not sure why; I guess he just doesn't like me. I've tried to get to know him. I've asked about work, about his family, and even about sports, but I never get more than a one-sentence response, like I'm bothering him or something. I can't wait to get out of this house.

All in all, it takes a few years for a blended family to solidify; it doesn't happen overnight, which is why it is important not to evaluate the new family too soon. After the first few blowups or shouting matches, it is easy to doubt the potential for long-term success, but this is premature. Often, the most difficult and the most important consideration in the creation of a new family is your expectations. You must be realistic. If you cling to an idealized fantasy of how the new family should be, it will be a miserable experience for everyone involved. Always remain willing to reevaluate your expectations.

Adolescence is a turbulent time in and of itself, so when the structure changes significantly, the turbulence increases—but so does the need for consistency. The only means for the adolescent to gain security about all this is to frequently test the limits, especially in the first couple of years. As always, be persistently patient and have faith.

Notes

1. For an in depth description of this process I recommend a novel by Roddy Doyle, *Paddy Clarke Ha Ha Ha*.

2. A San Francisco nonprofit organization, Kid's Turn, does an excellent job in educating families on the divorce process and how to deal with the associated emotions. Kids cope much better with divorce when they understand its terminology and landscape. For more information, visit their website: www.kidsturn.org.

3. A wonderful website and a book address the topic of blended families, or "bonus" families when it really works out: www.bonusfamilies.com and *Ex-Etiquette for Parents: Good Behavior After a Divorce or Separation* by Jann Blackstone-Ford and Sharyl Jupe.

20

Single Parenting

What are the unique difficulties in single parenting, and what is the best way to deal with them?

Single parenting is not tremendously different from parenting with a spouse—just exponentially more difficult and complex! First, single parents are continually "on" with their teenager. They can never simply turn to their partner, have them instantly understand, and retire to the bedroom for some rest and solitude while the crisis is addressed.

> Even though my husband passed away seven years ago, I still catch myself thinking "Go ask your father" when John interrupts me with an urgent request or question. It is such a pain to stop what I'm doing in order to give John my full attention, but whenever I give him less than full attention, I pay for it in the long run. For instance, a couple of weeks ago he came into the study on a Thursday night while I was working. He wanted to know if it was okay to go out to a party with Josh on Friday night and stay out an hour past curfew. He needed to know right then because Josh was waiting on the phone. By his voice, I could tell that there was something else hidden in the question, but I brushed it aside and let it pass, returning to my work after quickly giving my permission. Well, it was the next night when my inattentive attitude came back to haunt me. John "forgot" to tell me that Josh was driving (on his four-day-old license!), and that the party was in the next town! Of course, all this came to my attention twenty minutes before he was getting picked up. Needless to say, we had a very messy

scene, and when it was over I vowed (for about the hundredth time), to pay 100 percent attention to John's requests and hidden agendas, and most of all, to trust that parental voice in me that smells a rat.

Along with the pressure of always being "on," the single parent is also without the benefit of reflective conversation. Even after a couple has blown it in some way with their teenager, they still have the option to huddle with one another to learn from their mistakes, plan for the future, rethink strategies and approaches, and above all, support one another. Single parents do not have this shared, reflective experience. They have the solitude of their own thoughts, which as we have seen elsewhere, tend to focus on mistakes. Without this reflective dialogue, they have less of a chance of breaking out of or creatively understanding the cycle they're in with their kids. Finding other single parents to spend time with and to talk about various parent-adolescent concerns is immensely helpful, in fact essential. But often, you must actively invite others into these conversations.

Sarah's father left when she was in the first grade; since then it has been just her and me. Grammar school and middle school were fairly smooth, though the second half of eighth grade was tough. At one of her soccer games early in the fall, I introduced myself to a few of the other kids' moms and dads. It turned out that two of them were also single parents. Later that fall, as Sarah seemed to be changing faster than I could keep track of, I invited those two parents over for dinner. After some initial awkwardness, we started to talk fairly honestly about our relations with our kids. In a weird way, it was refreshing to hear that they were encountering many of the same difficulties that I was. It was also useful to hear how they understood and addressed the various problems. By the evening's end, I felt like my "bag of tricks" had been replenished. It was a great night! We all felt more hopeful and optimistic about our kids and ourselves. Since then, we've met for dinner every few months. It's strange; none of us are friends outside of these dinners, yet I count them as very important people in my life.

As a single parent, you may have plenty of friends and an active social life, yet at the same time spend little time with anyone who understands and appreciates the toll that single parenting takes on you. If you don't have access to other single parents for one reason or another, think seriously about seeing a local psychologist or family therapist for periodic consultations about parenting. Granted, this is a different arrangement and purpose than in most therapeutic relationships, but nonetheless one that many professionals are comfortable with—just be clear about what you want up front.

Obviously, single parenting requires a major sacrifice of personal time. From a simple logistics perspective, you do the job of two people by yourself. With time, you can teach your teenager to assume more and more responsibility, but no matter how good she is, the ultimate authority and responsibility always rest with you. With this increased responsibility comes a subtle trap: you invest too much of your personal esteem and identity into your adolescent's life. She becomes an extension of you, which, over the long run, leaves you uncomfortably vulnerable to her performance (in academics, sports, social life, drama, dance, the arts). Over time, this is a particularly seductive trap, because initially (prior to and during the initial stages of adolescence), it is so successful and rewarding. You sacrifice personal time for your daughter. She is openly grateful. You miss out on personal opportunities because you are a good parent. She openly flourishes as she grows with your added attention. You want more and more for her, mostly for her overall well-being and in part as a means to justify your sacrifices. She works hard, because she wants the same things for herself that you want for her. The two of you are following essentially the same blueprint. Her successes motivate you to sacrifice more; you begin to take and enjoy her successes personally. She continues to work hard, wanting to make you proud. Then she hits adolescence. You continue to bask in her various successes, but you also begin to take her inevitable "failures" personally. And worst of all, she is no longer open to your input. In fact, she is quite confused. You respond by directing her more precisely—you attempt to do a "better job." She resists. You insist. She rebels. You yell. And it all escalates quite quickly—in fact, more quickly and powerfully each time.

This is not a healthy pattern for either the adult or the teenager. (Single parents should read the next chapter carefully, as it applies doubly to them, and is the best antidote to this pattern.) Finally, as if all the preceding isn't enough, you're faced with increased economic pressure that not only affects your relationship with your adolescent, but also affects how you evaluate yourself as a parent.

> The worst is right before I go to sleep after we've had an argument. Not
> only do I play the fight over in my head about a hundred times—usually
> focusing on his faults in the first fifty versions and mine in the second

fifty—but then I move beyond the fight to include most of my other inadequacies as a parent. In that script, finances are a biggie! Somehow I feel like money should be a secure given. I mean, my parents couldn't have worried this much about paying bills, financing college, fixing the plumbing, and attempting to have a credible career, could they? Anyway, I do a real number on myself in this area. It basically comes down to this: if we have any economic crisis, I feel like a failure as a person and as an adult—I know, not too logical, but nonetheless . . .

From teenagers' perspective, having only one active parent means a 50 percent loss of parental diversity in their life, and the effects of this loss are far-reaching. Without another parent, it is easier for adolescents to get locked into one role with their remaining parent.

One of us always seems to be in Charissa's good graces while the other is the bad guy, though over time it seems to balance out. If one of us has been the bad guy for a long time, we make sure to switch roles. If my wife has been the bad guy, we'll make sure that I do the "reminding" about chores and the denying of extended curfew, while my wife gives her movie money and compliments her on her piano playing. This way she always feels safe with one of us should she need to confide in us.

Without two parents, the adolescent also loses the modeling of how two adults who love one another successfully fight: how they can disagree, argue, yell, and finally reach a successful resolution. Nor do teenagers experience how they can influence one parent about their perspective and see the other parent acquiesce in trust to the other parent and adolescent. Leaps of parental faith are more common with two parents than with one. Finally, with one parent, there is obviously only one gender present for the teenager to observe.

The solution to this is straightforward, though not simple: Get more adults involved in your adolescent's life. Teachers and coaches can play a vital role. Encourage your son to get close to a teacher, or encourage a coach to take a more active role in your daughter's life (see chapter 13). Look into summer experiences that place your son in proximity to caring adults: camps, youth programs, church organizations. The difficult part of this is to not get jealous when the strategy begins to work.

At first, it was great when William got close to Phil [the camp director at the local YMCA] when he worked as a counselor at the day camp. But after a while, I got tired of hearing "Phil" stories. Then I even began to get jealous. This guy was telling William the same things I had been telling him for fifteen years, yet this guy was a demigod and I was plain old mom! Ah well, such is parenthood.

In any single-parent family, the teenager inevitably assumes more responsibility than she would otherwise. This is not necessarily good or bad, but it does happen. (See chapter 19 for more on adolescents' increased responsibilities.) While most teenagers cannot acknowledge it during their adolescence, they are aware of all that you do for them (and do not do for yourself). It just takes time for that feedback to come around.

Dad
It's the man with the whistle
who made us spaghetti,
covered with hot dog bits.
He taught us life and basketball,
play for the team, box out,
but no foul outs. Bought us bikes,
mini-bikes, and snowmobiles to crash.
For years I've been witness to the chameleon golf swing,
back and forth across the grass
never reaching the green.
He drove me to St. Louis.
All of us went to the Arch
and stayed far from the airport.
He has given me material
which he impressed as trivial,
none have lasted like the lessons
he has taught us: compassion,
simple fun and a Family
grown from his saintly heart.
Somebody should call Hallmark
and create a new card day
for fathers who are moms.
Tim Riera

21

Parent
Mental Health

With all that is happening with our kids, what can we do to take care of ourselves during these years?

Taking care of your mental health is one of the best examples you can set for your teenagers. As noted earlier, by adolescence your kids are learning more by what you do than by what you say, as hard as that is to take. Without conscious attention, your spousal relationship, your continued intellectual and emotional growth, and your personal pursuits will all take resentful backseats to the trauma of adolescence. It is important to make and take time for these aspects of your life without abandoning your teenager. These aspects must be built into the fabric of your life. It's like saving money. You know the story: Unsuccessful savers typically pay their bills, spend the grocery money, allocate a certain amount of spending money, set aside some for unexpected expenses, and deposit the remaining two dollars in their savings account. Successful savers follow a completely different recipe. They pick an amount they are going to save every month and pay their savings account first. Then they deal with the rest. The same is true with your mental health: pay yourself first.

Ideally, you do something to feed your mental health on a daily basis, no matter for how short a time. My tai chi instructor, Lenzie Williams, calls this minimum and maximum practice routines. In studying tai chi, an ideal goal might be one hour of practice a day, which is ambitious. Typically, one would do quite well with this goal for, say, about five days—at which point you would miss a day, then practice well a couple more days before missing another day. Needless to say, after a few weeks you would miss more days than you practice. And after a few more weeks, you would probably give up on tai chi and move on to something else entirely—your guilt hangover due to missing multiple days has gotten the better of you. However, with minimum and maximum practice routines you can have the goal of ten minutes a day as a minimum practice and, say, one hour a day as a maximum practice, with anything in between ten minutes and one hour satisfactory (or at least guilt-free). Chances are that if you practiced in this way for the same four weeks you would have practiced more overall and, most important, still be interested in the activity. And, of course, you would have no guilt hangover. In fact, you would feel good about yourself. The same is true with your mental health and parenting. Do at least a minimal amount of whatever nurtures your mental health on a daily basis.

> I love to read. So every day I make sure I read at least a couple of pages of whatever novel I'm into at the time. Sometimes I get my pages in on the bus or at the Laundromat, but no matter what, I always get a few in every day. And it really makes a difference. When I have a stretch of an hour or so, I can really get lost in whatever I'm reading. Maybe it's an escape, but I prefer to see it as time purely for me, which, given everything else I do, seems more than fair.

And, even for people who don't have one special practice, this habit is healthy.

> There's actually no one thing I do daily, but every day I consciously do something for myself, no matter how small. For instance, when I have the time I work in the garden, or go for a jog, or go out for coffee with a friend, or smoke a cigar on the back porch. And when I'm short for time, I still manage something—maybe a walk down the street, or two minutes of listening to a favorite song, or maybe I'll just massage my feet for a couple of minutes before going to sleep.

For parental mental health, the mantra is "Don't take it personally." Remember, your teenager is in a phase different from all previous stages of development. Prior to this stage, most parents are quite willing, and even eager, to take their child's behavior personally. They bask in the joy and accomplishments of their kids through childhood, so the "don't take it personally" stance of adolescence is perplexing.

> I remember watching a close friend's five-year-old daughter crawl onto his lap, wrap her arms around him, take a deep sigh, and say, "Daddy, I love you. You're the smartest and nicest daddy in the world!" His heart practically came out of his chest. And I heard a little voice in the back of my head say, "Enjoy it now, but don't hold it against her when she is sixteen and doesn't think nearly so highly of you."

Most teenagers are critical of their parents—sometimes justifiably, but often not. With all that is going on with them (see chapter 2), they are usually just venting their frustration in a place they feel is safe. Very few teenagers, after an evening of arguing with their parents, come home to find the locks changed and a sign hanging on the door: "We're tired of your constant arguing. Go away and come back when you've grown up. Love, Mom and Dad." So in a twisted sort of way, their venting on you is a compliment. While teenagers aren't pleased with the arguing, it is the only "safe place" for them to sort through and make sense of their changing lives. It is also why clear structures and limits are crucial.

For your ongoing mental health as a parent, it is important to break down the isolation of adolescent parenting by making friends with the parents of other teenagers. Talk with other parents about what is really happening in your home, both the good and the bad. If you just focus on the good (and keep the negative silently to yourself), you'll walk away worse than ever, convinced that you really are an atrocious parent. If you only talk about the bad, you'll walk away depressed and hopeless, which isn't much better. By discussing the good and the bad, you will realize that what happens in your home isn't all that different than what happens in other adolescent homes. This in itself makes it easier to not take things so personally.

Finally, remember that a large part of your role as parent is to nurture your teenager's hope. At the same time, remember to take care of your own hope too. It is what will keep you going, even on the toughest of days.

22

Professional Help

What are the signs that professional help is needed for my teenager, and how do I go about getting it?

How to decide when help is appropriate is often a more difficult matter than actually getting the assistance. Of course, this task is obvious if your teenager approaches you with a request for help (and sometimes it happens that way), but more often than not, you decide that they (or both of you) need some assistance, with them initially resisting the idea.

> Whenever I mention the idea of seeing a therapist about the divorce, Thomas [adolescent son] just glares at me and walks away. Therapy has been essential for me, so I want him to get the same kind of benefit, but he absolutely refuses.

Professional help is indicated whenever you feel that health and safety are in jeopardy and you feel powerless to positively affect the situation. It is one thing for your teenager to get poor grades, but an entirely different matter to repeatedly come home drunk. The difficulty here is in allowing yourself to accurately assess the severity of the situation; once an honest assessment is made, the question of professional help is the next step.

> In retrospect, I can see that Shelly was in trouble for quite a while; it was just that we refused to recognize or believe it. She had lost a great deal of weight, wasn't going out with friends anymore, never ate in

front of us, and exercised obsessively. But it didn't all click until one of
her teachers called us, deeply concerned about her health. I can't believe
we didn't see it ourselves, but obviously we didn't.

I've noticed strange cuts on my daughter's arms, and I'm worried that she might be physically hurting herself. Am I crazy?

A strange first cousin to an eating disorder, only in an escalated version, is the
self-cutting that some teenagers start during adolescence. Typically, a teenager who cuts herself will do so on her forearms or thighs, and do her best to
keep them covered and keep the secret to herself. Most cutters are female.
Also, as with eating disorders, most of these teenagers are of above average
intelligence. Self-cutters feel relief when they hurt themselves, almost as
if the emotional pain becomes physical once they cut themselves and gives
them some sort of relief.

> It sounds strange, I know. But when I cut myself I feel at peace. Time
> stops and I relax. Sure it hurts, but it also feels good in a strange way.
> It's an escape.

Research on the prevalence of self-cutting varies widely, but generally
suggests that approximately 20 percent of adolescents have experimented
with some sort of self-injurious behavior and between 0.5 percent and 1 percent of teenagers self-cut on a regular basis. The majority of these self-cutters
are girls.

Self-cutters use this behavior as a coping mechanism. When they are in
some sort of anxious state or stuck emotionally, the cutting provides an out-
let. It is also a way to make pain physical instead of emotional—and therefore
much more concrete in their eyes. Others who have suffered abuse may cut
themselves to wake up to feeling again. Most of the teenagers who experiment
with this behavior only do it once or twice.

> My friend cuts herself all the time and it grosses me out, so one day I
> decided to try it myself. It was awful! And it hurt. I even shouted aloud
> when I made the cut, and it was tiny.

But, sadly, with others it can easily become an addiction.

> I remember the first time I cut myself. I was playing with a razor blade
> and gently ran it over my forearm, barely grazing the surface. Then I did
> it again, with more pressure. Then again and again. Before I realized it
> I had cut myself and was bleeding, but the pain was different than what
> I expected. It felt kind of good. I know, that's strange, but that's how it
> still feels today. Somehow it's real and it takes my mind off whatever
> is bothering me, which is why it is so addictive to me—cutting doesn't
> solve my problems, it just postpones them.

The existence of cutting or other self-injurious behavior is typically a sign
of deeper underlying problems, which is why, if you discover this behavior in
your teenager, you need to get her to a physician or psychiatrist/psychologist
right away. Stopping the cutting is much more than simple willpower or a res-
olute decision after the fact.

In any situation that may require professional intervention, accurate
assessment of the situation is the most difficult part. Parents, because they
want to believe the best about their kids, are in a difficult position to fully recognize what is going on. Because of this, other parents can be a great resource.
Also, feel free to call teachers and coaches just to check on how your teenager
is doing. (Don't ask them directly about the problem, since few are in the position to answer directly and with accuracy. Also, asking this undermines adolescents and the world they are developing away from home.) Serious problems
seldom limit themselves to one aspect of a person's life, so if something is
going on that requires outside attention, it'll usually show up in one of these
conversations.

> We were concerned about Byron's late-night activities, as we had found
> beer caps in the car on several occasions. Of course, he told us they were
> isolated incidents, and we were more than willing to believe him. We
> wanted to believe him, because to think otherwise was too overwhelm-
> ing. But after the third incident, I decided to call a few of his teachers,
> along with his baseball coach, just to get a general impression of how
> he was doing in their eyes. It turned out that of the four adults I called,
> two were very worried about him and another expressed concern. We
> clearly had to look at the situation much more closely, this time without
> our parent blinders on.

At bottom, there are three entrance points into assessing a problem area. The first focuses on education and discussion before a problem arises. This typically occurs at home and school. For example, a speaker comes into a health class to talk about alcohol and drug abuse. The students receive lots of information about the topic, hear a personal account, and have an opportunity for questions, discussion, and reflection.

The second entrance point occurs after a problem has been recognized but is still not debilitating to the person. Again, this happens at home and school, but is often augmented with professional assistance. An example is the mother who catches her teenager drinking or under the influence of marijuana. Something is definitely amiss, but it still might not be disabling. This situation requires honest discussion, a reexamination of family guidelines and agreements, information on drugs and alcohol (for both parents and adolescent), and possibly the services of a counselor.

The final point occurs after the problem has been established and has turned into a disability. This requires professional assistance and may, in extreme instances, include some sort of residential treatment. An example is the teenager who is so depressed that he doesn't have the energy to get out of bed for weeks at a time. At the minimum, this requires direct and ongoing professional intervention.

Once you make the decision that professional help is in order, be firm and insistent. Give your adolescent a choice in choosing who to see and under what circumstances, but not a choice as to whether you seek assistance. If he obstinately refuses to see a professional of your choice, the professionals usually have a variety of means of getting your teenager to come in or of working indirectly through you. I know of a counselor who met with an entire family minus the adolescent and simply sent him a summary letter of every meeting. Eventually, the boy insisted upon coming in, since the letters reflected a great deal of inaccuracies around his behavior, at least in his mind. Also, there are times when you might seek a professional consultation for yourself about parenting issues.

When you have determined that your teenager and you need professional assistance, keep several points in mind. First and foremost, remember that you have a great deal of choice. When you meet with professionals (whether they are psychologists, psychiatrists, family therapists, nutritionists, tutors, or gynecologists), remember that you are the consumer. Treat first meetings as part of the shopping-around phase. Beyond the education and skills of this person, you are looking for someone you can trust and respect. Give your teenager the same freedom.

Second, in your shopping-around period, ask the professionals any and all questions you have—don't worry about being rude. How much do they charge? Who do they meet with—the teenager alone, parents alone, everyone together? How confidential is what you say? What your adolescent says?

Third, the best sources for the names of helpful professionals are your friends, specifically the friends who also are parents of teenagers. Most parents of adolescents have either made use of or know of somebody who has gotten professional help. Don't be shy about asking; it doesn't mean you're a failure as a parent. Also, make use of the personnel at your school; deans, vice principals, and counselors all have referrals. In these cases, after securing their confidentiality, make sure to give them enough information so they can help, especially in determining the type of professional assistance you require.

> When I realized what was happening with Celia, I didn't know where to turn. For lack of a better starting point, I called her guidance counselor, who directed me to the school counselor. She was very helpful in describing the various types of professional help available and suitable for what was happening with Celia. On top of that, she gave me several names to call and the titles of a couple of books to read. She was very helpful.

Never forget that as a parent you know your child best. This means that when your intuition tells you that something is amiss, you need to pay attention. In my experience, a parent's intuition is the best indicator that something is amiss, and from there the challenge is assessing what is going on beneath the surface.

> I know that teenagers are moody, sulky, and defensive by nature. But with Natalie, it seemed like all that, only more extreme. I couldn't put my finger on it, but there seemed to be a sadness that permeated everything else. All her teachers said she was fine, but none of it sat well with me. Finally, I mentioned something to her pediatrician prior to her annual physical. Well, it turned out she was suffering from depression. And now, ten months later, she is back to herself, and we all see the difference.

I cannot say enough about trusting your intuition, not as a final diagnosis but as an indicator to get other opinions, and especially in the case of depression, the input of a counselor or physician.

23

Back to the Relationship

Given how important friends are to teenagers, how do we make sure they know and are in accord with our family values?

The bad news first. As your kids move into and through adolescence, their peers influence their daily behavior more than you do. Whether it's the clothes they wear, the music they listen to, or the parties they choose to attend or not attend, peers matter most when it comes to behavior.

> It's strange, but now that I'm a junior I feel like my friends are raising me more than my parents. It's weird. I still love my parents, but when I think about doing something or not doing something, the first thing I think about is what my friends will think and say.

There is, however, good news that is vital to hold onto. When it comes to *attitudes*, parents have much more influence over their children than peers. This is great news. Parents would do well to never lose sight of this reality. That is, over the long run behaviors come and go, but attitudes are lasting and over time carve the path of one's life. For proof of this, think back to your own adolescence. During that time your values and behaviors were probably farther from your parents than at any other time during your life. But now, as an adult, I would wager that your values, even if they are still different from your parents', are much closer than they were when you were a tenth grader. The same is true for your kids. In the long run, your attitudes will prevail over the behaviors they are currently trying out.

This means that the most important tool you have during and after adolescence is your relationship with your sons and daughters, so you need to stay vigilant on what you cultivate in this relationship. Try this:

- Take a moment to consider three aspects of one of your children that, if you had Harry Potter's magic wand, you would change in an instant: three things that drive you crazy that you would want to improve. Just three!
- Now take another moment to consider three aspects of that same child that you cherish: behaviors that stop you in your tracks and fill you with joy and pride.
- Reflect on a typical week in your home—what do you communicate most often—what you want to change or what you cherish?

While this is not meant as an exercise in guilt, it does have that effect on most of us. As products of our society, we are quite self-critical and other-critical, especially when it comes to our children.

If you asked your child to predict how you would answer the questions above, most will do well on the first question—what you would change about them. However, most would do poorly on the second question. Sadly, this means many have internalized their deficiencies but not their strengths. (And please understand that I am in no way advocating false praise.) The irony staring us in the face on this one is that, if our children already know what we would like to see them change about themselves, why on earth do we keep telling them, over and over again?

Actually, there is a more subtle and perhaps more profound way we influence our children that goes beyond our praise or our criticism: our expectations. In a famous study conducted by Robert Rosenthal, and discussed in length in his book, *Pygmalion in the Classroom*,[1] he showed the self-fulfilling prophecy effects of positive expectations on the part of a teacher toward his or her students. Known as the "Oak School Experiment" all students were given an IQ test and then 20 percent were randomly selected and put into the test group. Remember, this group was selected randomly, so there was no correlation between these students and high IQ scores. The teachers of these students were informed that they had "unusual potential for intellectual growth," and, furthermore, that the teachers should expect these students to "bloom" academically over the course of the year. At the end of the school year, all the students were again tested and indeed the 20 percent labeled with positive expectations performed and had improvements significantly better than the other 80 percent of students. Thus, the Pygmalion Effect: students who were expected to perform better lived up to those expectations.

While there is no magic wand in parenting children over the ages, the Pygmalion Effect is something to bear in mind. Especially as children get older, they are often simply looking to essentially borrow from us the confidence in them that they themselves lack.

In my years in schools, I have seen too many parents coast when it comes to the relationship they have with their teenagers. It is as if they think that, because they did a great job through the early years, their child can take it from here, or that because they are the parent and because they love their child, the relationship is automatically good. Wrong. The parent-child relationship is unique, wonderful, and full of love, but without conscious effort, it does not thrive. And be clear, I am not in any way advocating trying to be friends with our kids—as I've said in an earlier chapter, they will have plenty of friends throughout their lives but only two parents.

As parents, we need to keep in clear view both the development of our teenagers in terms of behaviors, habits, and attitudes and the well-being of our relationship with them—sometimes despite what is happening with their behavior.

> Sean [age 12] had been a model student up until seventh grade when his behavior began to shift for the worse: not turning in homework assignments, talking in class, teasing other kids. It was nothing over the top but a definite shift from the wonderful student he had been up until then. At first, we got all over him for these changes, and it made a difference—in the beginning. But over time our words, warnings, and consequences made less and less of a difference. We were lost as to what to do.
>
> One night it occurred to me that our relationship with Sean had also changed for the worse since he entered seventh grade. I tried to put myself in his shoes and imagine what it was like for him. Didn't take long for me to see that from his perspective he might feel that we

were abandoning or rejecting him when he was less than perfect. That insight took my breath away.

The next morning on the drive to school, I told Sean that for the rest of the week we would not discuss any of the trouble that he was getting in at school. Not because we didn't care, but because we cared so much. We all needed a break from letting troubles define our relationship to each other.

This mom hit the bull's eye in her diagnosis and treatment of what was happening at the relationship level with her son, so it's no surprise that over the next week—when her son came to trust she would not bring up all the troubling behaviors—their relationship went through a profound transformation. And surprise of all surprises, weeks later, once the relationship was again on solid ground, the troubling behaviors magically went away—with no commentary from Sean's parents.

Your job as a consultant parent is to pay as much attention to the quality of the relationship you have with your teenager as you do to the particulars of his or her behavior. Make it a priority to keep the relationship healthy, honest, and compassionate.

Note

1. Robert Rosenthal and Lenore Jackson, *Pygmalion in the Classroom: Teacher Expectation and Pupils' Intellectual Development* (New York: Crown House Publishing, 2003).

24

Concluding Remarks

This book has probably stirred feelings for you—of your own youth and your own past and future as a parent. The adage "What goes around comes around" is in many ways the cornerstone of the parent-adolescent relationship. Inevitably, aspects of the relationship are messy—just like good education. Thus, parents needn't expect themselves to get it right the first time through. In fact, you'll probably blow it at least as much as you succeed, like any decent therapist, who constantly needs "correcting" by the client. Trust me, you'll have another chance; it'll always come around again. (In fact, when you mess up on Tuesday, it'll probably come around again before the weekend!) This book is very much for the reflective parent—something to refer to after you've blown it and need to think it through again in order to rectify earlier performances.

If nothing else, I hope this book has conveyed the fact there are no tried-and-true prescriptions for successfully parenting teenagers. There are, however, attitudes and understandings that are crucial. Personally, I believe the horizons described in chapter 2 are most useful in understanding most adolescent behaviors and for appreciating the context of the adolescent years. And during adolescence, context is just about everything. The horizons also allow you to stay involved, creative, and curious with your teenager, so you will try different approaches and behaviors with your child rather than trying the same things over and over with fewer and fewer successes.

It is useful to remember that, like it or not, you are much more of a consultant than a manager for your teenager (except when it comes to health and safety issues). Thinking in terms of influence is much more useful and sane than thinking in terms of control.

Parenting adolescents is uniquely difficult because they are alternately (and sometimes simultaneously) in two different stages of life: childhood and adulthood. Your job is to provide the environment that lets them grow into adulthood in a healthy way rather than regress back to childhood in unhealthy ways. After all, adolescence is about passion and about learning how to use that passion in constructive and conscious ways. Probably the best you can do here is to maintain consistency, love, hope, and a deep faith that they'll get through it all. In short, love them for what they are, not for what they have the potential of becoming.

But it is also clear that parenting is an art. And like any art, it is limitless in its possibilities. Like any art, the more proficient you become at parenting the more room you see for improvement. At the same time, then, parenting is a craft, something you can always learn to do better.

Finally, I offer the words of Robert Pirsig, author of *Zen and the Art of Motorcycle Maintenance*, on, of all things, the instructions for putting together a rotisserie.

> These rotisserie instructions [read: parenting instructions] begin and end exclusively with the machine [read: the adolescent]. But the kind of approach I'm thinking about doesn't cut it off so narrowly. What's really angering about instructions of this sort is that they imply there's only one way to put this rotisserie together—their way. And that presumption wipes out all the creativity. Actually there are hundreds of ways to put the rotisserie together and when they make you follow just one way without showing you the overall problem, the instructions become hard to follow in such a way as not to make mistakes. You lose feeling for the work. And not only that, it's very unlikely that they've told you the best way. . . . And when you presume there's just one right way to do things, of course the instructions begin and end exclusively with the rotisserie. But if you have to choose among an infinite number of ways to put it together, then the relation of the machine to you, and the relation of the machine and you to the rest of the world, has to be considered, because the selection from among many choices, the art of the work is just as

dependent upon your own mind and spirit as it is upon the material of the machine. That's why you need the peace of mind.

On a practical note, many of us have taken weekend workshops and courses to learn to "think outside the box." Well, most teenagers live outside the box, and we're doing our best to get them in the box without losing the ability to go outside the box when they need to. When we stay curious about them and their world, they are free to exercise that creative thinking way outside the box, and best of all, they often open the door for us and our own creativity if we are paying attention.

Carl Jung offers a slightly different perspective: "Consciousness is not achieved without pain." From this viewpoint, raising a teenager provides numerous opportunities for leaps of consciousness. And this is difficult (but worth remembering) when your teenager's room is empty at 2:00 a.m., when the phone isn't ringing, when the vice principal is asking for a meeting, when you are buying a gown for the prom, when you are not buying a gown for the prom, after you have found an empty beer can in the car. When all is said and done, they need and want you as allies, not enemies, during this confusing and vital phase of life. You need to know this deep in your heart because most teenagers won't say it aloud.

BIBLIOGRAPHY

Alan Guttmacher Institute. *Sex and America's Teenagers*. New York: AGI, 1994.

Allen, Joseph P., Joanna Chango, David Szwedo, Megan Schad, and Emily Marston. "Predictors of Susceptibility to Peer Influence Regarding Substance Use in Adolescence." *Child Development* 83 (January 2012): 337–50.

Allen, Joseph. "Why A Teen Who Talks Back May Have a Bright Future." *All Things Considered*. NPR. January 3, 2012.

Applegate, Elizabeth. *Encyclopedia of Sports and Fitness Nutrition*. New York: Prima Lifestyles, 2002.

Blackstone-Ford, Jann, and Sharyl Jupe. *Ex-Etiquette for Parents: Good Behavior after a Divorce or Separation*. Chicago: Chicago Review Press, 2004.

Chandra, Martino, Steven Martino, Rebecca L. Collins, Marc N. Elliott, Sandra H. Berry, David E. Kanouse, and Angela Miu. "Does Watching Sex on Television Predict Teen Pregnancy? Findings from a National Longitudinal Survey of Youth." *Pediatrics* 122, no. 5 (November 2008): 1047–54

Colvin, Geoff. *Talent Is Overrated: What Really Separates World-Class Performers from Everybody Else*. New York: Portfolio, 2008.

Davidson, Cathy. *Now You See It: How the Brain Science of Attention Will Transform the Way We Live, Work, and Learn*. New York: Viking, 2011.

Doyle, Roddy. *Paddy Clarke Ha Ha Ha*. New York: Viking, 1993.

Dreikurs, Rudolf. *Children: The Challenge*. New York: Hawthorn/Dutton, 1964.

Fairchild, Betty, and Nancy Hayward. *Now That You Know: What Every Parent Should Know about Homosexuality*. San Diego, CA: Harcourt Brace Jovanovich, 1979.

Furman, Ben, and Tapani Ahola. *Solution Talk: Hosting Therapeutic Conversations*. New York: W. W. Norton, 1992.

Greenberg-Lake: The Analysis Group, Inc. *Shortchanging Girls, Shortchanging America*. Washington, DC: American Association of University Women, 1991.

Inaba, Darryl S., and William E. Cohen. *Uppers, Downers, and All Arounders*. Ashland, OR: CNS Productions, 1993.

Kinsey, Alfred C., Wardell B. Pomeroy, Clyde E. Martin, and Paul H. Gebhard. *Sexual Behavior in the Human Female*. Philadelphia: W. B. Saunders, 1953.

Kinsey, Alfred, Wardell Pomeroy, and Clyde E. Martin. *Sexual Behavior in the Human Male*. Philadelphia: W. B. Saunders, 1948.

Kübler-Ross, Elisabeth. *On Death and Dying*. New Haven: Yale University Press, 1968.

Laumann, Edward O., John H. Gagnon, and Robert T. Michael. *The Social Organization of Sexuality*. Chicago: University of Chicago Press, 1993.

Levine, Mel. *A Mind at a Time*. New York: Simon & Schuster, 2002.

Lidz, Theodore. *The Person: His Development Throughout the Life Cycle*. New York: Basic Books, 1968.

Mamlet, Robin, and Christine VanDevelde. *College Admission: From Application to Acceptance, Step by Step*. New York: Three Rivers Press, 2011.

Mayher, William S. *The Dynamics of Senior Year: A Report from the Frontlines*. Tarrytown, NY: Hackly School, 1989.

Pirsig, Robert. *Zen and the Art of Motorcycle Maintenance*. New York: Quill/William Morrow, 1974.

Riera, Michael. "A Phenomenological Analysis of Best-Friendship in Preadolescent Boys," PhD diss., California Institute of Integral Studies, San Francisco, 1992.

Rosenthal, Robert, and Lenore Jackson, *Pygmalion in the Classroom: Teacher Expectation and Pupils' Intellectual Development*. New York: Crown House Publishing, 2003.

Shedler, Jonathan, and Jack Block. "Adolescent Drug Use and Psychological Health: A Longitudinal Inquiry." *American Psychology* 45 (May 1990): 612–30.

Shoda, Yuichi, Walter Mischel, and Philip K. Peak. "Predicting Adolescent Cognitive and Self-Regulatory Competencies from Preschool Delay of Gratification: Identifying Diagnostic Conditions." *Developmental Psychology* 26, no. 6 (November 1990): 978–86.

Singh, S., and J. E. Darroch. "Trends in Sexual Activity among Adolescent American Women: 1982–1995." *Family Planning Perspectives* 31, no. 5 (1999): 211–19.

Sonenstein, F. L., K. Stewart, L.D. Lindberg, M. Pernas, and S. Williams. *Involving Males in Preventing Teen Pregnancy: A Guide for Program Planners.* Washington, DC: The Urban Institute, 1997.

Stewart, D. L. "On Being a Dad: A Teen's Lesson in Lurching." *San Francisco Chronicle*, August 21, 1991.

White, Michael, and David Epston. *Narrative Means to Therapeutic Ends.* New York, W. W. Norton, 1990.

ADDITIONAL RESOURCES

Bruner, Jerome. *Actual Minds, Possible Worlds*. Cambridge, MA: Harvard University Press, 1986.

Coburn, Karen, and Madge Treeger. *Letting Go: A Parent's Guide to Today's College Experience*. Bethesda, MD: Adler and Adler, 1992.

Elium, Jeanne, and Don Elium. *Raising a Daughter*. Berkeley, CA: Celestial Arts, 1994.

Gilligan, Carol. *In a Different Voice*. Cambridge, MA: Harvard University Press, 1982.

Grollman, Earl A. *Straight Talk about Death for Teenagers*. Boston: Beacon Press, 1993.

Heron, Ann. *One Teenager in Ten: Writings by Gay and Lesbian Youth*. Boston: Alyson Publications, 1983.

McNaught, Brian. *On Being Gay: Thoughts on Family, Faith, and Love*. New York: St. Martin's Press, 1988.

INDEX